city-lit

BERLIN

Oxygen Books

Published by Oxygen Books 2009

This selection and commentary copyright © Heather Reyes 2009

Copyright Acknowledgements at the end of this volume constitute an extension of this copyright page.

A CIP catalogue record for this book is available from the British Library.

ISBN 978–0–9559700–4–7

Typeset in Sabon by Bookcraft Limited, Stroud, Gloucestershire

Printed and bound in India by Imago

Praise for *city-lit* series

'Brilliant ... the best way to get under the skin of a city. The perfect read for travellers and book lovers of all ages'

Kate Mosse, best-selling author of *Labyrinth*

'An inviting new series of travel guides which collects some of the best writing on European cities to give a real flavour of the place ... Such an *idée formidable*, it seems amazing it hasn't been done before'

Editor's Pick, *The Bookseller*

'This impressive little series'

Sunday Telegraph

'An attractive-looking list of destination-based literature anthologies ... a great range of writers'

The Independent

' ... something for everyone – an ideal gift'

Travel Bookseller

'A very clever idea: take the best and most beloved books about a city, sift through them for the pithiest excerpts, and then compile it all into a single volume for the literary-minded tourists'

Jeremy Mercer, author of *Books, Baguettes and Bedbugs*

' ... the excellent *city-lit* series, which uses descriptions of a city penned by writers, both living and dead, to illuminate the metropolis in question'

Giles Foden, *Condé Nast Traveller*

'The perfect books for the armchair traveller as well as those of you visiting cities around the globe'

Lovereading

'A breath of fresh air ... each volume offers what it says on the tin: *city-lit – perfect gems of city writing*'

Mslexia

Editor's Note

A first visit to Berlin can be like finally meeting a relative you've heard stories about all your life – a relative with something of a 'reputation'. Despite warnings you are drawn to her complexities and contradictions, her insouciant self-confidence masking insecurity, and the fact that she so clearly wears her past on her sleeve.

What we hope *city-lit BERLIN* provides is a way of beginning to get under the skin of this amazing, chameleonic city that embodies so much of twentieth-century history – both the good and the bad – and that has picked itself up after its disasters and turned itself into a vibrant centre of culture and fun as well as serious reflection. We are also using it to promote German writing previously unpublished in English, with nearly twenty extracts chosen by my co-editor in Berlin, translator and 'lovegermanbooks' blogger Katy Derbyshire.

city-lit BERLIN contains a wide range of texts and genres, from German classics like Theodor Fontane's *Effie Briest* and Alfred Döblin's *Berlin Alexanderplatz* to blogs by enthusiastic visitors like Simon Cole. It doesn't shy away from the past (see Rachel Seiffert's *The Dark Room* and Anna Funder's *Stasiland*), but also gives a portrait of the Berlin of today (as when Tobias Rapp takes us clubbing). Alongside well-known texts like Christopher Isherwood's *Goodbye to Berlin* sit recently published works like Chloe Aridjis' *Book of Clouds*. Big historical events are told both through fiction (Beatrice Collins' *The Luminous Life of Lilly Aphrodite*) as well as by veteran reporter John Simpson. There is the ferocious humour of Thomas Brussig's *Heroes Like Us* and the anguish of Eva Figes' *Tales of Innocence and Experience*. Writers of a dozen national origins include young Kashmiri Nitasha Kaul, Indian writer and journalist Salil Tripathi, and Turkish author and actress Emine Sevgi Özdamar.

Inevitably there are omissions: we began with a collection of extracts roughly twice as long as the finished book. We would like to have included a piece from Erich Kästner's children's book *Emil and the Detectives* but found it didn't sit happily among the adult texts. The work of Kurt Tucholsky is missing, and we only have a small sample of the many spy-and-thriller novels set in Berlin. Recommendations for 'further reading' would include the books of Peter Schneider, and Martha Gellhorn's account of her time in Berlin. We have tried to introduce readers to new names, or old names in new contexts. A collection to be used as a starting point for further exploration.

Above all, Katy Derbyshire and I hope your pleasure in reading this collection matches the rich experience we have had in putting it together.

Heather Reyes

Oxygen Books would like to thank the Goethe Institute, London for supporting our commissioned translations of German texts.

Contents

Rory MacLean, 'Introducing Berlin' 1

'Come to the cabaret ... '

Paul Verhaeghen, *Omega Minor* 5
Philip Kerr, *March Violets* 5
Christabel Bielenberg, *The Past is Myself* 6
Elias Canetti, *The Torch in My Ear* 6
Christopher Isherwood, *Goodbye to Berlin* 8
Joseph Roth, *The Wandering Jews* 10
Peter Gay, *Weimar Culture* 12
Sebastian Haffner, *Defying Hitler* 14
Ian Walker, *Zoo Station* 16
Rolf Schneider, *Berlin, ach Berlin* ('Berlin, oh Berlin') 18
Tobias Rapp, *Lost and Sound: Berlin Techno und der Easyjetset* 21
Simon Cole, *Berlin Blog* 25
Wenonah Lyon, 'The first time I saw Berlin ... ' 25

Out and About

Cees Nooteboom, *All Souls' Day* 31
Anna Winger, *This Must Be The Place* 33
Chloe Aridjis, *Book of Clouds* 37
Cees Nooteboom, *All Souls' Day* 38
David Hare, *Berlin* 39
Chloe Aridjis, *Book of Clouds* 40
Salil Tripathi, 'Learning by the book' 41
Alfred Döblin, *Berlin Alexanderplatz* 44
Chloe Aridjis, *Book of Clouds* 46
Anna Winger, *This Must Be The Place* 47
Ralf Rothmann, *Hitze* ('Heat') 47
Anna Funder, *Stasiland* 49
Christiane Rösinger, *Das schöne Leben* ('A Nice Life') 50
Katja Lange-Müller, 'Sklavendreieck' ('The Slave Triangle')
     in *Neues aus der Heimat* ('News from home') 52
Philip Hensher, *Pleasured* 53
Paul Verhaeghen, *Omega Minor* 54
Simon Cole, 'Running the Berlin Wall' 56

'Ich bin Berliner'

Philip Kerr, *The Pale Criminal* 58
Jakob Hein, *Gebrauchsanweisung für Berlin* ('Berlin: a user's manual') . . . 59
Paul Verhaeghen, *Omega Minor* 61
Thomas Brussig, *Berliner Orgie* ('Wild Berlin') 61
Jeffrey Eugenides, *Middlesex* 63
Geert Mak, *In Europe* 64
Ian Walker, *Zoo Station* 65
Beatrice Collin, *The Luminous Life of Lilly Aphrodite* 66
Elias Canetti, *The Torch in My Ear* 67
Ian Collins, 'Marlene Dietrich: RIP' 70

Contents

Mikka Haugaard, 'Hans Christian Andersen in love' 73
Ian Walker, *Zoo Station* 76
Tobias Rüther, *Helden: David Bowie und Berlin*
   ('Heroes: David Bowie and Berlin') 78

'Money, Money, Money ... '

Beatrice Collin, *The Luminous Life of Lilly Aphrodite* 82
Christopher Isherwood, *Goodbye to Berlin*. 83
Christabel Bielenberg, *The Past is Myself* 85
Beatrice Collin, *The Luminous Life of Lilly Aphrodite* 87
Paul Verhaeghen, *Omega Minor* 89
Dan Vyleta, *Pavel and I*. 90
Chloe Aridjis, *Book of Clouds* 91
Vladimir Kaminer, *Russian Disco* 92
Inka Parei, *Die Schattenboxerin* ('The Shadow-boxer') 93
Bernd and Luise Wagner, *Berlin für Arme* ('Berlin for the poor'). 95
Chloe Aridjis, *Book of Clouds* 96
Simon Cole, *Berlin Blog* 97

The past is another country

Daniel Kehlmann, *Measuring the World* 99
Theodor Fontane, *Effi Briest*. 102
Gertrude Bell, *The Letters of Gertrude Bell*. 103
Karl Baedeker, *Guide to Berlin* 105
Beatrice Collin, *The Luminous Life of Lilly Aphrodite* 107
Christopher Isherwood, *Mr Norris Changes Trains*. 109
Christopher Isherwood, *Goodbye to Berlin*. 111
Volker Weidermann, *Das Buch der verbrannten Bücher*
   ('The book of burnt books') 114
Philip Kerr, *March Violets*. 116
Thomas Wolfe, *You Can't Go Home Again*. 117
Philip Kerr, *March Violets*. 121
Beatrice Collin, *The Luminous Life of Lilly Aphrodite* 121
Paul Verhaeghen, *Omega Minor* 122
Inge Deutschkron, *Ich trug den gelben Stern* ('I wore the yellow star') ... 123
Eva Figes, *Tales of Innocence and Experience*. 126
Philip Kerr, *March Violets*. 127
Geert Mak, *In Europe*. 128
Rachel Seiffert, *The Dark Room*. 129
Hans Fallada, *Alone in Berlin* 130
Rachel Seiffert, *The Dark Room*. 130
Christabel Bielenberg, *The Past is Myself* 133
Anonymous, *A Woman in Berlin*. 133
Dan Vyleta, *Pavel and I*. 136
Tamsin Walker, 'Old Woman' 137
W. G. Sebald, *The Rings of Saturn* 139
Dan Vyleta, *Pavel and I*. 141
Thomas Pynchon, *Gravity's Rainbow* 142
Ian McEwan, *The Innocent*. 143
Dan Vyleta, *Pavel and I*. 145
Paul Beatty, *Slumberland*. 146
C. S. Richardson, *The End of the Alphabet*. 147

Contents

A Tale of Two Cities

David Hare, *Berlin* 151
Len Deighton, *Funeral in Berlin* 151
John Simpson, *Strange Places, Questionable People* 155
Ian Walker, *Zoo Station* 155
Philip Hensher, *Pleasured* 156
Michael Wildenhain, *Russisch Brot* ('Russian Bread') 159
Kate Adie, *The Kindness of Strangers* 161
Ian Walker, *Zoo Station* 165
John le Carré, *The Spy Who Came In From The Cold* 167
Len Deighton, *Funeral in Berlin* 168
Ian Walker, *Zoo Station* 168
Chloe Aridjis, *Book of Clouds* 170
Rayk Weiland, *Ich schlage vor, dass wir uns küssen* ('I suggest we kiss') . 172
John le Carré, *The Spy Who Came In From The Cold* 173
Monika Maron, *Animal Triste* 175
Philip Hensher, *Pleasured* 176

And the Wall came tumbling down

John Simpson, *Strange Places, Questionable People* 178
Thomas Brussig, *Heroes Like Us* 182
Philip Hensher, *Pleasured* 184
Steffi Badel and Mtislav Rostropovich, *Mein 9 November: Der Tag an
    dem die Mauer fiel* ('My 9 November: the day the Wall fell') 185
Yadé Kara, *Selam Berlin* ('Salaam Berlin') 187
Anna Funder, *Stasiland* 188
Jan Morris, *A Writer's World* 188
Anna Funder, *Stasiland* 190
Simon Cole, *Berlin Blog* 192
Anna Funder, *Stasiland* 193
Rory MacLean, *Stalin's Nose* 196

Berlin: *Weltstadt*

Robert Harris, *Fatherland* 198
Iain Bamforth, *The Good European: Essays and Arguments* 201
Geert Mak, *In Europe* 206
Paul Verhaeghen, *Omega Minor* 208
Geert Mak, *In Europe* 209
Fridolin Schley, 'The Heart of the Republic' 209
Emine Sevgi Özdamar, 'My Berlin' 214
Ian Walker, *Zoo Station* 218
Rory MacLean, *Berlin Blog* 219
Nitasha Kaul, 'Letter' 220

Goodbye to Berlin

Chloe Aridjis, *Book of Clouds* 223
Ian Walker, *Zoo Station* 225
Thomas Wolfe, *You Can't Go Home Again* 227

Index 230
Acknowledgements 236

Introducing BERLIN
by Rory MacLean

Why are we drawn to certain cities? Perhaps because of a story read in childhood. Or a chance teenage meeting. Or maybe simply because the place touches us, embodying in its towers, tribes and history an aspect of our understanding of what it means to be human. Paris is about romantic love. Lourdes equates with devotion. New York means materialism. London is forever trendy.

Berlin is all about volatility. Its identity is based not on stability but on change. No other city has repeatedly been so powerful, and fallen so low. No other city has inspired so many artists and witnessed so many murders. It's a capital city made up of villages. An island long adrift on a foreign sea. A city where history broods. Its legends, both real and imagined, stalk the streets: Lenin drinks at the same café as Bowie's heroes, Wim Wender's trench-coated angels wing above torch-lit Nazi processions, Speer conjures myths from the same canvas as Georg Grosz, Dietrich shops alongside Sally Bowles at Ka De We, le Carré's George Smiley watches the packed trains leave for Auschwitz.

I was once a baby-boom Canadian 'doing' Europe, a child of the most liberal and stable of nations. During a happy, footloose summer I climbed the Eiffel Tower, tripped down the Spanish Steps and made love under the stars on an Aegean beach. Then on the last week of the holiday I saw the Wall. The sight of that brutal barrier shook me to my core. At the heart of the continent were watchtowers, barbed wire and border guards who shot dead 'defectors' because they wanted to live under a different system. I knew the history. I understood what had happened. But I couldn't conceive how it had happened. The individuals whose actions had divided Germany and Europe – the wartime planners, the Soviet commissars, the Grepo – weren't monsters. They were ordinary men and women. I ached to understand their motivation, how they came to act as they did, yet at the same time I was repulsed by their crimes and needed to give voice to their victims' suffering. A decade would pass before I began doing that, putting pen to paper, writing my first book as the Wall fell, then another fifteen years and six more books before I settled in the city.

Berlin's unpredictable undercurrents long attracted artists. The historian Peter Gay wrote that living in the city in the Golden Twenties was the dream of 'the composer, the journalist, the actor; with its superb orchestras, its 120 newspapers, its forty theatres, Berlin was the place for the ambitious, the energetic, the talented. Wherever they started, it was in Berlin that they became, and Berlin that made them famous.' During the Weimar years it was the world's most exciting city. Here Walter Gropius conceived the Bauhaus, Weill penned 'The Ballad of Mack the Knife' and Isherwood immortalized the cabaret. Nabokov, Kafka, Auden and Spender were inspired in its cafés. At Babelsberg Studio Fritz Lang filmed 'Metropolis' while von Sternberg and Dietrich created 'The Blue Angel'. For ten breathless years, artists and intellectuals danced on the edge of a volcano. When their vision of a new world was rejected by Germans in 1933, the year Hitler became Chancellor, Berlin's exiles carried their new modernity abroad.

Situated on a long plain of marshes stretching as far as Warsaw, medieval Berlin was an uncultured spot. Christianity did not take root here until the twelfth century. Robber barons and the plague besieged the primitive outpost as late as the fifteenth century. It was the Hohenzollern princes who wrested a capital from the swamps with hard work and immigrants. But the princes' obsession with military power also laid the foundations for the bullish force of Prussia, the 'army within a state' which aspired to European domination. It's no wonder that Goethe loathed the place, equating it with the Devil's world. At the outbreak of the First World War, Berlin was a grandiose capital dominated by pomp, parades and overbearing buildings of immense ugliness. 'Groups of people everywhere, and in addition, soldiers marching out of the city, showered with blossoms as they went. Every face looks happy: we have war!' cheered the actress Tilla Durieux in 1914. But within a year disillusionment had set in and, by 1918, some 350,000 young Berliners had been killed in action. The ignominy of defeat and the vindictive Versailles Treaty made the returning troops ideal candidates for radicals on both the left and right. Revolution, insurrection and political assassinations characterised the next desperate years and – along with the wild inflation of 1922–23 – shattered respect for tradition. Then, in 1924, the American-led Dawes Plan stabilised the mark, fuelling a bubble of prosperity and stimulating a remarkable cultural flowering that bridged east and west and transformed Berlin into the international capital of modernism. Almost overnight the population boomed, industrial output soared above pre-war levels and Germany became second only to the US in value of world exports. The city pulsated with life and easy money. Hungry for experimentation, artists from Britain, France, America and Russia moved to Berlin, attracted by creative and sexual freedom, as well as by the least repressive censorship laws in Europe. Heinrich Mann called it 'a city of excitement and hope'. But for all its frenzied, prodigious output, the decade was golden for only a small minority, many of whom were outsiders. In 1926 a young Jospeh Goebbels – another of many ambitious story-tellers – arrived at the Anhalter Bahnhof, determined to 'take the city' for an aspirant Hitler. At the time there were fewer than 200 Nazi Party members in Berlin, while the Communists boasted a member-ship of 250,000. In an audacious move Goebbels cast the Communists – along with the Jews – as the scapegoats for society's ills. He orchestrated hundreds of street battles against them to gain publicity. He took advantage of the resurgent financial crisis and, after 1929, of mass unemployment (one third of the city's labour force was out of work towards the end of the Great Depression). His Machiavellian mastery of propaganda exploited the suffering of Berlin's majority; like most Germans they embraced the Nazi's radical solutions in response. In the month following Hitler's accession to power over 50,000 Berliners joined the Party.

The minority left-wing avant-garde was easily destroyed. German literature went up in smoke in the 1933 book burnings. Bertolt Brecht, Alfred Döblin, Mann and many other writers fled the country, along-side Lang, Einstein and Mies van der Rohe. With the Nazis' arrogant triumph Hitler proposed rebuilding Berlin as 'Germania', the new capital of the populist, nationalistic 'Thousand Year Reich'. 'In ten years no one will recognise the city' he boasted. During the Second World War more bombs fell on it than on the whole of England. By 1945 three-quarters of the city lay in ruins.

The victorious Allies divided Berlin into four sectors. Stalin's secret intention was to draw it – and then the whole of Germany – into the Communist orbit. In 1948 he blockaded the city as a means of driving the Americans out of Europe, but the Allies retaliated by launching the Berlin Airlift to sustain its freedom. With the brutal suppression of the 1953 uprising, hundreds of thousands of East Germans began moving west, forcing the Communists to close their escape route by building the Wall. Behind it East German literature flourished, though not necessarily in print due to strict censorship. In the encircled western sectors writers struggled to come to terms with the recent past, handicapped by both widespread denial and young men moving to West Berlin only to escape military service, their spirit of refusal emasculating criticism and engendering self-indulgence. The return to literature of quality – influenced by the residencies of Heinrich Böll, Wolf Biermann, Günter Grass and Uwe Johnson as well as Ryszard Kapuscinski, Cees Nooteboom and Susan Sontag – was accelerated by reunification. The city has emerged from its dark anger to become again a creative capital of Europe: cool, experimental, bohemian, with cheap rents and an irony-free exuberance that attracts aspiring scribblers and the international cultural elite alike. East and west, German and foreign, meet once more, as illustrated in the work of Thomas Brussig, Bernhard Schlink and Uwe Tellkamp, Jeffrey Eugenides, Jonathan Franzen and Imre Kertesz.

Today I ride my bicycle past the site of the wooden observation stand where I decided to become a writer, across the former death strip, to the glittering glass and steel phoenix of Potsdamer Platz. Near to it is the Holocaust Memorial, the undulating labyrinth of concrete plinths which commemorates the murdered European Jews. The black husk of the Kaiser Wilhelm Memorial Church, destroyed by Allied bombs in 1943, casts a long shadow along buzzy Kurfürstendamm. At my son's school an old brick wall is still pockmarked from machinegun fire. A young German painter told me recently, 'I do not want to say that they – the SS officers, the guards by the Wall, the Stasi interrogators – are like us. It is different, worse I guess. They are us – and we would have been them, in our respective times. It does not mean that I think we – the Germans – are likely to ever become Nazis again. Germany is a profoundly different land now, its identity reshaped forever by cataclysmic events. But it is the potency of us, them, me, to have been part of such events that is the horror today.'

Of all human characteristics change is ever the most constant. Germans no longer shy away from acknowledging the darkness in their past. Convinced of the Freudian idea that the repressed (or at least unspoken) will fester like a canker unless it is brought to light, Germany has subjected itself to national psychoanalysis. Past atrocities are unearthed and confessed, as a condition of healing, as if the psychic health of a society depends upon it. This courageous, humane and moving process is inspiring painters and authors at home and abroad, illuminating legends real and imagined, galvanizing again this volatile, ever-changing city ... for a time.

Rory MacLean, Berlin 2009

Rory MacLean, author of the much acclaimed *Stalin's Nose* and *Under the Dragon*, lives in Berlin where he is writing a book on the city and its ghosts.

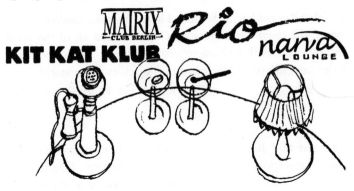

'Come to the cabaret ... '

So, 'WILLKOMMEN IN BERLIN' ... Welcome to Berlin.

I love this sprawling town. I love the anarchy of stone and flesh visible only at night. The city is a web. The city is my mother. I love her. I love her wide boulevards, I love her open squares. I love the radical proletarian style that she has adopted; I love how she can shine with splendour underneath the grime. I love her penchant for slumming, her nightly quest for an authentic and purifying anarchy of body and soul – unlike Paris, Berlin will never be serenaded in poetry or depicted in delicate watercolours. This city is a snapshot; you need the fleetingness of newsprint and a theatre of moving images to do her justice. Berlin is the New York of the old world; the only true New York of the old world, a city with enough *cojones* to dance on the dangerous edge of splendour and doom.

Paul Verhaeghen, Omega Minor

✳ ✳ ✳

Berlin. I used to love this old city. But that was before it had caught sight of its own reflection and taken to wearing corsets laced so tight that it could hardly breathe. I loved the easy, carefree philosophies, the cheap jazz, the vulgar cabarets and all of the other cultural excesses that characterized the Weimar years and made Berlin seem like one of the most exciting cities in the world.

Philip Kerr, *March Violets* in *Berlin Noir*

* * *

I did not find Berlin a beautiful town, but an exciting one; without question a capital city, as different from Hamburg as London from Liverpool. Its particular spell grew on you, so they said, but it had an immediate attraction for me in that the buoyancy of its climate made nonsense of such little indulgencies as 'feeling tired'. I also discovered to my pleasure that the irrepressible Berliners were utterly indifferent as to what impression they or their massive chunks of Wilhelminian architecture made on outsiders. You could take Berlin or you could leave it [...]; the inhabitants themselves, the *Ur-Berliner*, could think of no better place in the world to live.

I wanted to live there too, but by making up my mind that, for the sake of the children, I must have a house with a garden, and by deciding rather rashly that Berlin-Dahlem would suit me nicely, I added a private problem to the many others which were keeping my head buzzing. For I also discovered in Berlin that it was not only the sparkling air which differed from the misty haze of the north German seaport; something of the essential nature of the political issues at stake stood out there with a crystal clarity which at first took my parochial breath away.

Christabel Bielenberg, *The Past is Myself*

* * *

Elias Canetti (1905–1994) – probably best known today for his novel Auto-da-Fé *– was bowled over by his first visit to the city as an impressionable 23-year-old.*

So here I was in Berlin, never taking more than ten steps without running into a celebrity. Wieland knew everyone and introduced me to everyone right away. I was a nobody here and quite aware of this; I had done nothing; at twenty-three, I was nothing more than a hopeful. Yet it was astonishing how people treated me: not with scorn, but with curiosity, and, above all, never with condemnation. I myself, after four years under Karl Krauss's influence, was filled with all his contempt and condemnation and acknowledged nothing that was determined by greed, self-ishness, or frivolity. All objects to condemn were prescribed by Krauss. You were not even allowed to look at them; he had already taken care of that for you and made the decision. It was a *sterilized* intellectual life that we led in Vienna [...].

And suddenly, the very opposite came in Berlin, where contacts of any sort, incessant, were part of the very substance of living. This brand of curiosity must have agreed with me, though I did not realize it; I yielded naïvely and innocently, and just as I had strolled into the maws of tyranny right after my arrival in Vienna, where I had been kept nicely aloof from all temptations, so too, in Berlin, I was at the mercy of the hotbed of vice for several weeks. [...]

Everything was equally *close* in Berlin, every kind of effect was permitted: no one was prohibited from making himself noticeable if he didn't mind the strain. For it was no easy matter: the noise was great, and you were always aware, in the midst of noise and tumult, that there were things worth hearing and seeing. Anything went. The taboos, of which there was no lack anywhere, especially in Germany, dried out here. You could come from an old capital like Vienna and feel like a provincial here, and you gaped until your eyes grew accustomed to remaining open. There was something pungent, corrosive in the atmosphere; it stimulated and animated. You charged into everything and were afraid of nothing.

Elias Canetti, *The Torch in my Ear*
translated by Joachim Neugroschel

❊ ❊ ❊

*For many Anglophone readers, Christopher Isher-
wood's Berlin novels provide their first literary experience of the city in the last days of the Weimar Republic,
just before the disaster of National Socialism destroyed
it. Who can think of Berlin without recalling the stage
show and film* Cabaret, *with Liza Minelli playing Sally
Bowles, and such songs as 'Money, money, money'
and the title song itself, inviting us to 'come to the
cabaret'? The rule-flouting cabaret performances of
the time had become a magnet for the free-thinking
world – though, by the end, not all were as glamorous
as a young man had come to expect ...*

A few days later, he took me to hear Sally sing. The Lady Windermere (which now, I hear, no longer exists) was an arty 'informal'
bar, just off the Tauentzienstrasse, which the proprietor had
evidently tried to make look as much as possible like Montpar-
nasse. The walls were covered with sketches on menu-cards,
caricatures and signed theatrical photographs – ('To the one and
only Lady Windermere.' 'To Johnny, with all my heart.'). The
Fan itself, four times life size, was displayed above the bar. There
was a big piano on a platform in the middle of the room.

I was curious to see how Sally would behave. I had imagined
her, for some reason, rather nervous, but she wasn't, in the
least. She had a surprisingly deep husky voice. She sang badly,
without any expression, her hands hanging down at her sides
– yet her performance was, in its own way, effective because of
her startling appearance and her air of not caring a curse what
people thought of her. Her arms hanging carelessly limp, and a
take-it-or-leave-it grin on her face, she sang:

> *Now I know why Mother*
> *Told me to be true;*
> *She meant me for Someone*
> *Exactly like you.*

There was quite a lot of applause. The pianist, a handsome young man with blond wavy hair, stood up and solemnly kissed Sally's hand. Then she sang two more songs, one in French and the other in German. These weren't so well received.

After the singing, there was a good deal more hand-kissing and general movement towards the bar.

Sally seemed to know everybody in the place. She called them all Thou and Darling. For a would-be demi-mondaine, she seemed to have surprisingly little business sense or tact. She wasted a lot of time making advances to an elderly gentleman who would obviously have preferred a chat with the barman. Later, we all got rather drunk. Then Sally had to go off to an appointment, and the manager came and sat at our table. He and Fritz talked English Peerage. Fritz was in his element. I decided, as so often before, never to visit a place of this sort again. [...]

Last night, Fritz Wendel proposed a tour of 'the dives'. It was to be in the nature of a farewell visit, for the Police have begun to take a great interest in these places. They are frequently raided, and the names of their clients are written down. There is even talk of a general Berlin clean-up.

I rather upset him by insisting on visiting the Salomé, which I had never seen. Fritz, as a connoisseur of night-life, was most contemptuous. It wasn't even genuine, he told me, the management run it entirely for the benefit of provincial sightseers.

The Salomé turned out to be very expensive and even more depressing than I had imagined. A few stage lesbians and some young men with plucked eyebrows lounged at the bar, uttering occasional raucous guffaws or treble hoots – supposed, apparently, to represent the laughter of the damned. The whole premises are painted gold and inferno-red – crimson plush inches thick, and vast gilded mirrors. It was pretty full. The audience consisted chiefly of respectable middle-aged tradesmen and their families, exclaiming in good-humoured amazement: 'Do they really?' and 'Well, I never!' We went out half-way through the cabaret performance, after a young man in a spangled crinoline and jewelled breast-caps had painfully but successfully executed three splits. [...]

'Ever been to that communist dive near the Zoo?' Fritz asked me, as we were walking away from the Salomé. 'Eventually we should cast an eye in there ... In six months, maybe, we'll all be wearing red shirts ... '

I agreed. I was curious to know what Fritz's idea of 'communist dive' would be like.

It was, in fact, a small whitewashed cellar. You sat on long wooden benches at big bare tables; a dozen people together – like a school dining-hall. On the walls were scribbled expressionist drawings involving actual newspaper clippings, real playing-cards, nailed-on beer-mats, match-boxes, cigarette cartons, and heads cut out of photographs. The café was full of students, dressed mostly with aggressive political untidiness – the men in sailor's sweaters and stained baggy trousers, the girls in ill-fitting jumpers, skirts held visibly together with safety-pins and carelessly knotted gaudy gipsy scarves. The proprietress was smoking a cigar. The boy who acted as a waiter lounged about with a cigarette between his lips and slapped customers on the back when taking their orders.

It was all thoroughly sham and gay and jolly: you couldn't help feeling at home, immediately.

Christopher Isherwood, *Goodbye to Berlin*

❊ ❊ ❊

A different kind of cabaret experience. Austrian writer Joseph Roth (1894–1939) recalls stumbling into a traditional Jewish cabaret in pre-Nazi Berlin.

I stumbled upon the cabaret by chance, wandering through the dark streets on a bright evening, looking through the windows of small prayerhouses, which by day were no more than shopfronts, but in the morning and evening, houses of worship. [...]

The cabaret I saw was set up in the yard of a dirty old inn. It was a rectangular, glassed-in yard, whose walls were windows, giving onto corridors and passages, revealing such domestic details as beds, shirts, and buckets. A stray linden tree stood in the middle of it, representing nature. Through one or two lit-up windows you could see inside the kitchen of a kosher restaurant. Steam rose from cauldrons. A fat woman with bare and flabby forearms wielded a wooden spoon. Directly in front of the windows and half-obscuring them was a platform from which one could go straight into the main hall of the restaurant. This platform was the stage, and in front of it sat the musicians, a troupe of six men, said to be the six sons of the great Mendel from Berdiczev, whom the oldest European Jews can still remember and whose violin playing was so beautiful that no one who heard it – in Lithuania, Volhynia, or Galicia – ever forgot it.

The actors who were about to appear went by the name of the Surokin Troupe. Surokin was their director, producer, and treasurer, a fat, clean-shaven man from Kovno who had sung as far afield as America; a cantor and tenor; star of synagogue and opera, pampered, proud, and condescending; in equal parts entrepreneur and comrade. The audience sat at small tables, eating bread and sausages and drinking beer. They went to the kitchen to fetch food and drink, enjoyed themselves, howled and laughed. They were made up of small merchants and their families, not Orthodox but "enlightened", as those Jews are called in the East who shave (even if only once a week) and wear European clothes. Those Jews observe the religious customs more out of pious habit than religious need; they think of God only when they need him, and, given their luck, they need him fairly frequently. They range from the cynical to the superstitious, but in certain situations all of them are apt to be maudlin and touching in their emotionalism. Where business is concerned they will deal with one another and with strangers with complete ruthlessness

... but one needs only to touch a certain hidden chord within them and they will be selfless, generous, and humane. Yes, they are perfectly capable of shedding tears, especially in an open-air theatre like this one.

The troupe consisted of two women and three men – but when it comes to their performance, I hardly know what to say. The entire programme was improvised. First to appear was a small, skinny fellow. [...] He sang old songs and made fun of them by giving them unexpected and unsuitable twists. Then the two women sang an old song together, an actor told a funny story of Shalom Aleichem's, and at the end, Herr Surokin, the director, recited Hebrew and Yiddish poems by recent or contemporary Jewish poets; he would recite the Hebrew verses followed by the Yiddish translation, and sometimes he would sing two or three stanzas as though he were alone in his room. And then there was a deathly hush, and the little merchants made big eyes and propped their chins on their fists, and we could hear the rustling of the linden leaves.

Joseph Roth, *The Wandering Jews*
translated by Michael Hoffmann

❊ ❊ ❊

But it isn't just cabaret culture that pre-war Berlin is famous for. In Weimar Culture, *historian Peter Gay reminds us that it was also a vibrant centre for all the arts ... classical music, painting and literature – with the publication of Thomas Mann's remarkable novel* The Magic Mountain *'the' literary event of 1924. But he also gives a vivid portrait of the seedier side of the city as it tries to grapple with spiralling inflation.*

Mann's *Zauberberg* was the literary event of 1924; in its first year, it sold fifty thousand copies – a vast number for a bulky two-volume novel in those days. And it was in the same year that another event took place, less widely publicized but equally significant: Bertolt Brecht, already a well-known playwright, and halfway between his nihilistic and Expressionist experiments and a new cool, highly personal lyricism, moved from Munich to Berlin.

The move is significant because it symbolizes the growing power of Berlin in the golden mid-twenties. As Germany's largest city, as the capital of Prussia and the Empire, Berlin had been the only possible choice for capital of the Republic. And Berlin came to engross not merely government offices and party headquarters, but the leaders of culture, at the expense of the provinces. Other major cities like Munich, Frankfurt, or Hamburg struggled to keep excellence in their universities, took pride in special institutes, cultivated continued high quality in their theatres and liveliness in their Bohemian quarters. But Berlin was a magnet. After years of resistance, Heinrich Mann gave way and moved there. 'Centralization', he said in humorous resignation, 'is inevitable'. The city drew strength from its illustrious immigrants, and in turn gave strength to them. 'Beckmann is unthinkable without Berlin', one of his admirers noted in 1913, while, in 1920, another admirer turned the observation around: 'Beckmann', the critic Meirer-Graefe said, 'is the new Berlin.' The old Berlin had been impressive, the new Berlin was irresistible. To go to Berlin was the aspiration of the composer, the journalist, the actor; with its superb orchestras, its hundred and twenty newspapers, its forty theatres, Berlin was the place for the ambitious, the energetic, the talented. Wherever they started, it was in Berlin that they became, and Berlin that made them, famous: young Erich Kästner, who became notorious with his impudent verses before he became famous for his children's books, was fired from his post on the staff of a Leipzig newspaper and so in 1927, he recalls, he 'went off, penniless, to conquer Berlin'. [...]

Berlin, it is obvious, aroused powerful emotions in everyone. It delighted most, terrified some, but left no one indifferent, and it induced, by its vitality, a certain inclination to exaggerate what one saw. Stefan Zweig was one who projected his horror at later events onto his horror of Berlin in the time of inflation: 'Berlin', he writes, 'transformed itself into the Babel of the world.'

Bars, amusement parks, pubs shot up like mushrooms. What we had seen in Austria proved to be merely a mild and timid prelude to this witches' sabbath, for the Germans brought to perversion all their vehemence and love of system. Made-up boys with artificial waistlines promenaded along the Kurfürstendamm – and not professionals alone: every high-school student wanted to make some money, and in the darkened bars one could see high public officials and high financiers courting drunken sailors without shame. Even the Rome of Suetonius had not known orgies like the Berlin transvestite balls, where hundreds of men in women's clothes and women in men's clothes danced under the benevolent eyes of the police. Amid the general collapse of values, a kind of insanity took hold of precisely those middle-class circles which had hitherto been unshakable in their order. Young ladies proudly boasted that they were perverted; to be suspected of virginity at sixteen would have been considered a disgrace in every school in Berlin.

Peter Gay, *Weimar Culture*

* * *

In Defying Hitler, *Sebastian Haffner pays tribute to those heroic people who took a stand against Nazism – including a cabaret master of ceremonies who wasn't afraid to use humour as a weapon against a humourless regime.*

Chance had led us to the Katakombe, and this was the second remarkable experience of the evening. We arrived at the only place in Germany where a kind of public, courageous, witty and elegant resistance was taking place. That morning I had witnessed how the Prussian *Kammergericht*, with a tradition of hundreds of years, had ignobly capitulated before the Nazis. In the evening I experienced how a small troop of artistes, with no tradition to back them up, saved our honour with grace and glory. The *Kammergericht* had fallen but the Katakombe stood upright.

The man who led this small group of actors to victory – standing firm in the face of overwhelming, murderous odds must be counted as a victory – was called Werner Fink. This minor cabaret master of ceremonies has his place in the annals of the Third Reich, indeed one of the very few places of honour there. He did not look like a hero, and if he finally became something like one, it was in spite of himself. He was not a revolutionary actor, had no biting satire; he was not David with a sling. His character was at bottom harmless and amiable, his wit gentle, light and capricious. His jokes were based on double entendre and puns, which he handled like a virtuoso. He had invented something that could be called the hidden punch-line. Indeed, as time went by it became more and more necessary for him to hide his punch-lines, but he did not conceal his opinions. His act remained full of harmless amiability in a country where these qualities were on the liquidation list. This harmless amiability hid a kernel of real, indomitable courage. He dared to speak openly about the reality of the Nazis, and that in the middle of Germany. His patter contained references to concentration camps, the raids on people's homes, the general fear and general lies. He spoke of these things with infinitely quiet mockery, melancholy and sadness. Listening to him was extraordinarily comforting.

This 31st of March was perhaps his greatest evening. The house was full of people staring at the next day as if into an abyss. Fink made them laugh as I have never heard an audience laugh. It was dramatic laughter, the laughter of a newborn defiance, throwing off numbness and desperation, feeding off the present danger. It was a miracle that the SA had not long since arrived to arrest everybody here. On this evening we would probably have gone on laughing in the police vans. We had been improbably raised above fear and danger.

Sebastian Haffner, *Defying Hitler*
translated by Oliver Pretzel

* * *

From the 70s onwards, Berlin once again became famed for its pubs and clubs and cabarets. Ian Walker takes us on a night out in 80s Berlin.

'The weather was better under communism,' I said to Astrid as we reached the door to the Djungel. She rang the bell.

The same woman had been on the door at the Djungel since 1979. She wore a black leather mini-skirt. She opened the door just wide enough to get a decent view of prospective customers. Faced with strangers, she looked them up and down expressionlessly for a few seconds before making her decision. It was like facing the guards at the border except that here the dress code was stricter. To those that the girl in black leather deemed too old, too unfashionable, too poor or too fat, she shook her head and said *private* or *full*. […]

Outside the Djungel stood a small group of West German teenagers in rain-sodden pastel casuals. They had been refused admission.

Acknowledging Astrid with a miniscule movement of the eyebrows, the face-check girl opened the door and a flood of noise poured out.

'Every time I come here I swear I'll never come again,' Astrid said, picking her way through the crush till she was able to place one hand on the chrome rail of the bar. 'But where else is there to go?'

She ordered two beers from the skinhead barmaid, who looked about forty and wore a black vest. The harsh-lit bar was long and narrow and led to a small dark dancefloor.

Next to a fountain was a circular steel staircase, permanently clogged with people like bits of cork in a corkscrew. The staircase connected to a champagne bar where the richer clientele sat at white tablecloths and peered down through chrome railings to the throng below.

I met some familiar faces at the bar. A 29-year-old American called Dan briefly interrupted his conversation with the lead singer of Einstürzende Neubauten to say how you doing? Dan had come to Berlin on holiday four years ago and never gone home. He was working as a window-cleaner and still hoping to become a pop star. The lead singer of Neubauten wore a clerical collar and black coat and had a hairstyle like a palm tree. Another Sunday night regular, he was telling Dan about a forthcoming tour of Britain. Neubauten had been popular for some time in both East and West Berlin and were now beginning to attract a following among the disaffected avant garde of other cities. The band made music with industrial tools, pneumatic drills for example.

Neubauten were one of a few dozen West Berlin bands producing a form of alienated white noise known locally as Mauersound, Wallsound, the soundtrack composed in the shadow of a cliché. Mauersound was a homegrown reaction to the syncopated rhythms overlaid by Anglo-American lyrics that provided the background to public life all over West Berlin, the pop music singles flaunting cultural supremacy in a love song. The Internationale lasted three minutes and had a catchy chorus.

A dark-haired girl of about seventeen strode towards the dancefloor wearing a T-shirt that said, after the style of merchandise sold by pop groups on tour, ADOLF HITLER, EUROPEAN TOUR 1939. The list of countries which followed (Austria, Czechoslovakia, Poland, etc.) was written in black and red on white, the colours of the first German flag. [...]

Astrid was on the dancefloor. I stood at the bar talking about nothing in particular to the window-cleaner who wanted to be a pop star. 'Waiting For My Man' was succeeded on the turntable by 'Suffragette City'. Its author, David Bowie, a man with a green and a blue eye, had sought refuge in this town between 1976 and 1978, a period of residence which had breathed new life into the notion of decadent Berlin. Marlene Dietrich, Checkpoint Charlie, David Bowie, the jumbled-up names somehow summarised the city for the millions abroad who vaguely supposed modern Berlin was *Cabaret* plus fifty years, *Cabaret* redesigned against the glamorous backdrop of the Wall.

Ian Walker, *Zoo Station*

✳ ✳ ✳

Before we move on to trendy post-Wall Berlin, Rolf Schneider takes us into a good old-fashioned Berlin pub, or 'Kneipe'.

In the Berlin districts of Wedding, Prenzlauer Berg, Friedrichshain, Kreuzberg, and Neukölln there are still a few street intersections which have a pub – a *Kneipe* – on every corner, though there used to be many more. As a local saying puts it, the typical Berlin street crossing has four corners and five corner pubs.

Berlin corner pubs are Spartan institutions. Their interiors are just as uncomfortable as Vienna coffee houses are in their own way, with profoundly uncongenial interior furnishings, despite all kinds of affirmations to the contrary in song and story.

A Berlin corner *Kneipe* looks like this:

The bar is located opposite the entrance door, often positioned diagonally in the square room, and it is referred to as the "counter" in the pub visitor's vocabulary. This counter is the most important fixture of the *Kneipe*; it is the altar on which sacrifices are carried out, and from it the blessings of all religions – ecstacy and intoxication – are bestowed, produced in

18

this case by means of the fermented juices of malt, hops, grain, potatoes, and herbs. Any extra liquid is drained away through the holes of the counter's perforated chromium (occasionally brass) surface. A wet brush for cleaning glasses protrudes from the washing sink – an arrangement which doesn't look very hygienic. In the middle of the counter, standing like a crucifix, is the beer tap, fitted out with two spigots, one for drawing light beer and the other for strong beer. In the base of the counter there are chilling compartments for bottles of liquor. The glasses, at least those visible to the customers, are stored on a wall shelf directly behind the counter.

A really well-stocked corner *Kneipe* has a glass display case to one side of the counter holding cold *Frikadellen*, the fried balls of ground meat which are Berlin's equivalent of the meatball. Increasingly less common are the three large open glass containers set on the cabinet or on the counter itself, which contain pickles, pickled eggs and pickled herring.

In front of the counter there are between two and four stand-up tables with surfaces of pale, scrubbed wood, each with an ashtray in the middle bearing an advertising logo, and a stack of beer coasters.

In a corner *Kneipe*, there is always a poster for the next major football match hanging on a wall near the entrance. Next to the poster, framed or embossed on a wooden plaque, is a silly, sentimental saying set out in rhyming verses.

Among the glasses on the wall shelf behind the counter, a small radio sits broadcasting popular tunes, which are generally ignored by the customers.

If there is enough room, there may also be tables with seating, plus a pinball machine, slot machine, and jukebox. Sometimes there is an additional separate space with card players, a table for the regulars (identified by an appropriate metal sign), and a leather-bound menu listing standard dishes: potato salad, goulash and roast pork

The master of all this, the priest behind the counter-altar, is the proprietor, also the landlord and barman, a character who is often full-bellied and bald, a cigar-smoker, his bare arms planted on the counter surface, on his face the expression of petty, well-fed power.

The clientele is predominantly male. When women are present, they have the air of colourful birds. The men have shoved their caps back against their necks and are talking, gesticulating as they speak. They hold stinking cigarettes in their hands, they try to drown out the others. What might sound like an argument is actually not disagreement but a mixture of sanguinity and bad alcohol. The themes of the day – sport, politics, economics, private matters – are discussed using brash expressions in the barking Berliner accent. If one of the tipplers has drunk too much, to the point of staggering or picking a fight, he will be led to the door (against his protests) where a few compassionate individuals have turned up to accompany the ailing party home.

Once upon a time the corner *Kneipe* in Berlin functioned as a news exchange, centre of communications, pawn shop, and a transfer point for thieves and fences. It was the living memory of the district and a source of strength and revival. But its function changed with the decline of extreme material deprivation. Because the pub's role arose in the depths of misery, its spare furnishings befitting this poverty, it became problematic and pointless over time, with the result that it is gradually dying. Pizzerias, ice cream parlours, and bakeries are moving into its orphaned rooms. Nowadays in the city districts named above, there are many corners, four to each street crossing, which no longer have a *Kneipe* at all.

> Rolf Schneider, *Berlin, ach Berlin* ('Berlin, oh Berlin')
> translated by Susan Thorne

✳ ✳ ✳

And on to the clubbing present with Tobias Rapp.

A new Berlin is being invented here. This is neither the West Berlin of the 70s, the battleground of alternative culture that has left its signature on Ton Steine Scherben records and Seyfried comics, nor the dark Kreuzberg of the 80s, brought to global fame by the radical left, Mayday riots and the Einstürzende Neubauten; the incomparable village in the shade of the Wall that still showed the signs of the burden of history, which Sven Regener describes in his *Berlin Blues*. And it's not the East Berlin of the 90s either, the adventure playground that graduated from gaudy dancers on walls to the backdrop of the Love Parade. It's certainly not the Berlin of the Aggro rappers, the city of no mercy where everyone looks out for himself and crime lies in wait on every street corner. And it has nothing to do with the neo-Wilhelminian fantasies regularly raising their heads from soap-boxes since reunification.

This new Berlin that attracts thousands of clubbing tourists every weekend is the party capital of the Western world. It's a city where the rents are low and the authorities are extremely liberal. Where the reality principle of other cities is suspended in favour of a comprehensive lust principle. No one here really has to work – apart from on some kind of art or music projects – new clubs are opening up all the time, and you actually spend all your time at parties. That especially.

Be it Berghain or Bar 25, Tresor or Watergate – the clubs in the new party zone have made Berlin a place of pop-cultural desire. A city that convinces a lot of people that it's not everywhere that freedom has been sacrificed to security. That you can do things differently. [...]

The Berghain has a number of similarities to a cathedral, not just in terms of architecture. It really is a temple to techno. And whether intentional or not, the long wait in the queue is the prelude to an initiation rite that continues with the inevitable tingling feeling as you shuffle closer to the door. You see people being turned away ahead of you. You try to work out the criteria. It's usually fairly simple: groups of young lads always have it tough, even tougher if they're tourists, heteros or obviously drunk. But these are just probabilities. No one can help laughing when a punk isn't allowed in and shouts out a loud, 'Fuck you, Deutschland! You're a load of tossers! I'm from Vienna!'

You don't want to party with just anyone, so you don't shed a tear for any of those turned away; at the same time you pay for the exclusivity with the risk of not getting in yourself.

Identification with the tormentor mingled with excitement and fear – a whole lot of contradictory emotions come together on the way into Berghain. And it has to be that way; it's the opening tension that lifts when you finally enter the club.

The initiation rite continues with the careful drug check you pass through in the lobby – a ritual cleansing. After that you make your offering, another religious act. Only to land up in the cloakroom, a huge room dotted with sofas and dominated by a giant mural by the Polish artist Piotr Nathan. It's called 'Rituals of Disappearance'. The light architecture underlines the feeling of an initiation: it's dark outside, dimly lit in the lobby, bright in the cloakroom. Once you've stepped over the final threshold and entered the large hall from which you've already heard thumping beats, it suddenly goes dark again. You cross the room, walk up the large steel staircase, and even if you know what you're letting yourself in for in the hours to come, it's always a brief shock to stand by the dancefloor, shrieked at by the music. For a few seconds until your eyes have adapted to the flashing strobes, you stumble around half blind. It's not unlike a slap in the face – not only do you have to shove your way more or less sober through a mass of sweating bodies that have all been here a few hours. The sound waves of the music assault you physically too.

Something to drink to start with.

There are a total of six bars on the three levels. One in the right-hand side room next to the large dancefloor, a room you can imagine like the side aisle of a gothic cathedral. Just as the old master-builders staged a clever interplay of windows and slim columns to emphasise the direct link heavenwards, the spotlights here are set to make the already high ceiling appear even higher. Another bar is slightly hidden to the left of the dancefloor, near the darkrooms. From there, a staircase takes you up to the Panoramabar, slightly smaller and slightly brighter than Berghain itself. Upstairs is house and hetero, downstairs is hard and gay. (...)

You go to Berghain late, sometimes very late: plenty of Berliners now come bright and early in the morning to avoid the tourist rush-hour up to eight a.m. And you stay a long time. Often, you can't quite remember what you did in the hours in between. Not just because you may have been under the influence of various uppers and downers in the meantime – Berghain opens up its own space-time continuum. With other clubs, you go in, stay a while and then go somewhere else. Here, you stay. The rest of the world disappears. In Berghain, you're out of area. You have to be into it. You can feel very lost as the only sober person in the middle of hundreds of people determined to get high. Especially as the place is huge – 3000 people probably get hustled through on a good night. But every room has such a confident underlying feeling for proportion that you feel – well, feeling at home would be overdoing it. Like a fish in water is more like it. You're here precisely because it's not home, after all.

Taking photos is not allowed in Berghain, not even with the camera on your mobile phone. Because a lot of guests don't want to be photographed living out their sexual fantasies, they tell you at the door if you ask. That may well be, but above all every photo would be a bridge to the outside world, a reminder that the outside world even exists. No other club manages to seal itself off from the outside world as perfectly as Berghain. The sun may be high in the sky outside – inside, there is only ever that permanent half-darkness that feels like dawn. [...]

Then you walk around, look around here and there, have a drink, go to the toilet and look out of the window above the urinal onto the strange little stream snaking its way through the wasteland behind the Panoramabar. You meet all kinds of people; some you know, others you don't. While you're waiting to be served at the bar a French guy in his early twenties tells you he's a techno DJ from Montpellier, come to Berlin like the Muslims go on a pilgrimage to Mecca. On the staircase you bump into a huge, half-naked skinhead who tells you with a smile that there's no other club like this, "not even in Russia." Next to the dancefloor you pick up the thread of a conversation on dub reggae you dropped there a couple of weeks ago.

And then you dance. [...]

And at some point it's over; Berghain's a classic club all the way, not an after-hours club. You go to the cloakroom and hand in your token, not a slip of paper with a number on it like everywhere else but a metal tag on a strap – another indication of the club's detail-obsessed perfectionism – that you can hang around your neck or fasten elsewhere. No matter how trashed you may be at the end of the night, you'll always get your jacket back. They think for you here. That's important when no one's quite on the level mentally.

So you stumble out of the door into the light, nod your farewells to the doormen, who you don't actually know but who you somehow feel obliged to; you have to do something to symbolically round off the night. You look around, feel the fresh air on your skin, notice how sweaty you really are, hear the slight whine in your ears mingling with the chirping of the birds, the murmuring of the people sitting around in some corner or other drinking one more beer, and the quiet rattle of the sound system emanating from the building.

Now you can go home. Or stop by at Bar 25.

Tobias Rapp, Lost and Sound. Berlin Techno und der Easyjetset
translated by Katy Derbyshire

✳ ✳ ✳

Journalist Simon Cole is one of the best of Berlin blog-gers. Here's a snippet from one of his entries (more later ...) on the pleasures of the city.

One of the delights of Berlin is just wandering the streets. Today it's Friedrichshain, which is squashed between Karl Marx Allee and the Spree river and one of many sub-centres of this diffuse city. Berlin feels like an ever-shifting urban canvas, and leaving the new style bars behind in the avenues, we find esoteric treasure in the side streets and alleyways.

Like a plane crash survivor, Berlin embraces the now and all the possibilities of existence that brings, yet can never escape the memory of its trauma. Pasted on a garage wall, a riot of CMYK announces another rendezvous of the colourful-but-cool in a venue which will enjoy its moment in the sun, before returning to the tumbledown obscurity from whence it came. This is the city of the *Geheimtip*, the nod and the wink about a bar, cellar or even someone's front room which is temporarily the focus of the fickle and fashionable.

Simon Cole, Berlin blog at Bookpacking.com

✳ ✳ ✳

And finally an article by Wenonah Lyon recalling two contrasting visits to the city and praising the manner in which it has faced up to its problematic past.

The first time I saw Berlin, it was pure Isherwood. The second time, it was Günter Grass. Until we know a place very well, we experience it though filters that direct and interpret what we see; history and literature shaped my Berlin.

I was born in 1942. My understanding of Berlin was formed by two world wars and the Holocaust … almost current affairs, almost not-history. I read German fiction … Thomas Mann, Günter Grass, Bertolt Brecht.

I went to Berlin for the first time in 1996, to give a paper. The last day in Berlin was free, and I bought a day card for all forms of public transportation. I got off at different stations and wandered on foot wherever the U-Bahn took me.

I went into a park and at the back of the park, concealed by trees, saw a public toilet. I opened the door to the WC and saw a man kneeling on the floor. At first, I thought he was a workman. Then I noticed he knelt in front of a young woman sitting on a toilet with a rubber tube tied around her arm. The man was holding a hypodermic needle.

I apologized and said I didn't want to interrupt them.

He said, "No, no, come in."

There were two toilet stalls. It seemed rude to refuse.

So I went in, sat on the toilet and put my credit card and passport in my shoe.

The girl said, "It's very nice that you come in. Most people run away from us and are afraid."

I flushed the toilet and went out. I stopped at the door and looked at them. She looked about eighteen, long brown hair, thin. She spoke beautiful English.

I said, "You be careful, now."

She smiled and said, "You be careful, too."

There's a very good production of *Cabaret* playing in London these days … 2008. The play, like the movie and the short stories they are based on, depends on what lies outside the frame; what the audience brings into the theatre. Performers in the Kit Kat Club, with its S-M, its experiments in sexual diversity and gender-bending, seem like wilful children playing, enjoying shocking the petit bourgeoisie. But we know the Grown-Ups are outside with their crooked-cross armbands.

When I saw the London production of *Cabaret*, I remembered the girl in the park with the needle in her arm. I suppose she thought me naïve. I thought her very young, very innocent.

The second time I went to Berlin was to visit a friend, a Hungarian linguist. She lives in East Berlin and combines an Eastern European sense of humour (black) with a moral compass developed growing up in a Communist state. She was anti-Russian – you do not like people who occupy your country – but is also a good atheist, an antiracist, and sees public service as an obligation. She believes that satisfactory work is necessary for a happy life and is willing to pay high taxes to support those too feckless to work as well as those unfortunates unable to work. She would fit very well in a Rhode Island Unitarian Church if she could be lured anywhere near a place called "Church".

These days, she lives in Berlin and does not need to look for like-minded people. We spent the evenings wandering around her neighbourhood. It's full of art galleries that rent out for a day. Someone, or small group of someones, comes in at midnight, places the work on exhibition, opens in the morning and clears off before midnight so another someone can show their work the next day. There are theatres, cinemas, puppet shows – some are free. The shop windows are full of 4"x6" index cards, advertising things for sale, events, meetings – the Sex Workers' Collective, the Green Party, an anti-racist march, a parents' play group.

Berlin in 2007 must have been very like Berlin in 1929 in its tolerance and delight in creativity. The Berlin of Brecht and Isherwood seemed like a palimpsest under the rich, powerful stable Germany of 2007. There are darker echoes from the past as well. Turkish workers are attacked; a hostel for asylum seekers is burnt down. A Jewish cemetery has gravestones over-turned and painted with swastikas.

My friend worked during the day so I bought a 72-hour public transportation pass and went out alone. The first day, I went to Friedrichstrasse and walked down Unter den Linden; Imperial Berlin before the First World War, with museums and universities. I went to Checkpoint Charlie, a major tourist attraction, with all sorts of tat for sale. The Brandenburg Gate is very triumphal and the Reichstag is almost as beautiful as the British Houses of Parliament. Stone recreated the nineteenth and twentieth centuries.

The next day I went to Alexanderplatz and saw cinema rather than literature or history. I left the subway and blundered around a grey warren full of people knowing where they were going and why. Occasionally, people like me, strangers, bewildered, would ask me where something was. Sometimes I even knew – could point in a direction because I had been lost there.

Saturday, I used the working underground Alexanderplatz. I'm not sure how many levels Alexanderplatz-the-train-station has. At least three. But probably more. It was like falling into a computer game or a Grimm fairy tale. I took the train to Kurfurstendamm, the opposite of Alexanderplatz.

When I left the underground, I saw a plaque. Something in German, then, under it, a list of all the concentration camps. Just names.

The surrounding area was full of expensive stores, including the KaDeWe Department Store. My friend told me I must visit this store. Before the Wall fell, this was unique, the finest department store in West Berlin. Now, it's like Harrod's in London or Fenwick's in Canterbury or Nordstrom's in San Francisco: the same upmarket labels were arranged in little boutique-like sections of a floor, globalization in action.

Sunday, I went back to Alexanderplatz and left the train station for the area around. I went out onto the Platz, a great grey slab with a grey sky, both – if I turned to the right – going on and on. There were, on the edges, the usual multi-nationals. But one can turn one's back on them. I walked down Rathausstrasse and cut across the park. I sat on a park bench on a grey day in the middle of a lawn of soft green grass and the last of the roses and listened to a hurdy gurdy. Then to the DDR Museum Berlin. It's a very good folk museum, showing life as it was in East Berlin before re-unification. It was a mix of good and bad. Like everything. Do people from the old East Germany have any regrets, I wonder? Getting rid of an occupying force, the Soviets, of course, rejoice, rejoice ... but giving up East Germany?

The appeal of Communism, Socialism and the liberal demo-cratic welfare state is essentially moral and ethical. One might argue that capitalism is more efficient, more effective, but there is no moral or ethical argument to be made. How can you seriously argue that it is more important for rich people to have lots of money than poor people to have lots of food? Capitalism essentially makes political economy a moral free zone. Morality becomes an attribute of the private, personal sphere and has no role in public life. Germany fascinates me because it demonstrates so many of the moral choices of my era, my twentieth century, my twenty-first century. The central event of the 20th century, I think, was the Holocaust. It is central because it shows what we can do. It is not important that it occurred in Germany – it is important that it happened in a major European country, a civilized place, one that we can't dismiss. Technological progress does not involve ethical progress. The Holocaust is an example of what we can do – any of us.

In Germany in 1930, a small minority, I suspect, wanted actively to get rid of Jews, homosexuals, gypsies, communists. Another small minority risked themselves to protest or defend ... Most people were willing to accept anything for personal security. Isherwood described it. Grass wrote about the result; what happened after ...

History: the lesson of the twentieth century is that people in a group are capable of great evil – sometimes because they're afraid, sometimes because they're greedy, sometimes, I fear, because killing can become trivial and the dead are faceless.

If we don't understand, we can't prevent ... I think the Germany of my generation turned and faced their dead. Very few Americans of my generation faced their own dead in Vietnam.

Our grandchildren (German and American), are impatient with the Holocaust and Vietnam. It happened a long time ago and has nothing to do with them. They ignore history; perhaps literature and art can teach them differently.

Wenonah Lyon, 'The first time I saw Berlin ... '

Out and About

When you're out and about in Berlin, you can never, ever forget the city's history – as contemporary Dutch author Cees Nooteboom reflects at the opening of his novel All Souls' Day. *We join him in a ramble around the city, starting close to one of its best book shops.*

Arthur Daane was several steps away from Schoeller's Bookstore before he realized that a word had stuck in his head and that he had already translated it into his own language. His brain had registered the German word for history – *Geschichte* – but quickly turned it into the Dutch *geschiedenis*. Somehow it sounded less ominous in Dutch. He wondered if that was because of the last three letters, the suffix *nis*, which also meant "niche". A strange word. Short. Not mean and curt, as short words could be, but comforting. After all, a niche was a place to hide in, a place to find hidden things. Other languages didn't have that. He began to walk faster, hoping to rid himself of the word that way, but his little ploy didn't work, not here, not in this city, for every inch of Berlin was steeped in history. [...]

He turned around, which meant no to Kurfürstendammn, yes to Savignyplatz. It also meant passing Schoeller's again. [...]

The snow had started coming down faster. That's what happened when you worked with cameras, he thought – you were constantly looking at yourself when you walked. Not so much out of vanity as amazement. Amazement mixed with, well ... [...]

In one long sweep the camera registered Berlin's snow-covered Knesebeckstrasse, the majestic houses, the handful of pedestrians with their shoulders hunched against the snow. And he was one of them. That's what it was all about – the pure coincidence of that particular moment. The lone figure heading down the street, past Schoeler's Bookstore, past the photo gallery, that's you. [...]

At the corner of Savignyplatz he was almost blown off his feet by a sudden snow flurry. This was getting serious. A continental climate. Another reason he liked Berlin. It always made him feel that he was in the middle of a vast plain stretching deep into the heart of Russia. Berlin, Warsaw, Moscow – mere stops along the way.

He wasn't wearing gloves, and his fingers were feeling frozen. [...]

At the corner of Kantstrasse the light was red. He looked to the left, to the right, didn't see any cars, and was tempted to cross, but stayed where he was, feeling his body process contradictory commands: an odd kind of neural wave going to the wrong leg, so that one foot stayed on the curb while the other stepped off it. Through the snow he watched the silent group of people waiting on the other side of the crosswalk. At moments like these the difference between the Dutch and the Germans was plainly manifest. As a pedestrian in Amsterdam, you were an idiot if you didn't cross on red, and here you were one if you did, something the Germans didn't hesitate to point out: "Tsk, tsk, there goes another suicidal maniac."

He had asked Victor, a Dutch sculptor now living in Berlin, what he did when there were no cars in sight.,

"I cross the street, except when there are children around. Got to set a good example, and all that."

As for himself, he had decided to make use of those odd, empty moments by doing what he called "instant meditation." In Amsterdam no self-respecting bicyclist had headlights, stopped on red, or went the right way down a one-way street. Dutch people always wanted to decide for themselves whether or not a rule applied to them – a mixture of Protestantism and anarchy that produced a stubborn kind of chaos. […]

The light turned green. The six snowy figures on the other side of the street simultaneously set themselves in motion. Okay, you shouldn't generalize, but there is such a thing as a national character. How had it come about?

"From history," Erna had said.

What he found so fascinating about the idea of history was that it was based on a chemical compound of fate, chance, and design. The combination of these three elements produced a chain of events that produced another chain of events, which were said to be inevitable, or random, or to happen according to a secret plan that was not yet known to us, though by now things were getting pretty esoteric.

For a moment he considered going into the Tintenmaus to read the paper. At least it would be warm inside.

Cees Nooteboom, *All Souls' Day*
translated by Susan Massotty

* * *

In the first novel of American Berlin resident Anna Winger, Hope, newly arrived in the city, aims to get to know it through daily tours using the underground. But this turns into a cautionary tale: her naïve assumptions about travel being 'free' – after all, there are no ticket-barriers on the U-Bahn, nothing to stop you just walking into the station and onto a train – turn

*out to be ill-founded. And having abused the 'honour
system', she must pay the price … (You have been
warned!)*

Most days, Hope waited until rush hour was over to set out on
her trips around the city. Compared to what she had been used
to in Manhattan, rush hour in Berlin wasn't even that bad. On
the occasions that she set out too early or came home too late,
she still almost always got a seat on the subway. […]

Although she never set out without a plan, she knew that
another person (Dave, for example) might have said that her travelling lacked an organizing principle, might have suggested that
instead she make a list of important attractions or at least pick a
theme: graveyards, museums, modern architecture, flea markets,
parks designed by someone famous, World War II battle sites,
Cold War battle sites, soccer stadiums. But he would be missing
the point. The point was to figure out where she was. The point,
she thought, was to let the city unfold on its own. […]

As the U-Bahn pulled up above ground, Hope blinked into
the daylight thinking that it was possible to see every layer
of the city's history at once in any direction. A drive through
Berlin was like visiting a grand archaeological site, but unlike
that of a civilization from thousands of years ago – already
dug up and dusted off, set aside at a clinical distance – this one
was fully in use; it was up to visitors to excavate the remains,
to make sense of it for themselves. In New York, as soon as
one building came down, another went up so quickly as to
completely obliterate the memory of what had been there
before. In the other European cities, the past was glorified, the
architecture spruced up for tourists to the point of caricature.
But here, nobody seemed to be in any hurry one way or the
other. Buildings had been bombed and the city had been ripped
apart, but years later holes remained all over the place without
explanation or apparent concern. The city moved forward with
a lack of vanity that she found relaxing. […]

It was during one of the few crowded moments in the afternoon when the police came onto the train. Hope was standing up at the time, holding on, when she noticed a plainclothes man and woman, with official-looking badges hanging around their necks, making their way through from the other end of the car. The man was middle-aged and the woman was younger. As they addressed the passengers, each one nervously but obediently produced a little piece of paper for their inspection. One by one they looked closely at the papers, then passed them back. They appeared to be tickets of some kind, although unlike any other subway ticket or pass Hope had seen before. Most apparently passed muster, but those passengers in possession of the wrong kind of paper were rounded up by the door. After a while the man stayed back to guard the prisoners and only the woman continued up the aisle. The train, which had been loud with conversation at the previous stop, had fallen silent. People waited with their hands in their laps, little papers in their hands. Hope fished around in her pockets automatically, though she knew she didn't have a ticket because she didn't even know she needed a ticket. The understanding that the subway was free wasn't the only reason she had been riding it every day, but the sheer generosity of it had been very appealing. It had made her feel welcome, and the sudden realization that she had been wrong about this made her feel queasy. She backed herself into the closed doors at the other end of the car.

"*Fahrkarte*," said the female cop when she reached Hope.

Her eyes were a grayish-blue and small, her thin lips pursed. When Hope failed either to produce a ticket or to explain herself, she took her arm as if to pull her toward the other prisoners, but just then the doors opened and the crowd pushed past them in both directions. Hope pulled her arm free and backed onto the platform at Friedrichstrasse station, turned at the top of the stairs and ran down them.

It was drizzling outside the station. She ran up the sidewalk without looking back, intoxicated by the flight forward. She ran past the traffic that marked the northern end of Friedrichstrasse, past the construction sites and empty spaces, through puddles cast the murky yellow of streetlights at dusk, feeling the distance left behind by each footstep. But at the first corner past the station a hand, then two, landed on her back; then an arm around her waist. The cop, who had been chasing her, now hugged her from behind and Hope, no longer able to move forward, collapsed against her, panting.

"Where is your ticket?" She spoke basic, if heavily accented, English. "No good to run."

She released Hope from the hug but held on to one wrist.

"I didn't know I needed a ticket."

"There machines in every station."

"But no turnstiles." Her cheeks were wet. "Nobody checks."

"I check."

"Now? I've been riding the subway every day for ten days."

"Lucky for you, then. You should have paid. We have honour system here. Please show me your passport."

"An honour system for the subway," said Hope. "That's just a trap."

She was crying now. The rain came down harder.

"I don't have my passport with me."

"It is illegal to go out without identification."

"Illegal?"

Hope stared at the policewoman through a thick lens of tears, thinking that if they took her to jail and she were allowed one phone call, she would call Walter to bail her out, not Dave. It wasn't that Dave couldn't successfully negotiate with the German police; actually, he would relish the opportunity. It was that afterward he would ask her too many questions that she couldn't answer, while Walter would ask her none at all. He would bring a towel to dry her hair. He would take her home and make her tea.

"Then you pay sixty marks now." The policewoman pulled an official-looking pad of paper out of her pocket, rounding her body over it to protect it from the rain. "Fare is four. Penalty is sixty. Since you have not identification I cannot send you a bill. You must pay now."

"That's fifteen times the fare."

"You ride for long time already free. Penalty sixty."

"That's too much."

"This is a free country now. Be lucky. We have honour system now. Next time you buy ticket or worse."

She reached deftly for Hope's handbag and pulled out a pack of gum, a pen, Dave's copy of *Weimar Culture*. It was a small, attractive, yellow book; raindrops stained the cover immediately.

"You can't just go through my bag like that."

The policewoman removed a brown leather wallet from the bag, opened it, took out sixty marks and handed it back to Hope, along with the bag itself. Then she leaned over her pad and wrote out a receipt.

"I am the police," she said. "I do whatever I want."

Anna Winger, *This Must Be The Place*

✳ ✳ ✳

Someone else who enjoys the Berlin trains is the narrator of Chloe Aridjis' Book of Clouds.

In order to reach Savignyplatz, where the historian lived, I had to take the S-Bahn from Alexanderplatz, a seven-minute tram ride from my new home. Apart from the station itself with its grand steel arch and vintage red sign, I was inexplicably drawn to the 365-meter television tower, which, now that I was living back in the eastern part of the city, would serve as my beacon. Whenever I lost my way I'd need only search the sky for the massive metal sphere impaled on the tapering cement column and know that somewhere in its shadow lay my home.

As for the S-Bahn, it too was a wondrous thing, especially its elevated routes, and during each ride I'd fall into that limbo between origin and destination where thoughts are churned out in time with the wheels of the train but with far less purpose and linearity. It wasn't just the trancelike glide of the wheels, however, or the view out the window. It was the announcer's voice. I preferred this recorded voice to any other voice I had heard in my life, especially on days when I felt disconnected from the city, attached by the thinnest of strings.

"*Nächste Station: Friedrichstraße.*"

All it took were a few words to retighten the bond.

"*Ausstieg links,*" the announcer would add for those ignorant of which side to disembark.

There was a spring to his utterances, a buoyancy packed and delivered in anticipation of every stop, and I would put away my book or newspaper and sit back and listen to the stations as they were rolled off, one by one, uninterrupted – that is, if other presences didn't interfere, such as plainclothes ticket inspectors or junkie musicians, their pleas for attention like dark blood clots in the city's circulation.

Chloe Aridjis, *Book of Clouds*

❋ ❋ ❋

And so to some of the city's most famous sights. First, in the company of Cees Nooteboom, a brief winter visit to the exquisite Charlottenberg Palace.

He neared the vanilla walls of Charlottenburg Palace. The cloakroom attendant held his coat as if it had dog shit on it. He peered through the windows in the back, which looked out over the highly regimented ornamental gardens. The circular fountain that children sailed their boats in during the summer wasn't working now. Instead, a hopeless half-erection of gray ice was hanging crookedly from the spout. The path was lined with bushes in planters, now covered up against the winter cold – snowmen in battle array. A bit farther, where Prussian order had less of a hold on nature, tall trees stood like sentries, while an army of greyish black ravens flew back and forth.

Cees Nooteboom, *All Souls' Day*
translated by Susan Massotty

* * *

Playwright David Hare wonders if the reunification of Berlin has really turned out to be 'the greatest architectural opportunity of the century' as was predicted. Here he takes us to one of the city's most recent and now world-famous sights.

Admittedly, there is the famous Memorial to the Murdered Jews of Europe, over which views are much more evenly divided. What other nation, asks the novelist Martin Walser, as if his patience were finally snapping after sixty years, feels the need to memorialise its own disgrace? 2,711 identical concrete slabs are laid out over an area of 204,400 square feet. A decision was made and approved: no text, no images. Why not? Because anything the architect might want to say, any decoration he might wish to add would be – hey! What was it Adorno said? – 'Too much and not enough.'

'I like to think people will use it for short cuts,' said the architect Peter Eisenman when the Memorial was opened in 2005. At the start he'd even encouraged people to leave graffiti on the bare stones, slow, it seems, to realise just what the graffiti were likely to be. But the chemical agent he then used to make the Memorial graffiti-proof turned out to be made by a company called Degussa, which was part of a group with another company called Degesch, who had, in their time, manufactured the gas Zyklon B.

Oh yes, it's the usual human mess. Hard to disentangle the past, isn't it? The right intentions? The wrong result? In that sense, Berlin's a truer city than most, truer because it's a city without set pieces. Where are the great views? The great vistas? What hill can you climb and see it all?

David Hare, *Berlin*

* * *

And Chloe Aridjis takes us through the powerful experience of visiting the same memorial at night.

"Let's go somewhere else," he said at around midnight.

The moon was nearly full that night, and because it was nearly full there was only one place, Jonas said, one place we had to visit.

We walked down Unter den Linden, the trees atwinkle with white holiday lights, and past the regally lit Brandenburg Gate, a different creature from that evening in 1986, then turned left before arriving at a sea of upright concrete slabs, which I recognized immediately as the new Holocaust memorial. I had yet to visit the place but had read about the controversy surrounding it, some people saying it was too vulnerable and exposed, others complaining it was only dedicated to the murdered Jews and not to other victims of the Nazis, others criticizing the barrenness of the place and its lack of so-called aesthetic principles, and yet others said it was *too* aestheticized and didactic. Each time there was a new memorial voices of all tenors would start clamouring, always in disagreement, even about whether these monuments were necessary in the first place.

Once inside the new memorial, the space, which at first seemed so open and exposed, closed in on us with each step we took, the 2711 concrete slabs like a stalled army converging from all sides. Despite the hundreds of possible exits and entrances it was hard not to feel an immediate wave of claustrophobia and disorientation, and wherever I looked I saw dark pillars, some only half a meter high, others looming overhead. The sloping ground made it hard to secure a foothold and every few meters I found myself grabbing onto the slabs to steady myself, although I had the feeling that at any moment they might treacherously tilt away. It was the topography of the place that threw me off balance, not the tequila from the bar, and before long everything was undulating and vertiginous and the only steady presence was the moon, whose beams washed the stones, skimmed the tops and dissolved.

The plinths seemed to lean in a million directions as I followed Jonas, keeping an eye on his black cap lest the rest of him disappear. I couldn't even fathom whether our movements were upward or downward since the ground robbed me of any surety. It was like walking among 2711 upended sarcophagi, 2711 souls awaiting judgment, in an ad hoc graveyard devoid of markings or inscriptions.

Chloe Aridjis, *Book of Clouds*

* * *

Another moving recognition of the city's destructive past – the site where Nazi enthusiasts made bonfires out of books – is visited by author and journalist Salil Tripathi.

On a warm night in Berlin in early September, my friend Kean Wong, a Malaysian writer, and I walked along a strangely quiet avenue, where the only sound you could hear was the tinkling bells of bicycles. We were headed towards Bebelplatz, an open square surrounded by imposing buildings: on one side the sturdy Faculty of Justice, on the other, an officious building wrapped by a *tromp l'oeil* exterior, advertising an organic lemonade. A bank and a hotel formed the third side of the square, and the fourth was the opening to Unter den Linden, beyond which lay the university.

The glow from the ground was visible, unmistakeable. It cast a straight halo, pointing skywards, looking like the steady flame of an eternal candle. The closer you got, the more granular the image became and what seemed like a straight cone revealed its true self: the particles were not marching in a straight line, following orders; they continued their random Brownian motion.

While the light was not blinding in its intensity, it was sharp and bright. When you looked through the glass, the stark whiteness hit you square in the eyes. It was like being deafened by eloquent silence, if such a thing is possible. Or being blinded by the afterglow of luminosity that mortal flames could not extinguish. The glow was straight, as if trying to impose symmetry on an amorphous mass of particles.

There was a time when such symmetry was not an illusion but a fearsome manifestation of an imperial ambition. We were at the site where, a little more than 75 years ago in May, Adolf Hitler's youth ransacked libraries, brought books – by one count, more than 20,000 – and made a bonfire. Among the authors whose works they turned to ashes were Thomas Mann, Erich Maria Remarque, Karl Marx and Heinrich Heine.

The choice of Heine was particularly poignant. In his 1821 play *Almansor*, Heine had written: "Das war ein Vorspiel nur. Dort, wo man Bücher verbrennt, verbrennt man am Ende auch Menschen" ('That was mere foreplay. Where they have burnt books, they will end in burning human beings.')

When you looked under the square glass – that source of light – you saw rows of empty bookshelves in white. At first glance, they looked cheap and kitschy, the kind you can buy at Ikea and assemble within an hour. They acquired value only when filled. And the Nazi youth had destroyed the very books that gave meaning to those shelves.

The Nazi bonfire was not some insane Taliban escapade, where they burnt any book that was not the Quran. The Nazi youth burnt specific books by specific authors – if they were Jewish, Socialist or Communist. And Heine was prescient about what would happen in his country a century later: five years after the book burning, in November 1938, on a single night, Nazi youth destroyed hundreds of synagogues in Germany. World War II started 10 months later; the Holocaust and its horrors – where they burnt people – were revealed six years later.

You could disagree with a book, argue with it, challenge it, and defy it. But burn it? Germany was the culture of Mann and Schopenhauer, of Kant and Hegel, Nietzsche and Goethe. Ideas clashed with each other and wisdom flourished.

But the Nazi youth wanted to streamline ideas and force them to march in one specific way. If you stepped out, if you looked different or thought differently, you were struck down. They wanted to tear down the past they did not like.

But we are an ingenious lot. If forced to burn our words and thoughts, as the Nazis tried at Bebelplatz, we find other ways to remember them. The Soviet Union could not silence Solzhenitsyn; Suharto's Indonesia could not keep Pramoedya Ananta Toer quiet. Samizdat literature was born from the principle that when you don't trust the printed word, you believe in the spoken word.

Our desire to remember vanquishes their insistence that we forget. In Ray Bradbury's novel *Fahrenheit 451* (the temperature at which paper burns), after the dystopian society has burnt all possible books, we come across an island where men and women talk to themselves, reciting words from books that have been burnt, remembering them so they don't disappear from our collective consciousness.

Later that night, Kean took me to another part of Berlin and showed me another commemoration – the plaques in the city's sidewalks. The sculptor Gunter Demnig has been going around German cities, hammering in tiny plaques with names of former Jewish residents who lived on particular streets and in specific homes, fixing the date they were taken away and, if known, the date of their passing in a death camp.

They stand apart on the street, but only slightly; they look like stumbling blocks, but only marginally; but that's Demnig's point. He calls them *Stolpersteine*, German for stumbling block. It is an individual's tribute against collective madness, a memorial against the folly, giving dignity to those who died in anonymity.

At Bebelplatz, many Germans burnt the thoughts of fine thinkers. Burning people was the next step. In the same city, one man has been going round placing plaques, remembering them. Those plaques give the city its permanence, its solidity, its continuity.

At Bebelplatz, the bookshelves are empty – the empty space reminding us of what Germany lost. By fixing those plaques, Demnig shows how Germany is becoming whole again.

Salil Triphati, 'Learning by the book'

✳ ✳ ✳

Alexanderplatz (or 'the Alex') is one of the many locations that changed drastically in the course of the twentieth century. Even in the 1920s it was undergoing radical transformation for the construction of the underground system – recorded here in one of the most famous Berlin novels, Alfred Döblin's Berlin Alexanderplatz. *(It's worth at least sampling Fassbinder's 15½-hour film of the novel.)*

On the Alexanderplatz they are tearing up the road-bed for the underground. People walk on planks. The tram-cars pass over the square up Alexanderstrasse through Münzstrasse to the Rosenthaler Tor. To the right and left are streets. House follows house along the streets. They are full of men and women from cellar to garret. On the ground floor are shops.

Liquor shops, restaurants, fruit and vegetable stores, groceries and delicatessen, moving business, painting and decorating, manufacture of ladies' wear, flour and mill materials, automobile garage, extinguisher company: the superiority of the small motor fire extinguisher lies in its simple construction, easy service, small weight, small size. – German fellow-citizens, never has a people been deceived more ignominiously, never has a nation been betrayed more ignominiously and more unjustly than the German people. Do you remember how Scheidemann promised us peace, liberty, and bread from the window of the Reichstag on November 9, 1918? And how has that promise been kept? – Drainage equipment, window-cleaning company, sleep is medicine, Steiner's Paradise Bed. – Book-shop, the library of the modern man, our collected works of leading poets and thinkers compose the library of the modern man. They are the great representatives of the intellectual life of Europe – The Tenants' Protection Law is a scrap of paper. Rents increase steadily. The professional middle-class is being put on the street and strangled. [...]

Boom, boom, the steam pile-driver thumps in front of Aschinger's on the Alex. It's one storey high, and drives the stakes into the ground as if they were nothing at all.

Icy air, February. People walk in overcoats. Whoever has a fur coat wears it, whoever hasn't, doesn't wear it. The women have on thin stockings and are freezing, of course, but they look nice. The tramps have disappeared with the cold. When it gets warmer, they'll stick their noses out again. In the meantime they nip a double ration of brandy, but don't ask me what kind of brandy, nobody would want to swim in it, not even a corpse.

Boom, boom, the steam pile-driver batters away on the Alex. [...]

Across the street they are tearing down everything, all the houses along the city railroad, wonder where they get the money from, the city of Berlin is rich, and we pay the taxes. [...]

Alfred Döblin, *Berlin Alexanderplatz*
translated by Eugene Jolas

* * *

*The bombing of much of 'the Alex' during the Second
World War led to a massive rebuilding programme
during the Soviet era – including the construction of the
iconic television tower which has become inescapably
identified with the Berlin skyline. Like many of the city's
open spaces, today's Alexanderplatz is annually taken
over, from late November, by one of the ubiquitous
German Christmas markets where hot spiced wine and
cheerful lights and colours provide some welcome relief
from the bleak and bitter cold of a Berlin winter.*

I waited until the next day of clement weather – we'd had a spell
of crystalline skies but piercingly chilly afternoons – and alighted
from the tram at Alexanderplatz, now the site of one of the dozens
of Christmas markets that had recently appeared across the city.
Starting in late November these markets would spring up in every
square and empty lot, and here, to accompany the competing
stands of gluhwein, sausages and kitschy carved ornaments, an ice
rink blasting disco music had been set up in front of the department store. The last of the cranes had been carted off, clearing the
space for something even less scenic, I was sorry to see, for the rink
was not only a repugnant sight, dozens of red-nosed kids elbowing
ahead of one other, shoving and screaming and falling on their
rumps, but with its loud, tinny music it was also an assault on the
ears, turning the entire square into a cheap amusement park. […]

In addition to the Christmas markets, winter made itself felt
in other ways. Marzipan bears with raisin eyes winked from
the windows of my bakery. The trams filled with bronchial
coughs and sneezes programmed to erupt just as the name of
each stop was announced. In anticipation of the early dusk the
streetlights hummed on at ten past four. Some people put up
a fight and clung to their autumn wardrobe, but for the most
part there was a proliferation of hats and coats and gloves.

Chloe Aridjis, *Book of Clouds*

* * *

At the Christmas Market by the Gedächtniskirche, vendors were already heating up their grills. The greasy smell of bratwurst came into the car. Tourists were eating kale and bacon for breakfast. The working stiffs at the Europa Center hurried into work in beige overcoats. The mothers soldiered up the sidewalk in groups of two or three, while tucked deep into their strollers, the next generation watched the storm clouds gathering overhead, breathing in Berlin's fresh winter air like a drug.

Anna Winger, *This Must Be The Place*

* * *

Cold wind with the scent of brown coal on it drives sleet across the asphalt and generates a rustling in the trees, old oaks, giant horse chestnuts, the hollows and holes filled in with concrete. Where a street lamp stretches into the branches, the leaves have stayed hanging on and are still green here and there.

Dark too the kiosk on the corner, but the newsagent had already opened up, reached into the delivery box and was piling the news into his lean-to. On the board in front of the hatch was a thermos flask, and next to the cashbox for the float were his sandwiches for breakfast, a gold-wrapped chocolate perched on top. Behind the brush of the little park a car door slammed. An ambulance drove across Urbanstrasse. No light inside.

'Holy moley,' said the man and rubbed his hands together. He was wearing a hat with earflaps. 'It's cold enough to freeze your parts off. And they say the climate's warming up. I reckon the Siberian ice wind's coming over here.' [...]

DeLoo crossed the road by the shut-down fountain, boarded up for the winter, and pushed open the door of the café. A rush of heat, cigarette smoke and the stink of the oil heater took his breath away a moment. Behind the waist-level dividing wall, the pots full of gravel and silk flowers, quiet voices, a murmur of heavy tongues. But at the front, at the standing tables and fruit machines, no one left. The counter was almost cleared out; only two plates with a dab of pasta salad and a skinless chicken drumstick were left behind the glass. Next to the kebab spit, coffee steamed away in a bulbous pot, and a couple of Turkish pastry rolls seemed to be sweating honey.

Hannelore threw the net from the deep fryer into the sink and turned around. In her mid-forties and not very tall, she had the doughy pale skin of a native Berliner, hair dull as straw and shadowed, slightly protruding eyes in which one thought one read sheer horror whenever she laughed at a joke. She never said hello, only saying what was absolutely necessary – 'Mayonnaise? Ketchup? Roll?' – and even now, two vertical wrinkles above the base of her nose, she just raised her chin. 'What?'

He gestured at the coffee. She looked at the clock on the wall, reached into the shelf and blew something out of the Friesian-patterned mug before she filled it up. To the rim. With her tea towel, she wiped the drips from its base and put it down on the coin DeLoo had placed on the counter for her, and turned back to the sink. [...]

Thin snow on the pavements by the canal, between the spokes of the market stalls, and not a tyre mark, not a foot-print anywhere. DeLoo paused on the bridge, leaning on the old balustrade, leaves of steel, where the flakes fell past him to the depths without generating the slightest quiver on the smooth black water; but between the blocks howled the wind and drove them almost horizontally across the street.

Ralf Rothmann, *Hitze* ('Heat')
translated by Katy Derbyshire

This extract from Anna Funder's Stasiland *combines the Berlin cold, the television tower and a view of the famous East Berlin 'Palast der Republik' which, while awaiting its fate, became a lively centre for 'creative' events – gigs of every kind, from Wagner to 'Riverdance' ... (once they'd removed the asbestos, that is).*

I take my cup to the living-room window. In the park there is snow on the ground and the trees, light on light. My breath mixes with coffee steam on the glass. I wipe it away. In the distance lies the city, the television tower at Alexanderplatz like an oversized Christmas bauble, blinking blue.

I can't see it but I know that just near there, on the site of the old Palace of the Prussian Kings pulled down by the Communists, is the parliament building of the GDR, the Palast der Republik. It is brown and plastic-looking, full of asbestos, and all shut up. It is not clear whether the fence around it is to protect it from people who would like to express what they thought of the regime, or to protect the people from the Palast, for health reasons. The structure is one long rectangular metal frame, made up of smaller rectangles of brown-tinted mirror glass. When you look at it you can't see in. Instead the outside world and everything in it is reflected in a bent and brown way. In there, dreams were turned into words, decisions made, announcements applauded, backs slapped. In there could be a whole other world, time could warp and you could disappear.

Like so many things here, no-one can decide whether to make the Palast der Republik into a memorial warning from the past, or to get rid of it altogether and go into the future unburdened of everything, except the risk of doing it all again. Nearby, Hitler's bunker has been uncovered in building works. No-one could decide about that either – a memorial could become a shrine for neo-Nazis, but to erase it altogether might signal forgetting, or denial. In the end, the bunker was reburied just as it was. The mayor said, perhaps in *another* fifty years people would be able to decide what to do. To remember or forget – which is healthier? To demolish it or to fence it off? To dig it up, or leave it to lie in the ground?

Anna Funder, Stasiland

❊ ❊ ❊

The Palast der Republik – now demolished – was just one among hundreds of venues all over Berlin (with the highest concentration possibly in the Mitte district) hosting music, readings, poetry slams, multimedia events and just about any kind of entertainment you can dream up. How to cope with this wealth of opportunities? Christiane Rösinger offers some advice on 'intelligent going-out' ...

In this situation, as so often, things were better in the old days; almost everyone ran a club, a bar disguised as a gallery or some kind of dive, at least one night a week; the rest of the week everyone visited each other, and everyone drank for free at each other's places.

The net effect was that you never paid for drinks, and of course you made nothing running the bars either, but everything equalled itself out in the nicest possible way. Everyone was always everywhere and no-one had to pay.

Today things are very different; the industry has been professionalized.

Simply drinking less is clearly not an option, and the invention born of youthful necessity (smuggling plastic bags into the disco, containing alcohol of supermarket origin) somehow seems sad when you are over eighteen. And with so-called 'preheating' – imbibing alcoholic beverages at home in order to set out for the night with a head-start – things can quickly go downhill. So how can you carry on living it up yet still economize? There are only two alternatives: staying at home, or intelligent going out.

Intelligent going out begins with merciless self-examination: Do I really want to see this punishing band tonight, this DJ no-one has heard of?

Do I really want to pay to get into a stuffy room and stand around consuming lukewarm, over-expensive badly-served drinks? If the answer is no, the self-analysis continues. What is it which is really important to me? The answer is, going out, standing around on the street, meeting people, and talking.

And here the summer months provide countless opportunities.

You will recall the ancient wisdom which observes that standing outside the venue is the real going out. Next to every cool underground bar, electro club and rock cellar in this city is a take-away selling beer, a lonely Cuban bodega or a dive bar. There you can set up camp and prove that people who are content in themselves can establish a scene anywhere, without having to rely on sceny venues.

You get something to drink and say hello to everyone going past; some of them join you. The people who leave early tell you what the concert/DJ/art installation was like and thus you experience the whole evening *en passant*, have company, and miss nothing.

When it comes to illegal pharmaceuticals, to avoid having to tighten your belt you might want to exploit the benefits of whole-sale ordering or the advantages of bulk-buying co-operatives.

With a friendly 'do you have a cigarette? My packet got stuck in the machine,' much unnecessary nicotine expenditure can be avoided.

Anyone seeking to save even more and go out even more intelligently, should stay at home, because anyone who watches television is never alone; the daily series in particular lend our empty days meaning and form, rendering going out super-fluous.

Christiane Rösinger, *Das schöne Leben* ('A Nice Life')
translated by Steph Morris

✳ ✳ ✳

*Berlin is full of contrasts, and not too far away from
the trendy venues of Mitte, in the middle section of
the Tiergarten – the green lung in the middle of Berlin
– is a place without clubs or poetry: just a shopping
paradise for the poor.*

Straight through the middle of the part of Tiergarten by the
name of Moabit runs the tolerably famous Turmstrasse, a
leisure and shopping paradise for the poor, with three porn
cinemas, four amusement arcades, Penny and Plus supermarkets, a Rudis Resterampe seconds store and two Aldis.

In October last year, on one of the mellow autumn days so
frequent in Berlin, I crossed this very Turmstrasse rather late
in the morning towards Aldi II; and there was plenty going
on there again. Music played from wide-open windows, Elvis
and Turkish male choirs, bikes dozed in the sun outside the
copy centre, one coach lined up after the next, not a parking
space between them. Out of Aldi wound the languid tail of a
snake of people, children sucking at colourful coke cans, dogs
straining and wailing at lampposts, bollards and post boxes
where their owners had tethered them. On the sill in front of
the window, plastered from inside with special offer posters,
sat – probably not *very* comfortably – three older ladies in
leisure outfits, observing the goings-on: people scurrying out
of the side exit of Aldi, pulled crooked by big angular plastic
bags, who – not without a certain measure of acrobatic skill –
manoeuvred unwieldy shopping trolleys piled high with dozens
and dozens of instant lemon tea jars and sangria tetra packs to
the coaches.

'Can't get in without a Polish passport,' said the one with
grey curls, dressed in an orange sweatshirt over an azure blue
pleated skirt. 'They could at least buy oats for their kids out
there in the woods,' answered the chubby one with the giant
butterfly bead appliqué on the front of her yellow angora dress.

'Tastes terrible, that sticky Spanish rubbish,' announced the grey-curled one, pointing a finger at the Sangria packs. 'Mind you, we didn't mind it twenty years ago,' commented the third woman in a deep, conciliatory tone, swathed in a flapping-sleeved, black something up to her pointed chin, and added with a sigh:

'Alright, I'll get us *one* beer.'

The ladies removed their behinds from the windowsill, briefly blocking the trolleys' path, each one of them dividing the queue in three different places, and disappeared from my view – turning around the corner of Turmstrasse and Gotzkowskystrasse one after another.

Katja Lange-Müller, 'Sklavendreieck' in
Neues aus der Heimat ("The Slave Triangle" in 'News from home')
translated by Katy Derbyshire

✳ ✳ ✳

Certain districts of Berlin have developed their own special identities and reputations. We visit some of them in the company of Philip Hensher and Paul Verhaeghen.

Kreuzberg was a place more talked about, perhaps, than lived in; it was a district better known to most Germans than whole towns twice the size. [...]

But even within the bounds of Kreuzberg, Kreuzberg was a place more talked about than real, somehow; the people who walked in the Oranienstrasse and sat in the Oranienstrasse bars seemed, if you judged by their conversation, to think that the streets might vanish, might never have existed, without the constant evoking of the name of the square mile or so. An overheard snatch of conversation between strangers always offered the word *Kreuzberg*, brought in at some length; a town of lovers, it sometimes seemed, separated from their beloved, fated to go on saying the beautiful name, in the street, in a bus, inside their narrow walls, in the open air, to anyone who would listen and many who wouldn't, until the streets seemed filled with the nutcracker-noise of the name, *Kreuzberg*, produced by a thousand tiny yelling voices, a crowd of dwarfs, the hundred European accents of those same blond children who had heard of the walled witchy town from their warning mothers, and remembered. When they talked of it, people often liked to think of it as something interior, imagined; not bricks and streets, but, as they said, a state of mind. There was something satisfied about the way they said this, and Friedrich never did. He had come there not because it was a state of mind, which he could have attained in Cologne, but because it was a place; a walled place; a quiet distant one. That was why anyone went there, and why no one was born there.

Philip Hensher, *Pleasured*

✳ ✳ ✳

The apartment buildings and churches of the Moabit district bathe in the last natural light of the day, a necropolis with silver windows and weathervanes that groan in the icy wind. I catch glimpses of the River Spree, gentle, tame and *orderlich*, yet its black waters seem still to be rippling with the memories of the deaths of Rosa Luxemburg and Karl Liebknecht, thrown into these waters in 1919. The Spree's inky surface mirrors the fraying edges of the palaces of the bourgeoisie and the billboards of the new Reich. The last remnants of the mist have disappeared, the clouds are shredded into ribbons, and the sun is setting in a dusk gathered out of a few last gasoline-soaked rags of indigo and some crimson-fingered dirty flames. In between the Tiergarten and Bellevue Stations, I catch a glimpse of the campy guardian angel of the city, proudly displayed on top of her two-hundred foot column at the Große Stern, holding up her wreath of laurels and her iron cross. She sends out her blessing in a glow forged partially from her own gold, partially from the last rays of the setting sun. Alone and sovereign, she spreads her wings over the park, ready to take off and crash. Far behind her, I can make out the silhouette of the *Fernsehturm*, the tower of East German Television, an enormous globe covered in blunt spikes of stainless steel, hoisted a thousand feet in the air on an impossibly slender stalk of concrete. In the dying light from the west, two rows of the globe's facets light up, one horizontal, one vertical, meeting in the sun's focal point, a broad cross of sparks, a crypto-Christian evening blessing over town and country, courtesy of the communist architects. [...]

Real estate developers are strangling the old city centre. The first glass-and-steel monsters of their visions have already been erected on Friedrichstraße: a counterfeit city that popped up almost overnight, dizzy with deathly halogen light, each of its surfaces hard and cold – they reflect and reject every human touch, they chill every human heart; their design looks utopian only on computer screens of architects who know they will never have to live there. When evening falls, the street collapses. The worst is that one can't even absolve this new town of its artificiality, for it is itself without sin – where there is no soul, there can be no sin. I hardly spend any time there. I wander around the true city, around the old neighbourhoods that still have a heart. I love Kreuzberg and the Mitte, I love Prenzlauer Berg and Friedrichshain. I even feel affection for Wedding and Köpenick, for Spandau and Lichtenberg, and, on a very good day, I might even whip up some enthusiasm for Zehlendorf and Steglitz or gloomy Schöneberg. The city, quiet and buzzing, beautiful and ugly, is always an alembic close to boiling point.

Paul Verhaeghen, *Omega Minor*

* * *

And with a final burst of energy, we go for a run with journalist and blogger Simon Cole who set out to 'run the Berlin Wall'.

I arrive to a hot afternoon in Berlin. Everything is as it should be: the S-Bahn is half empty and its patrons park their bikes and pore over their books and newspapers. €2.10 buys me a hassle free journey through stations that resemble London – on a Sunday morning that is. Even the major hub of Fassbinder fame, Alexanderplatz, is quietly civilised and free of any interchange irritation. The U2 takes me to the familiar surrounds of Senefelderplatz in East Berlin, in the super cool *Szenebezirk* (literally "scene quarter" – think Shoreditch) of Prenzlauerberg. Arriving at the top-rated East Seven Hostel before 5 pm, this sunny evening seems an ideal time to get a quick training run in, and simultaneously reacquaint myself with my favourite part of Berlin.

And what a run. [...] Pounding the sunny Schwedter Strasse, past Lidl and heading north along Kastanienallee it's your quintessential summer evening idyll. The scenesters sun themselves over strong cold beers and strong hot coffees – none of this anaemic rubbish here thank you, and the smoking ban is for Wessis – and mums on bicycles ferry their kids on baby seats or pulling cute articulated trailers that make them look like mini maharajahs.

My feet feel unusually light, and I'm aware I'm running on my toes without having to think about it. Past the *Kino* (cinema) which is showing *Joy Division* this evening; then Morgenrot Café with its 'pay what you can afford' brunches; then left on Oderberger passing the retro and thrift shops that scatter their orange and brown kitsch-cool debris as if the pavement were just a natural extension of the cluttered inside.

Crossing the road on a red light, which immediately marks you out as a non-German and causes both frowning and bewilderment ("Why would anyone cross on a red?") and it's into the Mauer (wall) park. On May Day it's best avoided as anarchists and those left behind by gentrification let off steam, but tonight it's a picture of metropolitan delight as lovers, friends and bookworms range themselves along the south facing slope, soaking up the sunshine. Somewhat incongruously, two riot vans rest at its edge, but it still puts me in mind of San Francisco's Mission Dolores park. Berlin is so far the closest I've found to the SF vibe in Europe. [...]

In a few minutes I'm there, on the Bösebrücke. This bridge, part of Bornholmer Strasse, became famous on that night in 1989. Beseiged by a mob who weren't violent but weren't taking no for an answer, frazzled border guards opened the gates to relieve the overcrowding. Before they knew it, 20,000 impatient Ossis had streamed through after that afternoon's famous governmental gaffe. Pressed by journalists as to when the (just announced) loosening of travel restrictions would come into effect, a hapless government spokesman could only muster a response along the lines of "Er, now, I suppose?" Cue border bedlam.

If Himmler exemplified the banality of evil, perhaps this represents the haphazardness of history? Or the idiosyncrasy of the iconic? Still punning in my head, it was time to head back through tree-lined streets in an identikit housing estate as old couples shuffled along to the Imbiss on their evening constitutional. Crossing Bernauer Strasse, there was the Wall information centre where black and white films show that fateful day in 1961 when Berliners woke up to a city cut in half. On this street, desperate old ladies jumped from three or four floors up as people held blankets to catch them. Morose bricklayers soon sealed the windows, as Ulbricht's 'anti-fascist protection system' took shape.

Nearing home I pass the Zionskirche. It's stunningly silhouetted against a blue sky so pure that nothing could spoil it ...

> Simon Cole, 'Running the Berlin Wall',
> blog at Bookpacking.com

'Ich bin Berliner'

'If I were a stranger in Berlin, how would you describe the people of this city to me?'

I smiled. 'What's a Berliner, eh? That's a good question. […] They like to be made to feel exceptional, although at the same time they like to keep up appearances. Mostly they've got the same sort of look. A scarf, hat and shoes that could walk you to Shanghai without a corn. As it happens, Berliners like to walk, which is why so many of them own a dog: something vicious if you're masculine, something cute if you're something else. The men comb their hair more than the women, and they also grow moustaches you could hunt wild pig in. Tourists think that a lot of Berlin men like dressing-up as women, but that's just the ugly women giving the men a bad name. Not that there are many tourists these days. National Socialism's made them as rare a sight as Fred Astaire in jackboots.

'The people of this town will take cream with just about anything, including beer, and beer is something they take very seriously indeed. The women prefer a ten-minute head on it, just like the men, and they don't mind paying for it themselves. Nearly everyone who drives a car drives much too fast, but nobody would ever dream of running a red light. They've got rotten lungs because the air is bad, and because they smoke too much, and a sense of humour that sounds cruel if you don't understand it, and even crueller if you do. They buy expensive Biedermeier cabinets as solid as blockhouses, and then hang little curtains on the insides of the glass doors to hide what they've got in there. It's a typically idiosyncratic mixture of the ostentatious and the private. How am I doing?'

Philip Kerr, The Pale Criminal

✳ ✳ ✳

The above attempt to define Berliners is, of course, referring to Berliners of the past. Is it possible to pin down a typical modern Berliner? Here are two attempts – by Jakob Hein and Paul Verhaeghen.

I was once standing on the platform at Zoo Station, waiting for my train to Hamburg. As usual, Deutsche Bahn had generously granted all of us a few extra minutes' waiting time. By coincidence, I had positioned myself in front of the carriage location table, that handy graph that informs you of whereabouts the dining car and the first class carriages will be in the train you're waiting for. As these tables are extremely popular in Germany, I had the feeling almost every single passenger was paying their respects to this particular one. And I noticed just how easy it was to distinguish the inhabitants of Berlin from those of Hamburg. The Hamburgers were sporting neat haircuts, practical but high-quality and tastefully arranged clothing and suitcases that could just as well have been put on show in a shop window. The Berliners, on the other hand, had messy hair, were wearing any old clothes they had pulled out of the wardrobe, and their bags would have been hard to get rid of at a flea market.

The word 'normal' defines a circle containing everything that adheres to a certain set of agreed norms. Things outside of this circle are graded into 'not quite normal', 'not normal' and 'abnormal'. This definition of terms is absolutely fundamental for describing normality in Berlin. Essentially: anyone can feel at home in this city. That means if you pop out for a paper in shiny silver leggings, a cropped top, curlers and pink fluffy slippers, you might cause somewhat of a stir in Gera or Münster, whereas in many Berlin boroughs you'd probably meet a whole lot of people at the paper shop who look exactly like you. The lady with twenty cats in a bedsit, the granny with multiple piercings, the student bringing up a baby and a colony of lizards in his basement flat in Wedding, the long-haired geezer in his mid-forties who walks through the organic food store in cropped jeans and Jesus sandals even in November – none of them stand out in Berlin. For most people, that's a good thing. Gays and lesbians stroll around the city holding hands, transsexuals ride their bikes to the greengrocers with a whistle on their lips, and the last remaining teddy boys lean against their scooters, cool as cucumbers.

The word 'normal' is extremely broadly defined in Berlin. An old-age pensioner with backcombed, peroxide-blonde hair, a ton of makeup on her eyes, lips and cheeks – so much you're afraid she might topple over – a cropped imitation velvet T-shirt boasting the word 'Bitch' in bright pink letters; the whole ensemble finished off with a pair of white leggings sitting so low on her hips that the straps of her baby-blue thong cut visibly into her voluptuous flesh; between her fingernails, so long she must have used at least a bottle of nail varnish per hand, a golden cigarette holder, and in her right hand a dog's lead, at the end of which is a pampered poodle with pink-toned fur – in many of Berlin's boroughs, that's an absolutely normal sight.

That's why people who stuck out, who would be labelled as crazy, who were the eternal talk of their small town elsewhere love to move to this city. In Berlin, it might well happen that *they're* the ones staring at other people in amazement for the first few weeks. Some people can't actually cope with this new state of normality. An ambition awakes within them to carry on standing out, to be the most individual individual in this city full of individualists.

Jakob Hein, *Gebrauchsanweisung für Berlin*
('Berlin: a user's manual') translated by Katy Derbyshire

✻ ✻ ✻

The people who live in this city truly *live* in it, and each of them is truly alive. We Berliners are a multiform species. Rebels is what we are, rebels and agitators and jesters, and lunatics and dilettantes and noblemen and stoners and philosophers and bourgeois – and each of us is each of those. I am first and foremost an artist. But oftentimes I also feel like a court jester, a stoner, *etcetera*. Maybe I am least of all bourgeois, but yes, I am bourgeois too, deep inside, like every city-dweller. We belong in this city – that in itself makes us bourgeois. An agitator, certainly, that description fits me well – a rebel and an agitator in training. I don't need a megaphone for my protest – my protest does not scream, but scratches softly. There is much to protest against in this town.

Paul Verhaeghen, *Omega Minor*

✻ ✻ ✻

Among the inhabitants of any city there are always sex-workers. Berlin doesn't have a designated red-light district but, as Thomas Brussig points out, there is one particular street where you are more likely to find the 'colourful' figures of the local prostitutes.

Berlin is a generous city. Berlin doesn't have a restricted red-light area, and a whore could ply her trade anywhere she chooses to stand by the edge of the road. But Oranienburger Strasse has nevertheless emerged as the red-light district for streetwalkers.

Oranienburger Strasse is a road in the borough of Mitte, linking Berlin's trendy heart at Hackescher Markt with Oranienburger Tor, where Friedrichstrasse begins (or ends; Berlin is generous about these matters of interpretation). The tram stops three times along the street, not just passing the strictly guarded synagogue (the one shown burning in the now famous faked Nazi photo, which became a symbol of the 'Night of Broken Glass'), but also at least two dozen bars, restaurants and cafés and the 'Tacheles' art house, the institution that proves that even squatter artists inevitably end up just as petty and narrow-minded as the rest of us.

Fifty metres apart, there they stand on both sides of the street.

The reason why that street is Oranienburger Strasse is presumably historical, going back to the 1920s. As Oranien-burger Strasse was in the East when the city was divided, the red-light district stagnated up to 1990 (although there are plenty of people who insist on the legend that it was 'never dead'). But on the date of monetary union, the first of July 1990, the day when the East got real money again, the red-light district on Oranienburger Strasse celebrated its resurrection. As if it had never been away. From one day to the next, strangely artificial female figures lined the street: with skin-tight, neon pantaloons, with such over-dimensioned breasts that one couldn't help wondering how they kept their balance on their platform shoes, with long blonde wavy hair all the way down to their bullet-round arses. They looked like blow-up dolls, like cultivated creations. Barbie has completed the laboratory phase and been released for initial outdoor testing. Then came the winters, and they intensified the impression that there was something very fishy about the streetwalkers. Never mind how cold the nights are – they're always standing on Oranienburger. They stand not on the road and not on the pavement, but in the gutter, between parked cars. One every fifty metres.

One what? *Prostitute* is the official term and suppresses the fact that they are human beings. *Hookers* sounds coarse; they once wanted to be called *whores* out of defiant pride, but the word still comes across as problematic. *Call girls* ignores their maturity and professionalism. *Doxies* are extinct, as far as I know. *Sex workers* is for academics and bores. *Women* is not bad, but then what should I call the women who aren't *women*? (After all, there are many more women than *women*.) I like the term *sidewalk swallows*; it has something fugitive about it, the element of trimmings. But *swallows* isn't quite right; too unspectacular. I like *sidewalk flamingos*. Yes, they are colourful birds on the edge of the street, and pink is a colour that's often shown and worn here, to say nothing of their long thin legs.

Thomas Brussig, *Berliner Orgie* ('Wild Berlin')
translated by Katy Derbyshire

✻ ✻ ✻

A member of Berlin's large and established Turkish community provides the protagonist of Jeffrey Eugenides Middlesex *with the pleasure of watching 'an artist of bread baking' as well as some food for thought about identity.*

Once again, in Berlin, a Stephanides lives among the Turks. I feel comfortable here in Schöneberg. The Turkish shops along Hauptstrasse are like those my father used to take me to. The food is the same, the dried figs, the halvah, the stuffed grape leaves. The faces are the same, too, seamed, dark-eyed, significantly boned. Despite family history, I feel drawn to Turkey. I'd like to work in the embassy in Istanbul. I've put in a request to be transferred there. It would bring me full circle.

Until that happens, I do my part this way. I watch the bread baker in the döner restaurant downstairs. He bakes bread in a stone oven like those they used to have in Smyrna. He uses a long-handled spatula to shift and retrieve the bread. All day long he works, fourteen, sixteen hours, with unflagging concentration, his sandals leaving prints in the flour dust on the floor. An artist of bread baking. Stephanides, an American, grandchild of Greeks, admires this Turkish immigrant to Germany, this *Gastarbeiter*, as he bakes bread on Hauptstrasse here in the year 2001. We're all made up of many parts, other halves. Not just me.

Jeffrey Eugenides, *Middlesex*

* * *

And now a few individual Berliners worth knowing about – native, adopted, and temporary. One of the most prestigious claiming to 'belong' to the city was, of course, President John F. Kennedy, whose imperfect grasp of the German language led him to declare, in his famous speech of solidarity while visiting the newly divided city, "Ich bin ein Berliner" – meaning 'I am a doughnut' (he should have left out the 'ein'). Happily, the Berliners in the following portraits prove to be more substantial than doughnuts. First, a good German policeman ...

The great hero of Berlin's police museum is Detective Ernst Gennat. It remains a mystery why no television series has yet been based on his life, for no premise could be more perfect. Ernst Gennat weighed 135 kilos and, together with his faithful secretary Bockwurst-Trüdchen, solved almost 300 murder cases between 1918–39. His size inspired confidence and awe, and he despised all forms of physical exertion. For his work in the field he had a special car built to serve as mobile police department and forensics lab. Gennat was also the founder of 'forensic undertaking', by which mutilated and half-decayed corpses could be reconstructed. He was absolutely opposed to the use of force: 'Anyone who touches a suspect is out on his ear. Our weapons are our brains and strong nerves.' Shortly before his death he married, to make use of the police department's pension benefits for widows – but Trüdchen was not the lucky girl.

Geert Mak, *In Europe: travels through the twentieth century*
translated by Sam Garrett

* * *

*The grandfather of one of Germany's many great
composers was a great Berliner in his own right.*

We were walking past the Opera Café.

'Before the war,' Wolfgang said, 'there were fifty cafés
between Friedrichstrasse and the Unter den Linden. How is the
Kurfürstendamm these days? Is that not nice?'

No, I said. It was just an expensive tourist hang-out: chintzy
bars, car showrooms, porno nightclubs, street hustlers. He
nodded, his mouth downturned. He was in an odd mood. He
said he was going to take me to the sight of a Jewish school
opened by his hero, Moses Mendelssohn, on 4 January 1786,
he had the exact date in his mind. We left the main drag and
fifteen minutes later were walking down a narrow alley past
Salon Wagner, the premier gay hairdresser's of East Berlin.
Homosexuality was legalised in East Germany in the fifties.

Moses Mendelssohn arrived penniless in Berlin in 1743, made
his fortune and established his reputation as one of the leading
lights of German rationalism. A friend of Lessing, he believed
that Jews should stop regarding themselves as a separate people
and should play their part in German intellectual life. (He set in
train the process which terminated in Jewish intellectuals like
Georg Karger having no truck whatsoever with their inherited
Jewish identity.) Moses Mendelssohn's salon attracted the most
famous talents of his time and made Berlin an animated forum
of the European Enlightenment. His daughter, Dorothea, was
a feminist who followed the example of her father and ran a
literary salon. His grandson, Felix, became the well-known
composer, conductor and pianist.

The day Moses Mendelssohn walked through the city gates
the customs officer wrote in his logbook: 'Today there passed
six oxen, seven swine and a Jew.' Mendelssohn was now
remembered by one street in East Berlin, none in West Berlin.

Known only by its surname, there was no way of divining whether Mendelssohnstrasse honoured grandfather, daughter or grandson. Maybe it was killing three birds with one stone.

Ian Walker, *Zoo Station*

* * *

One of the saddest of the many political assassinations that took place in Berlin during the rise of Nazism was that of the much-loved foreign minister Walter Rathenau.

Rathenau was assassinated. The foreign minister and millionaire industrialist was gunned down as he drove to work in his open-topped car. The reason suggested was that he was part of a Jewish conspiracy.

There had already been three hundred and seventy-six political assassinations since the war. Most of the victims were liberals; almost half were Jewish. More than three hundred fifty murders were carried out by right-wing groups; around twenty by the left. The average prison sentence for left-wingers, however, was fifteen years; the average for the right wing, four months.

And yet workers left their factories and took to the streets of every city in Germany to protest Rathenau's murder. The labour unions declared a day of mourning. His body was laid in state in the Reichstag. Over a million mourners were recorded on the streets of Berlin, several million more in Hamburg and Frankfurt. It was an outrage, everyone agreed, a travesty, a crime of cowardice and misguided prejudice. Two of the assassins were tracked down; one was shot, the other shot himself. Thirteen years later, however, Himmler laid a wreath on their graves.

Although his mother claimed to have English roots, Edvard was a German of Jewish descent on his father's side. Like Rathenau, he had fought in the war and been decorated. He was, however, heartened by the public's collective outrage.

'You see,' he told Hanne. 'It is a random act by schoolboy fanatics. Everyone knows that there is no such thing as a Jewish conspiracy. Germany is the Fatherland. I feel perfectly safe here.'

And, sitting in his drawing room, where decorative paintings and Venetian-glass mirrors still covered every wall – where the heavy oak furniture looked as if it had been there since the beginning of time and the clock ticked the smooth, peaceful hours away – it was impossible to imagine that in one short decade, all of it would be gone and that, only a few years after that, Edvard would be dead from a hole he himself had fired into the soft, cultured recesses of his very large brain. It was impossible to imagine. But it would happen.

Beatrice Collin, *The Luminous Life of Lilly Aphrodite*

✻ ✻ ✻

Pre-war Berlin was the place to be if you wanted to hang out with the famous. Awash with writers, artists and composers, the city was perfect for an ambitious young man like Elias Canetti: he describes two memorable meetings that left a lasting impression on him.

The first thing that struck me about Brecht was his disguise. I was taken to lunch at Schlichter, the restaurant in which the intellectual Berlin hung out. In particular, many actors came there. They were pointed out; you recognised them on the spot: the illustrated magazines made them part of your image of public things. However, one must admit that there was not much theatre in their outward appearance, in their greetings and order, in the way they bolted down their food, swallowed, paid. It was a colourful picture, but without the colourfulness of the stage. The only one I noticed among them all – and because of his proletarian disguise – was Brecht. He was very emaciated. He had a hungry face, which looked askew because of his cap. His words came out wooden and choppy. When he gazed at you, you felt like an object of value that he, the pawnbroker, with his piercing black eyes, was appraising as something that had no value. He was a man of few words; you learned nothing about the results of his appraisal. It seemed incredible that he was only thirty. He did not look as if he had aged prematurely, but as if he had always been old. [...]

He did not care much for people, but he put up with them; he respected those who were persistently useful to him; he noticed others only to the extent that they corroborated his somewhat monotonous view of the world. It was this view that increasingly determined the character of his plays, while, in his poems, he started out far more vividly than anyone else in his day; later on, with the help of the Chinese (but this does not belong here), he found his way to something like wisdom. [...]

Why did I expect so much from Grosz? What did he mean to me? Ever since Frankfurt, when I had seen books of his displayed at the Bookstore for Young People – that is, for the past six years – I had been admiring these drawings and carrying them around in my head. Six young years are a long time. His drawings had struck me to the core at first sight. They expressed precisely what I felt after the things I saw around me during the inflation [...]. I liked the strength and recklessness I saw in these drawings, the ruthlessness and dreadfulness. Since they were extreme, I regarded them as Truth. A truth that mediated, that weakened, that explained, that excused was no Truth for me. [...]

Grosz was dressed in tweed, he was strong and tan in contrast to Wieland, and he sucked at his pipe. He looked like a young skipper, not an English one, he talked a great deal, he seemed more American. Since he was extremely open and cordial, I did not regard his costume as a disguise. I felt free with him and I let myself go. I was enthusiastic about everything he showed us. He was delighted by my enthusiasm, as if it were very important to him. He sometimes nodded at Wieland when I said something about a graphic. I sensed that I was on target; and while I couldn't open my mouth in front of Brecht without triggering his sarcasm, I aroused Grosz's interest and delight. He asked me whether I knew the *Ecce Homo* folder. I said no: the set had been banned by law. He went over to a chest, raised the lid, and removed a folder, which he then handed me as if it were nothing special. I thought he wanted me to have a look, and I opened it up; however, I was quickly enlightened: he said I could take it home, the folder was a present. "Not just anybody can get one," said Wieland, who knew how impulsive his friend was. But he did not need to say it. No act of magnanimity has ever eluded me, and I was overwhelmed by this one. [...]

The folder had been banned as obscene. There is no denying that certain things in it could appear obscene. I took it all in with an odd mixture of horror and approval. These were dreadful creatures of Berlin's night life that you saw here, but they were here because they were viewed as dreadful. I regarded my disgust at them as the artist's disgust. I knew very little about all this, I had been in Berlin for only about a week. [...]

Now, however, I had brought home the *Ecce Homo* folder. It inserted itself between me and Berlin, and from then on, it coloured most things for me, especially all the things I saw at night. Perhaps it would otherwise have taken these things a lot longer to penetrate me. My interest in the freedom of sexual matters was still not great. Now these unbelievably hard and ruthless depictions threw me into the sexual world, and I regarded this world as true. I would never have dreamt of doubting its truth. And just as one sees certain landscapes only through the eyes of certain painters, so too I saw Berlin through the eyes of George Grosz.

Elias Canetti, *The Torch in my Ear*
translated by Joachim Neugroschel

✳ ✳ ✳

Although she abandoned her country in disgust with the rise of National Socialism, Marlene Dietrich is often thought of as the quintessential Berliner. Journalist Ian Collins reflects upon Marlene's extraordinary life when he visits her grave. (And Marlene fans can visit a collection of memorabilia at the Deutsche-Kinemathek – Museum für Film und Fernsehen on Potsdamer Straße.)

A stifling summer day in Berlin. Light glares, noise blares, heat blazes. But cool calm pervades a certain cemetery. Outside the gates I buy a single rose and am guided to the grave I seek by a series of signs with the legendary slogan *Marlene Dietrich*.

This trim burial ground, in an elegant corner of the German capital, is screened and shaded by towering trees. Birdsong fills the air. The resting places of some of the city's most prosperous citizens are bright with bedding plants and pompous with ornate stone noting details of birth, death and status. Near the edge of this assembly is a simpler grave, planted with the chrysanthemums and bizzy-lizzies beloved of Berlin housewives: only the theatrical flourish of a vase of white lilies and red roses hints that Marlene Dietrich branched beyond her cosy, narrow bourgeois roots. The black headstone is crudely painted with the name, but there are no dates. The screen goddess and cabaret singer, who died exiled in Paris, had for decades claimed to be younger than records suggested. Then, a few months before her death, she snubbed 90th birthday greetings with the retort that she was, in fact, 91. Contrary to the end.

Beneath the name on the stone there is the inscription ' … *wann wird man je versteh'n*' or 'when will they ever learn?' The line, from the German version of *Where have all the flowers gone?* – a Dietrich torch song – sums up why I am here to honour a woman who for the last 15 years of her life shunned the world, but who now receives a stream of visitors.

We live in an age when it is more profitable to knock people down than to build them up, and the fatal blows of character assassination rain most heavily when death has removed the protection of libel laws. Marlene Dietrich's demise prompted a flood of stories about an imperious monster who, after bedding half of Hollywood in her bisexual younger and middle years, turned prudish and cantankerous – tearing up every available photograph of herself as Lola, the heartless star of *The Blue Angel* film which gave her fame in 1929. Her hatred of the "vulgar" classic was said to be greater than that of any other film in her "kitsch" cinematic career. Yet when Madonna was lined up to play Lola, in 1988, Dietrich furiously denounced the upstart usurper of *her* role. Wisely, Twentieth Century Fox dropped the remake idea.

Shortly after her death Sotheby's auctioned a cache of correspondence between the star and her ex-manager, Michael Benedict, in which the poor employee was harried by an apparent harridan. ("Do NOT ever slip notes for MD through THE DOOR … There is a thing called the telephone.") And yet almost everyone who worked with Dietrich has acknowledged that, in her ruthless quest for artistic perfection, she was hardest on herself. How else could she have toured in her one-woman stage shows until well into her 70s – maintaining her mystique and glamour despite a series of falls and fractures which would finally leave one of her celebrated legs in a steel calliper?

But the demolition industry is fuelled by biographies and memoirs. If a book by Dietrich's only daughter, Maria Riva, disappoints those hoping for a Mommie Dearest-type attack, the revelations of a former secretary, Bernard Hall, may be more sensational. For my part, I am simply charmed by a woman who, while not the greatest actress or singer in the world – whose material was rarely better than lacklustre – contrived to be one of the most charismatic performers of our century.

But I salute Marlene Dietrich most of all because she had truly heroic personal qualities. This daughter of a Prussian military officer grew up in a world where patriotism was considered the highest virtue. She knew, however, that decency was something different, and more deserving. Lured to Hollywood after *The Blue Angel*, she resisted Hitler's attempts to woo her back. He offered her a colossal salary and control over her work, if only she would consent to be a Nazi icon. As she said later: "He promised me a triumphal entry into Berlin. I'm afraid I laughed." At that time work was scarce and many would have succumbed. Several actresses gave the Nazis dire Dietrich imitations (even Hitler was embarrassed by the calibre of his puppets).

When Marlene made her Hollywood comeback, in the Western *Destry*, her salary went on bribes and fares to get people out of Germany. Some were known to her, others not. And in June 1939, she took American citizenship – declaring that *her* Germany had vanished.

During the war she entertained allied troops from Greenland to Africa, singing songs like *Lili Marlene* and *Falling in Love Again*, and playing the musical saw. Once she had to be rescued from the advancing Germans – if captured she would certainly have been shot. She also sang for prisoners of war, which must have been doubly poignant. Her own sister was then being held in less comfortable circumstances in Belsen (after the war, it was Marlene's care and money which got her back to health).

In 1945 she entered Berlin in enemy uniform, and for her courageous stand was booed during a final concert tour in 1960. Later she said: "I want to be buried in France, leave my heart in England, and to Germany – nothing." Only when the Berlin Wall had fallen did she relent, deciding to be buried near her mother in the Wilmersdorf cemetery next to her childhood home.

Even then there were fears that old enmities would be revived after the funeral – angry letters to German newspapers, alleging that Dietrich had "betrayed" her country, raised the spectre of neo-Nazi attacks. But the respectful people I saw by the graveside seemed to agree with the Green Party, whose wreath had carried the words: "You were the real Germany".

And on the wall, at the end of a list of notables buried in this rather beautiful site, someone had added: "Marlene Dietrich – the most wonderful woman in the world."

Ian Collins, 'Marlene Dietrich: RIP'

* * *

Among the many famous temporary residents and visitors to the city was Hans Christian Andersen … though his experience of Berlin was less than happy. That, however, was not Berlin's fault. Novelist Mikka Haugaard paints a picture of a man in love.

In the winter of 1845 Hans Christian Andersen the poet, playwright, writer of libretti, novelist and author of fairy tales came to Berlin because he was in love. He was forty years old and at the height of his fame, a fame of an extraordinary kind. He knew everyone and everyone wanted to know him. The son of a shoemaker and a sad alcoholic, he had been born on the island of Fynen in Denmark. His sister who had less gumption and a more conventional turn of mind became a prostitute and his aunt ran a brothel. But this was not for him, nor did he want to fulfil his mother's dream of becoming a respectable tailor. Fourteen years old he arrived in Copenhagen with the ambition of becoming a dancer, actor and singer. For a time he was all three, as well as an artist's model. But by 1845, he had achieved success as a dramatist, novelist and poet.

But he came to Berlin because he was in love. He arrived by that new method of travelling, the steam train. He had been to Berlin before in 1831 and had been impressed by the soldiers, particularly their legs. "The first soldier I saw," he wrote in 1831, "I fell in love with. What body, what legs." As for Berlin, he had found 'the streets straight and dull'. He was a man who loved the backstreets of Rome and their crumbling grandeur.

So he came here not for the city but for love. He stayed at The British Hotel on Unter den Linden. He had a room with a view, but, like a lot of travellers, was disappointed in the real thing and felt it was 'better in a picture'. Perhaps the noise bothered him. Carlyle who stayed in the same hotel a few years later wrote:

> *Hotel British Unter den Linden, October first. I am dead stupid; my heart nearly choked out of me and my head churned to pieces. Berlin is loud almost as London but in no other way great … about the size of Liverpool and more like Glasgow.*

Immediately he arrived Andersen sent a message to the woman he loved, Jenny Lind, the famous Swedish opera singer. Shy, he asked her for a ticket to hear her sing.

> *She replied that if there were any then I could have one. Didn't hear more. Had supper alone. Went out at six o'clock. It was raining and horrible. Arrived at the opera, tickets for the upper balcony only. Disgusting people: a soldier and a drunk Frenchman. I stood by the door, listened to Jenny, intended to be angry with her but she touched me. The theatre is really magnificent but I didn't notice. I was only there for Jenny. As in a dream I heard her. I don't love her, as one should, I know that. I am not happy and yet this is a pleasant room. I am so alone in Berlin.*

The last was more metaphor than reality. He was in a whirlwind of company from the King of Prussia to the brothers Grimm. Every day brought visitors and he was invited to dinner or he ate at the fashionable Café Royal. But this is nothing for a man in love.

> *Saturday December 27th: Letter from the Countess von Moltke and read my fairy tales to the King of Prussia, a sad and tedious affair. In the paper it says*

> *I belong more to Germany than Denmark. Spent the*
> *evening with the brothers Grimm.*
>   *Sunday December 28th: Rain and wind, awful*
> *weather. Booked to see the Princess of Prussia at 11.*

One gets the impression of a man pursued and thrown off course by adulation. In his own pursuit of the elusive Jenny he was less lucky. She claimed not to be at home when she clearly was. And like all men or women in love, it took him some time to get the message but even he couldn't fail.

> *Haven't heard anything from Jenny. I feel insulted and*
> *upset. She has not treated me like a sister in Berlin. If*
> *I was a stranger to her, then she should have told me*
> *and I would have behaved like one. She did fill my*
> *heart – I don't love her any more. In Berlin she cut*
> *out my sick flesh with a cold knife.*

This, of course, didn't stop him from trying to see her and finally on Friday December 26th he finds her at home.

> *Visited Jenny who had a Christmas tree. She gave*
> *me soap in the shape of a piece of cheese and some*
> *perfume. She was so wonderful, patted me, and*
> *called me a child. Told me she didn't want to return*
> *to Sweden, felt at home in Germany. Said I was such*
> *a kind person and a brother. The king invited me to*
> *dinner at the castle.*

When a woman gives you soap in the shape of cheese and tells you that are a child and a brother, then you know that she does not love you.

> *Wednesday December 31st: Visited Jenny who lit the*
> *tree for me. She sang a few songs and we had a friendly*
> *conversation. She asked me about my new play* Giving

Birth and said that she found it difficult to believe I had written it because I was a child and this was satire.

One senses the contempt. Shortly afterwards Andersen left Berlin having been made a Knight of the Red Eagle by the King of Prussia. Jenny stayed to sing, and to see the people she wanted to see. Among them was Felix Mendelssohn the composer, a married man with five children – but rumour has it that he sent her a letter suggesting they elope to America . If she refused, he would kill himself .

Mikka Haugaard, 'Hans Christian Andersen in love'

✳ ✳ ✳

Of the many people to have adopted Berlin as their home, among the most infamous is Ulrike Meinhof. Ian Walker's friendship with another Ulrike (who, like her better-known namesake, had a sister) prompts him to consider the life and 'career' of the woman whose activities on behalf of the RAF (Red Army Fraction) once made her a household name in Germany.

Ulrike Meinhof had been a writer and maybe that was why she had managed to script her life like a thriller; SUCCESSFUL JOURNALIST TIRES OF TRYING TO CHANGE THINGS BY WRITING, TAKES UP GUN INSTEAD! Born in 1934, she grew up in Jena, east of Weimar, the daughter of two free-thinkers belonging to the only church which had not fallen under Nazi control. She had a sister three years older. Her father, the director of Jena museum, died when she was six. After the war her mother drove her two daughters in a truck from the Russian zone to Oldenburg in Brit-ish-occupied Germany. Her mother died when Ulrike Meinhof was fifteen. She was adopted by her mother's best friend.

Sometimes I called Ulrike and Uschi The German Sisters, after the title of a film by Margaret von Trotha about the Red Army Fraction. In retaliation Ulrike called me The English Boy.

Sitting in the languorous garden with the sisters from Heidelberg, I wondered if Berlin had somehow contributed to the lethal rage of Ulrike Meinhof. She came to West Berlin with her twin daughters in the Christmas of 1967, having decided to divorce her husband, Klaus Rainer Röhl, the publisher of *Konkret*, the Hamburg-based magazine in which she had made her reputation. She found a small flat in Dahlem, later moving to Kufsteinerstrasse, nearer the centre. Her face became known to the public through her work on television. She hung out at the Republican Club on Wielandstrasse where the radicals paid for their food and drink by chucking money into a bottle on the bar.

'Everyone here is so loving,' she wrote in a letter to a friend.

When she took the irrevocable decision, she had just finished writing a television play called *Bambule*, based on her research at the Eichenhof orphanage for girls in West Berlin. One of the girls she befriended there, Irene Goergens, the illegitimate daughter of an American soldier, became an accomplice, a teenage member of the RAF. *Bambule* was scheduled for transmission on 24 May 1970 at the peak time of 8.15 p.m. It was never shown. Ten days earlier Ulrike Meinhof and Irene Goergens, wearing wigs and carrying guns in their briefcases, had with three others freed Andreas Baader from the German Institute for Social Questions in Dahlem. WRITER TURNS OUTLAW!

Convicted for setting fire to a Munich department store in 1968, Baader had been released pending appeal after fourteen months and had fled to Paris and Zurich whence he returned to Berlin. He had been re-arrested after an abortive search for weapons which he thought were buried in a cemetery in Rudow close to the Berlin Wall. Locked up in Tegel prison, he had been given permission by the prison authorities to research a book at the German Institute for Social Questions. In the getaway car, a silver Alfa Romeo, police found a tear-gas pistol and a copy of *Introduction to Capital* by Marx.

Ulrike Meinhof went to Jordan for arms training, returning in August to West Berlin where a few weeks later three banks were robbed on the same day by different units of the RAF. SHE CARRIES A 9MM FIREBIRD PISTOL IN HER HANDBAG! The television face was now up on wanted posters all over West Germany. After a spate of bombs at US Army headquarters in Frankfurt and Heidelberg in early May 1972, Ulrike Meinhof masterminded the bombing of the Springer press building in Hamburg. Arrested a month later, she was sentenced in November 1974 to eight years' imprisonment for her part in the freeing of Andreas Baader. The authorities at Stammheim maximum-security jail alleged she committed suicide by hanging herself on 9 May 1976. She was buried in the Protestant cemetery of the Church of the Holy Trinity in Mariendorf, West Berlin. Four thousand mourners attended her funeral.

Ian Walker, *Zoo Station*

✻ ✻ ✻

No gallery of famous people associated with Berlin would be complete without a sketch of David Bowie. His Berlin period was particularly productive and Tobias Rüther tries to reconstruct what Bowie's life would have been like during his Berlin years.

When he wasn't in the studio he rode around town. He soon bought himself a bicycle: a classic English Raleigh with three gears. Once Bowie had had his breakfast of coffee and Gitanes at Café Anderes Ufer, he cycled down Hauptstrasse towards the Hansa Studios on Potsdamer Platz.

Back then, cycling was a rather relaxed affair; hardly anyone can remember traffic jams in the West Berlin of the 1970s. So Bowie cycled off and past Kleistpark underground station; from here on the four lanes are no longer called Hauptstrasse but Potsdamer Strasse. On the left followed the Allied Air Safety Centre, housed in the building where the 20 July conspirators were tried before the so-called People's Court. Then Bowie passed the construction site of the so-called 'social palace', a twelve-storey residential machine on top of the ruins of the Sportpalast, where Goebbels invoked 'total war' in 1943 and now 514 concrete flats were being built [...]. A couple of blocks further and across the Landwehr Canal on Reichpietschufer, Bowie passed Mies van der Rohe's New National Gallery on the left and the next building site on the right: Hans Scharoun's State Library. It was completed in 1978. Bowie could virtually watch it being built as he recorded *'Heroes'*. Here, he will have turned off to the right to get to Köthener Strasse along the Landwehr Canal. House number 58 is the Hansa Studios. The building faces the Wall, directly on Potsdamer Platz [...].

And when he didn't cycle, as it is said to have rained often that autumn of 1976, then perhaps he simply took the bus. 'He valued and used the public transport system,' says Eduard Meyer (Bowie's studio technician at Hansa).

But what a route he took every day! It goes right across his formative programme. Bowie begins two or three blocks away from the house where Marlene Dietrich was born. Then he passes right by one of the headquarters of the Cold War, with its technique of brinkmanship – bringing a situation to the brink of escalation to gain capital out of it, as happened during the Berlin crisis of 1958 – which he had lived out in person in every one of his artistic undertakings. Immediately after that, Bowie passes one of the memorial sites of Goebbels' propaganda, which he once wanted to write a musical about, pushing on into the heart of the art of the very years that had fascinated him since his childhood, and from there cycling along the isolation turned to stone, into his own present day in the Hansa Studios. 'You could still tell,' says Eduard Meyer, 'how it fascinated him to be living in the place where Nazi history took place. He gave off that feeling to those immediately around him.' [...]

'There was a German school in Berlin at the beginning of the century called *Die Brücke* (the Bridge) – an expressionist school,' Brian Eno once said. 'Very rough, rough strokes – and they all have a mood of melancholy about them or nostalgia, as if they were painting something that was just disappearing. And all of that – the boldness of attack, the unplanned evolutionary quality of the images, and the over-all mood – remind me of the way David works.'

Anyone trying to read the traces of Eno's friend David Bowie in Berlin, anyone searching out eye witnesses and inscriptions and remains, looking for Bowie's brushstrokes from the time between autumn 1976 and spring 1979 at Hauptstrasse 155, is doing nothing other than what the man they are seeking did himself back then: Bowie was looking for himself in the city. He read himself in it. 'Berlin is a skeleton which aches in the cold,' writes Christopher Isherwood, 'it is my own skeleton aching.' And Bowie too no doubt identified with the city's strange fate. The fate of growing too quickly, politically and in urban planning terms, and having to suffer eternal growing pains; the architecture critic Heinrich Wefing once talked of Berlin's *partus praecipitatus*. Always having to be more, always having to wrestle with one's own role – Bowie recognised himself in this fate. And like Bowie, Berlin got high on itself and ruined itself through megalomania, and like Bowie, the city now had to make amends in a state of permanent hangover. Karl Scheffler's wretched dictum, quoted to death, that Berlin is condemned to be eternally becoming, never to be, gained a new dimension thanks to Bowie. Bowie was the embodiment of this statement. It was as if tailor-made for him. An ever-changing shape – that was what the theatre-maker Lindsay Kemp called his disciple David at the end of the 1960s. In Berlin, Bowie found a new master.

And how he threw himself upon Berlin and surrendered himself to the place! The city, he enthused, had been 'the artistic and cultural gateway to Europe in the twenties,' – 'virtually anything that happened in the arts happened there.' He spent hours walking by the Wannsee lake, cycling, visiting Nazi sites and having his photo taken there – at least he still did in the first few weeks. He crossed over to East Berlin over and again at Checkpoint Charlie to visit the Berliner Ensemble, Brecht's old theatre. Around the corner from there, he ate at Ganymed on Schiffbauerdamm with Iggy Pop and Tony Visconti, who called the wine restaurant a 'time machine', because the grey-on-grey other guests seemed to come from the fifties – but it was just East Germany's 'real existing socialism'. On the other side of the wall, in the neon West of Kurfürstendamm, Bowie is said to have regularly collapsed in the gutter after litres of pilsener – that must have been his own reverence to the drunken culture for which Berlin was known in the late seventies and early eighties.

But the city took him in and tolerated him, as it has tolerated every freak and interesting maniac that has tried their luck here: asking no questions, taking no interest, shrugging its shoulders. After Los Angeles, Bowie says, his paranoia was so huge for a while that he couldn't walk along a road without being afraid of people. Now no one looked at him longer than necessary. Some Berliners still pronounce his name 'Boffie' today; they had called Isherwood 'Issyvoo' in the thirties. Fame doesn't count for much in this city. 'Anyone could claim that,' is one of its maxims to this day. Even the local papers took a while in autumn 1976 to realise who was suddenly living in Schöneberg, had a regular table in the Exil restaurant on Kreuzberg's Paul-Lincke-Ufer and the Paris Bar on Kantstrasse, and disappeared backstage at Romy Haag's drag show in the evenings. Had the telephone cut off. And wanted to be alone. 'I thought I'd take the stage sets,' Bowie said, 'throw them away, go out there and live the real thing.'

Tobias Rüther, *Helden. David Bowie und Berlin*
('Heroes: David Bowie and Berlin') translated by Katy Derbyshire

'Money, money, money ... '

In late 1922, when a shipment of telegraph poles failed to arrive in France, French and Belgian troops invaded the Ruhr Valley and took over the steel factories, the coal mines, and the railways. To retaliate, the Weimar government ordered the workers to go on strike. Nothing was produced or ran in or out of the valley for months, and 150,000 people were forced out of their homes by the invading armies. The government started to print money to pay wages and cover living costs. Businesses were also allowed to print their own banknotes, and soon railways, factories, even pubs, were producing money. It was, however, soon worth less than it cost to print. One day a cup of coffee in a café might cost five thousand marks. An hour later it would have risen to eight thousand. You soon needed a suitcase of money to buy a sausage. At one point a dollar was worth over four billion marks.

In a matter of months, wealth that had taken centuries to accumulate became worthless. A former bank manager withdrew all his savings, used it to buy a U-Bahn ticket, and travelled round the city once before returning home to starve to death. A family of four who were used to dining at their mahogany table on beef stew and apple cake burned the table to keep warm and then drowned themselves in a lake. A local director borrowed money from a currency speculator and bought his own theatre. The show sold out every night but he still ended up with debts that would take several lifetimes of hard labour to repay.

Beatrice Collin, *The Luminous Life of Lilly Aphrodite*

✳ ✳ ✳

Such stories of the effects of spiralling German infla-
tion are well-known. Here's Christopher Isherwood
also observing the country's plunge into financial
turmoil.

Next morning, Frl. Shroeder woke me in great excitement:

'Herr Issyvoo, what do you think! They've shut the Darm-städter und National! There'll be thousands ruined, I shouldn't wonder! The milkman says we'll have civil war in a fortnight! Whatever do you say to that!'

As soon as I'd got dressed, I went down into the street. Sure enough, there was a crowd outside the branch bank on the Nollendorfplatz corner, a lot of men with leather satchels and women with stringbags – women like Frl. Shroeder herself. The iron lattices were drawn down over the bank windows. Most of the people were staring intently and rather stupidly at the locked door. In the middle of the door was fixed a small notice, beautifully printed in Gothic type, like a page from a classic author. The notice said the Reichs-president had guaranteed the deposits. Everything was quite all right. Only the bank wasn't going to open. […]

In the afternoon it was very hot. The details of the new emergency decrees were in the early evening papers – terse, governmentally inspired. One alarmist headline stood out boldly, barred with blood-red ink: 'Everything Collapses!' A Nazi journalist reminded his readers that tomorrow, the fourteenth of July, was a day of national rejoicing in France;

and doubtless, he added, the French would rejoice with especial fervour this year, at the prospect of Germany's downfall. Going into an outfitter's, I bought myself a pair of ready-made flannel trousers for twelve marks fifty – a gesture of confidence by England. Then I got into the Underground to go and visit Sally.

She was living in a block of three-room flats, designed as an Artists' Colony, not far from the Breitenbachplatz. When I rang the bell, she opened the door to me herself:

'Hillooo, Chris, you old swine!'

'Hullo, Sally darling!'

'How are you? ... Be careful, darling, you'll make me untidy. I've got to go out in a few minutes.' [...]

'Got a new boy friend?'

But Sally ignored my grin. She lit a cigarette with a faint expression of distaste.

'I've got to see a man on business,' she said briefly.

'And when shall we meet again?'

'I'll have to see, darling ... I've got such a lot on, just at present ... I shall be out in the country all day tomorrow, and probably the day after ... I'll let you know ... I may be going to Frankfurt quite soon.'

'Have you got a job there?'

'No. Not exactly.' Sally's voice was brief, dismissing this subject. 'I've decided not to try for any film work until the autumn, anyhow. I shall take a thorough rest.'

'You seem to have made a lot of new friends.'

Again, Sally's manner became vague, carefully casual:

'Yes, I suppose I have ... It's probably a reaction from all those months at Frl. Shroeder's, when I never saw a soul.'

'Well,' I couldn't resist a malicious grin, 'I hope for your sake that none of your new friends have got their money in the Darmstädter und National.'

'Why?' She was interested at once. 'What's the matter with it?'

'Do you really mean to say you haven't heard?'

'Of course not. I never read the papers, and I haven't been out today, yet.'

I told her the news of the crisis. At the end of it, she was looking quite scared.

'But why on earth,' she exclaimed impatiently, 'didn't you tell me all this before? It may be serious.'

'I'm sorry, Sally. I took it for granted that you'd know already ... especially as you seem to be moving in financial circles, nowadays –'

But she ignored this little dig. She was frowning, deep in her own thoughts:

'If it was *very* serious, Leo would have rung up and told me ... ' she murmured at length. And this reflection appeared to ease her mind considerably.

Christopher Isherwood, Goodbye to Berlin

✻ ✻ ✻

All cities have their very rich and very poor, but in Berlin's difficult times even the normally well-heeled had to take measures against starvation. Christabel Bielenberg remembers how the initial challenge of becoming poor soon lost its invigorating charm.

The snows came early and stayed put. Hard icy flakes battered the numbed and exhausted birds up against the window panes. God seemed to give up the unequal task of looking after them, and left it to us humans who were no better fitted for the job. Peter satisfied his childhood longing to be a farmer by setting us up with rabbits and hens, but when we went out one morning to feed our livestock, four rigid furry stones fell out of the rabbit hutch and we were obliged to transfer the hens, who occupied the floor below, to the coal cellar.

Our efforts at stock-rearing did not meet with much approval in the district. 'One might be living on an allotment plot!' Did we understand that Dahlem was a very respectable residential area? One particular lady, referred to by one and all as the *'Frau Baronin'*, took time off to give me quite a lecture on the subject. As the thermometer began its descent to unheard of depths, however, and the food rations (cut twice before Christmas) seemed bent on the same downhill path, the sepulchral cluckings from our cellar, which echoed regularly across the hedgetops, made havoc of our neighbours' status qualms. We noticed discreet wooden structures being erected in bushes and behind unused garages, and felt assured that by spring our corner of the smart residential district would greet the dawn as merrily as a busy barnyard.

There was something coldly unreal about those winter months of watching and waiting – watching the news we hoped would come from America, waiting for the Generals to act. They in their turn, we heard, were waiting for Hitler to attack in the West, he must burn his boats completely before they could be persuaded to make one move to get rid of him. But the expected attack in the West did not come. We were watching and waiting, they were watching and waiting, even Hitler seemed to be watching and waiting – nothing moved. It was as if the bitter, relentless cold had seeped its way into the very fibre of events. [...]

On market days I always had to bestir myself very early indeed, the reason being that I had not lived long enough in Berlin to have my *Quellen* – my sources of supply as they were called; and as soon as food rationing was introduced, everything that was not on the ration cards disappeared like magic from every shop counter and out of every shop window. Unless you were known to some shopkeeper, therefore, some wholesaler or better still farmer, and were able to come to a deal by dint of the ingratiating smile, the tender enquiry after wife and children, cows no longer had livers, hearts, kidneys or tails and hens had vanished off the face of the earth. *'Hamstering'* rapidly became an absorbing occupation, all absorbing for some; for contrary to my expectations (I still took German efficiency for granted) the rationing system in Berlin was chaotic. *Gemein-nutz geht vor Eigennutz* – community welfare comes before self interest. 'German women, your Leader and your country trust you.' Such pious slogans staring out hopefully from every other kiosk, every other billboard, made no impression whatsoever on the agile *Hausfrau* hell-bent on a fruitful scavenge.

My second reason for having to make an early start arose from the simple fact that I was very hard up. To serve the state in Prussia had always been considered an honour needing precious little encouragement financially. Peter's salary at the Ministry of Economics amounted to the princely sum of 486 marks and 20 pfennigs a month, equal to about £30, and when my allowance stopped abruptly on September 3rd, it left a very ominous void in our budget. To have no money was initially quite an adventurous affair, and the children and I would travel all over Berlin on the look-out for a shop or a market-stall where we could buy our wares a few pfennigs cheaper. However, after Peter had explained to me carefully that I was spending far more money on the bus trips than I was ever saving on the odd vegetable or piece of fish bought several miles away, I had stuck to home ground, or rather to home queuing and, as the weeks went by, much of the glamour went out of being poor.

Christabel Bielenberg, *The Past is Myself*

* * *

Starvation leaves no room for sentiment. Novelist Beatrice Collin fictionalises the kind of event that eye-witnesses of the time confirm as all too frequent among a population desperate to survive.

The cart horse swayed and then sank forwards to its knees. The boy with the reins in his hands and the sob in his voice started to shout, 'Come on! ... Gee up! ... Move! Why have you stopped? Move! Please move?' He hit the horse's ridged brown back with his whip, once, twice, three times. The horse flinched, showed the whites of its eyes, and then with a small moan, a letting out of breath, of steam, of life, it slumped and collapsed into a heap of angular bone and sagging skin.

Lilly wasn't the only one standing on Mariannenplatz who was watching. No sooner had the horse's head hit the cobbles than a dozen women appeared from doorways and alleyways armed with knives and bowls and cups. They ignored the boy's cries, his tears, his laments, and began to butcher the carcass, sawing through bone and slicing through veins to let the spurt of warm blood flow into their bowls. One woman, her face splattered with red, tried to hack off a ragged haunch with a penknife; another pulled out the tongue. In minutes, what was left of the horse would vanish completely. Lilly pushed to the front. All she had eaten for months was turnip – raw turnip, since there was rarely any coal to be had. She looked down at the skin and bone that remained and tried to convert it in her mind into something edible. She forced herself to think of stew, of soup, of meat. It was so long since she had eaten any, she had almost forgotten the taste. And yet she tried to make the connection. Horse ... food; food ... horse. The thought filled her mouth with bile and she had to resist the urge to gag. There was someone pulling at her skirt. It was the boy. Tears were streaming down his face.

'My mother,' he sobbed. 'What will my mother say?'

Lilly crouched down next to the bloody remains of the horse. An old woman was pulling out the horse's innards. She had the liver in her hands.

'Give it to the boy,' Lilly said.

The old woman, whose apron was already full, hesitated. Her eyes swivelled round to look at Lilly, to see if it was just a ruse. The sound of the boy's sobs was almost unbearable. Lilly held the old woman's gaze. And so, with much shaking of her head and cursing of the government, she pulled a piece of newspaper from her bag, wrapped up the horse's liver, and handed it over.

Beatrice Collin, *The Luminous Life of Lilly Aphrodite*

❊ ❊ ❊

Even the zoo animals weren't exempt from Berliners' desperate hunger. Just as during the Siege of Paris at the end of the Franco-Prussian war, the citizens' diet became exotic.

A bomb must have fallen on the zoo. A zebra mare wades through the moonlight on Unter-den-Linden, high on careful legs, shy, long-necked and thin as a giraffe. Her stripes are navy-on-sulphur; her ribs poke through her skin. A man grabs his pistol and takes her down. A small mob tears the flesh off the carcass with bare hands. Whoever eats that diseased animal's meat will die of rot in their guts. [...] A flight of holy ibises circles over the city. Holy ibises feast on cadavers; just breathing in the Berlin air is enough to satiate them. A herd of impalas jumps around on Opernplatz; they break their matchstick legs when they slip on the wet stones. We roam through the crowd that gathers around the animals. I apply my newly learned pickpocket skills and empty the wallets of the well-to-do citizens. They deserve it; they just watched Don Giovanni being dragged to a hell of his own making and they enjoyed it. Out of principle, I refuse to steal from the ones who have earned their money honestly, and so I choose only well-tailored gents, and ladies with shiny stones in their ample cleavage. A large proportion of the money I pilfer must come from the Aryanization of Jewish companies or the forced labour of my brothers in faith. I consider it a small form of restitution. A fight breaks out: a worker beats up one of his bosses over possession of an antelope thigh. The police intervene. Shots are fired. Dead bodies, human and animal, are carried away in moving vans.

Berlin, 1943. Our bodies are now fully inoculated with anti-bodies for imminent death.

Paul Verhaeghen, *Omega Minor*

∗ ∗ ∗

If defeat was hard for the remains of Hitler's army to bear, it was even harder for the destitute civilians of Berlin – especially the women (many of whom had been raped by the invading Soviet army), doing their best to ward off starvation in the appalling conditions of that first winter after the war. The narrator of Dan Vyleta's Pavel and I *knows the reality but comforts himself with a little wishful thinking.*

It was the winter of '46, Berlin, the city trussed up into twenty pieces like a turkey on Thanksgiving dinner, eight to the Russians and word had it not a woman there who had not been raped. A winter of death, people freezing in their unheated flats, impoverished, hungry, scraping together something less than a living from the crumbs that fell from their occupiers' tables. And yet, amongst the misery, the first stirrings of recovery: a nightclub in Schöneberg, a working man's brothel in Wedding; some bars around Zoogarten and in the December air the reek of the monkey cage. Small-time businesses, American customers, local staff. […]

It was the winter of '46, winter of death, people freezing while taking craps in the outhouse, you heard the spiel. Most cats in the city had long been eaten, their fur turned into gloves and collars, the black market awash with viola strings. Berlin that winter was dog-eat-dog and worse. […]

I have often wondered how much celebrating went on that winter, the winter of '46. On the whole I am inclined to be optimistic. Had the windows not all been frozen, I am sure we would have been able to make out a tree in every living room, a little shabby perhaps and more likely than not stolen from under their occupiers' noses. On their twigs: talc candles, wooden trinkets and, amongst the wealthy, fragile glass balls, hand-painted, and a silver star to top the crooked little bugger. I gather there wouldn't have been much in the way of presents, but perhaps they managed to procure something a little special for their dinner: a roast bird perhaps, or carp and almonds, a little torte for afters and a half-shot of something lively, just to toast the Christ-child on his coming. Call me sentimental, but I like to think they kept up their spirits, the Krauts, and forgot them for a night, those pangs of defeat.

Dan Vyleta, *Pavel and I*

* * *

Poverty is relative, of course – though always hard. In modern Berlin, those who frequent the flea markets are usually one above those who sell in them … though there are always tourists who find them 'colourful'.

Another Sunday had arrived, one more notch in the unrelenting parade of Sundays, bringing with it the prospect of a walk. Rather than set out aimlessly, I headed towards Boxhagener Platz, the site of an animated flea market I hadn't been to in months. It would be good to circulate in a crowd, I figured, prodded on by strangers too caught up in the visual onslaught to pay much attention to anyone in their midst.

The market was especially busy that afternoon. Long banks of furniture, outlandish clothes, a hodgepodge of crockery, vintage records: all was up for grabs, prices arbitrary (two euros for a skirt, twenty for a shabby belt) but negotiable. At the end of one row of stands sat a gaunt Russian, his face a familiar blend of boredom and melancholy, the ironed-on image of a Russian rock band fading from his T-shirt. Beneath his beige cap his nose stuck out like the muzzle of a malnourished fox. A thick, ruddy-cheeked woman stood near him, cigarette in one hand, baby carriage handle in the other. Like someone in a trance she pushed the carriage back and forth, back and forth, back and forth, but the baby inside, if indeed there was one, never made a squeak and all I saw when I peered in was a heap of blankets. Fanned out on the table before them lay an assortment of sad objects: a doorless birdcage, stuffed animals with missing eyes, a knapsack with a broken zipper, porcelain cups so thin they'd crumble between the lips.

After surveying a few other stands, mountains of junk with the odd gem thrown in, and getting shoved a little too often by zealous bargain hunters, I decided I'd had my fill for the day.

Chloe Aridjis, *Book of Clouds*

✳ ✳ ✳

Students are used to taking on all kinds of work to support their studies. Vladimir Kaminer tells us about a few unusual jobs done by a Ukrainian student studying at Berlin's prestigious Humboldt University.

Berlin is not exactly the city of the poor, but here as elsewhere there are increasingly disadvantaged sections of the population: students reading humanities subjects, single mothers, or street musicians with drug addictions. Not until you have completed your studies are you entitled to welfare. So graduates in theology are more often to be found talking to the social security office than to God. Even a student who is getting a grant of 800 marks a month, half of it needed for his rent, would be vegetating below the welfare level if it weren't for student jobs. But then, what jobs does a prospective humanities graduate get offered by the student job exchange? My friend Sasha from the Ukraine, who has been reading Slavic studies at the Humboldt University for two years, had a choice between dish-washing in an Australian crocodile steakhouse, cleaning the lavatories in the Beate Uhse Museum of Erotica, or helping with liposuction treatment at a beauty clinic. Though he is himself a vegetarian, Sasha opted for the crocodile restaurant, and was revolted from morning till night. Fortunately it was not long before he got to know Unter Wasser, a Russian rock band who also ran a removals service, and he went to work for them as a furniture loader.

Working in the removals sector strengthens a man's muscles and broadens his mental horizon. Every day you're meeting new people, entering new apartments, and making contacts. On one occasion, Sasha helped two women with their move. They ran a stand on Winterfeldplatz which bore the delightful legend Nuts from around the World and German Mushrooms from Saxony. The two women, who were raising a child together, took a liking to Sasha and promptly gave him a job as a vendor on the stand. Effortlessly he transferred from removals to selling nuts.

Vladimir Kaminer, *Russian Disco*
translated by Michael Hulse

* * *

To be poor in a big city means living in close proximity to other poor people, often in old, unhealthy buildings. In the 1990s whole swathes of East Berlin were in a state of decay. Here, a young woman describes her building in Mitte.

It was in January.

January in my third winter here, the harshest I can remember. The whole city is caught up in the brace of the cold. There are traces of snow everywhere, on fence posts, the tops of trees and in the gutters. Like today but just not melting, residues freezing stiff for endless days as the temperatures have fallen too low for more snow.

In the front building of number fourteen, Lehniner Strasse, a hard core of residents holds on that year, each of them sticking it out for a different reason despite the first cracks in the walls.

Two gay variety artistes live on the third floor with a four-metre-long brown and white spotted boa constrictor. I can see into their back room, which has been converted into a kind of terrarium and must be damp and humid, deteriorating the building's substance even more. I hear them arguing long and often over the great deal of housework their zoo requires. At night I see the glowing openings in their small stove, which has to be fed around the clock. They also keep tarantulas, a parrot and a docile-muzzled black mastiff. The dog follows them like a calf-shaped shadow when they carry their snake basket down the stairs towards the Friedrichstadtpalast on Mondays and Thursdays.

Opposite them lives a nun from an Indian sect, a subtenant of one of her fellow believers who has gone away to Southeast Asia. When she walks across the yard with her head held high early in the mornings, her orange habit shines out like a clear flame amidst the greys and browns of rotting urban substances. Now and then we chat in English. I find out she's actually Jewish and comes from Argentina. Giggling, she tells me about the stains she found under the carpet in her hallway, sniffing with her nose to the floor, the contours of the last tenant but one – a suicide whose putrefying body ruined the paint.

The third flat that is still inhabited is on the ground floor on the right and is the headquarters of a group of mainly homeless alcoholics. Some of them have keys, others ram bottles against the door at night until someone wakes from their alcoholic daze and opens up. The gas and electricity have been cut off; you can see them walking around in there with torches. The actual tenants are a bearded Saxon and his pointy-nosed, swollen-eyed female companion, half of whose body has strong shakes. They have a child, about six years old with a pointy nose of his own. Luckily, he only has to come here at weekends. In the brightly knitted threads of his plastic hat, his face always looks very pale. Mechanically and reluctantly, he takes pigeon steps between the childishly swaying adults.

Inka Parei, *Die Schattenboxerin* ('The Shadow-boxer')
translated by Katy Derbyshire

* * *

*From rags to (temporary) riches: a father and daughter
team give advice to the poverty-stricken Berliner –
and an amusing anecdote of how a computer error
gave them a taste of the high life.*

We would discourage shoplifting, for example. It does raise
the adrenalin levels and is good for the digestion, but the
unpleasantries are all the greater when it goes bottom-up. The
authors have had less than pleasing experiences with it, which
they would like to share with you here. When the male part
of the team first entered the 'Kaufhaus des Westens' department store – he himself came from the East – he was so overwhelmed by the magnificence and wealth of goods on sale
that he felt compelled to bring a present home for the female
part. Unfortunately, this was hindered by a lack of cash, so
that he attempted to put on the object of his choice – a pair
of pristine suede gloves – himself, which proved more difficult
than expected due to his rather too large hands. A store detective had observed this act and cornered the delinquent on the
escalator. How embarrassing when he was led off to the store
detectives' office and they there pried the gloves from his long
fingers, asked after his ID and, as he pretended not to have any
with him, his name. 'Thomas Richter,' he said, automatically
giving the name he had stored in his brain for cases of this kind
since his childhood. 'Address?' '19 Leninstrasse.' That was a
mistake, making the West Berlin cops suspicious, and when
they threatened a strip search he revealed his true identity with
his ID card.

But that's only the first part of the story. The second followed
after the thief had transferred a 50 DM penalty and subse-
quently received a letter from the store containing two invita-
tions to a gourmet meal in the KaDeWe gourmet department.
His ladyfriend called the store and asked whether the penalty

had been received. – 'No.' – 'But we've got a receipt.' – 'Oh, something must have gone wrong with the computer. You didn't get an invitation to a gourmet meal, by any chance?' – 'Not that I know of.'

The following Saturday, we donned our gladrags and arrived at the store at precisely 8 pm. Everything was illuminated, the men were dressed in heavy coats, the women in furs. The escalators were standing still; we were taken by lift to the fourth floor. What we experienced there, between lobster and oysters, artichoke hearts, foie gras and rosé champagne, we shall leave to the reader's imagination. It convinced us at any rate never again to descend to the depths of common shoplifting, and to purchase a golden customer card instead.

Bernd and Luise Wagner, *Berlin für Arme* ('Berlin for the poor')
translated by Katy Derbyshire

✻ ✻ ✻

Like city-dwellers everywhere, most working-class Berliners can't afford to live in the centre and usually end up in places like those described here by Chloe Aridjis.

I emerged from the Ring S-Bahn and entered the land of the Plattenbaus, which seemed even more looming and vast than those in Alexanderplatz and its immediate vicinity. Here the prefabricated concrete edifices overwhelmed the horizon, which was otherwise quite low, and had been repainted in playful colours with Rubik's cube patterns, alternating red and blue squares, or else in soft pastels, the lower half pink and the top half baby blue; yet others were bright red with green windows and balconies, but they all resembled huge Lego blocks, a delirium of squares or dice cast onto a flat, monotone terrain.

I turned off the main avenue, Landsberger Allee, and onto a curving street that branched off into different Plattenbau "communities" where, as far as I could tell, the mantra of Communist housing still felt very present in the layout. Each lot had three massive buildings enclosing a square equipped with a playground and a small communal space full of trees. Some even had a school and supermarket or miniature shopping centre, creating the impression that each area was self-ruling or self-sufficient, as if it had its own central nervous system and all you had to do was touch one nerve and every inch of the place would reverberate. I saw only one guy with a cocky strut but otherwise the people I passed simply looked like working-class folk getting on with their day, lots of women of different ages walking their dogs, young Vietnamese smoking cigarettes at the entrances to supermarkets, a group of elderly Russians gathered around a park bench. Dusk was falling but the silvery light suited the place, which seemed both frozen in time and strangely futuristic.

Chloe Aridjis, *Book of Clouds*

✳ ✳ ✳

So where do the better-off live? Previously one of the poorer areas of Berlin, Prenzlauer Berg is now a fashionable address for the city's upwardly mobile young professionals. Just one example of the constantly changing face of the capital. Blogger Simon Cole takes us for a quick visit.

It's difficult to imagine that Prenzlauer Berg was ever anything but a playground for the stylish young professionals of Berlin. Boutique shops sell the latest retro sportswear look for local hipsters, while tattooed 20-somethings brush the pavement outside low key bars that will later be filled with creative and media types sipping on premium beers. Yummy mummies drop into the local bakery for some of that richly fibrous bread that Germans adore and which makes them turn their noses up at anaemic British breakfast offerings.

There are kids everywhere in what was recently declared one of the most fertile spots in Europe; the ratio of children to adults shot up as it became the place to settle with your firstborn when suburbia is a wrench too far for the still young parent who has yet to leave books, bars and me-time behind. And it is very civilised. Having dodged HGVs in London's erratic and intermittent cycle lanes, it's a sight to behold these phalanxes of mothers – and the odd father – sedately crossing the boulevards on dedicated cycle paths with their own set of signals. You know for a fact that everything is recycled here.

And the art! The walls are a living canvas. Ironic exchanges of postcommunist banter: "Capitalism sucks" then the answering "Communism sucks" mix with the latest in stencil art. Huge dayglow pink letters on flyposters seem to challenge you to a fight as they announce "F*** Amerika". Dark stone buildings from another age have their gravitas subverted with rampant spray can colours and a plethora of pop art posters.

But these contradictions run deeper than the imposition of 21st century culture onto pre-war buildings, where parents obliviously push their single child under a sign for a club which shouts "B*stard". When I told a German girl I was going to visit my friend on Kastanienallee (Chestnut Tree Avenue) she immediately said: "Well she's not from the east then if she lives there." She smiled as she said it, but with that trace of a raised eyebrow that accompanies a point being made.

And indeed, my friend isn't. She's an academic who moved to Berlin and did reasonably well for herself, and so moved to the steadily-gentrifying Prenzlauer Berg to enjoy the fruits of her labour, in every sense. This was my first inkling, as someone new to Germany, that 'unification' is a small word for a long drawn out and incomplete process.

Simon Cole, Berlin Blog at Bookpacking.com

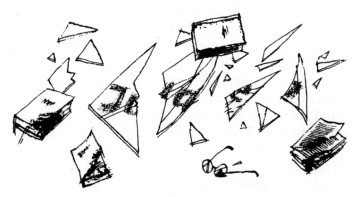

The past is another country

It's hard to imagine that Berlin was ever less than one of the most imposing cities of Europe. In Measuring the World *Daniel Kehlmann gives us a glimpse of a Berlin just beginning to take shape in the early nineteenth century.*

They reached Berlin the next day in the late afternoon. Thousands of little houses in a chaotic sprawl, a settlement overflowing its banks in the swampiest spot in Europe. The first splendid buildings were beginning to go up: a cathedral, some palaces, a museum to house the finds from Humboldt's great expedition.

In a few years, said Eugen, this would be a metropolis like Rome, Paris, or St. Petersburg.

Never, said Gauss. Horrible place!

The coach bumped over badly laid cobblestones. Twice the horses shied away from growling dogs, and in the side streets the wheels almost stuck fast in the wet sand. Their host lived in the Packhof at number 4, in the middle of the city, right behind the building site of the new museum. To make sure they didn't miss it, he had drawn a very precise plan with a fine pen. Someone must have seen them from a distance and announced their arrival, for a matter of seconds after they pulled into the courtyard, the main door flew open and four men were running towards them.

Alexander von Humboldt was a little old gentleman with snow-white hair. Behind him came a secretary with an open pad of writing paper, a flunkey in livery, and a young man with whiskers carrying a stand with a wooden box on it. As if rehearsed, they took up their positions. Humboldt stretched out his arms towards the door of the coach.

Nothing happened.

From inside the vehicle came sounds of hectic speech. No, cried someone, no! A dull blow rang out, then a third no! After which there was nothing for a while.

Finally the door swung open and Gauss clambered carefully down into the street. He shrank back as Humboldt seized him by the shoulders and cried what an honor it was, what a great moment for Germany, for science, for him personally.

The secretary was taking notes, and the man behind the wooden box hissed, Now!

Humboldt froze. This was Monsieur Daguerre, he whispered without moving his lips. A protégé of his, who was working on a piece of equipment which would fix the moment on a light-sensitive silver iodide plate and snatch it out of the onrush of time. Please hold absolutely still!

Gauss said he wanted to go home.

Just a moment, whispered Humboldt, a mere fifteen minutes, tremendous progress had been made already. Until recently it had taken much longer, when they tried it first he had thought his back wouldn't hold out under the strain. Gauss wanted to pull himself free, but the little old man held him with surprising strength and murmured, Bring word to the king. The flunkey was off at a run. Then, probably because that was what was going through his mind at that moment: Take a note. Check possibility of breeding seals in Warnemünde, conditions seem propitious, give me proposal tomorrow. The secretary scribbled.

Eugen, who was only just climbing out of the coach with a slight limp, made his apologies for the late hour of their arrival.

There was no late here, and no early, murmured Humboldt. Here there was only work, and the work got done. Luckily it was still light. Not to move.

A policeman entered the courtyard and asked what was going on.

Later, hissed Humboldt, his lips pressed together.

This was an unauthorized gathering, said the policeman. Either everyone went their separate ways or this would become police business.

He was a chamberlain, Humboldt hissed.

Excuse me? The policeman bent forward.

Chamberlain, Humboldt's secretary repeated. Member of the Court.

Daguerre ordered the policeman to get out of the picture.

Frowning, the policeman stepped back. First of all, anyone could claim the same thing, and secondly, the ban on gatherings applied to everyone. And that one there, pointing to Eugen, was clearly a student. Which made it particularly ticklish.

If he didn't immediately make himself scarce, said the secretary, he would find himself in difficulties he couldn't even begin to imagine.

This was no way to address an officer, said the policeman nervously. He would give them five minutes.

Gauss groaned and pulled himself free.

Oh no, cried Humboldt.

Daguerre stamped his foot. Now the moment had been lost forever!

Daniel Kehlmann, *Measuring the World*
translated by Carol Brown Janeway

✻ ✻ ✻

> *The protagonist of Theodor Fontane's famous novel*
> Effie Briest *(1895) leaves the provinces to enjoy life*
> *in Berlin where new buildings, confidence, and the*
> *ambition of its rulers were transforming the city.*

Friedrichstrasse station was crowded; but nonetheless, Effi
had recognized her mother from the compartment, and Cousin
Briest beside her. Their joy at the reunion was great, waiting
in the luggage hall was not too severe a test of their patience,
and in little more than five minutes their cab was trundling
alongside the horse tram rails into Dorotheenstrasse in the
direction of Schadowstrasse where the *pension* stood on the
first corner. [...]

The next day was a very fine one, and mother and daughter
went out early, first to the eye clinic where Effi sat in the waiting
room and occupied herself leafing through an album. Then
they went to the Tiergarten and on to the vicinity of the Zoo
to look for an apartment in that area. And as it happened they
did locate something eminently suitable in Keithstrasse, which
is where they had been thinking of from the outset, except that
it was a new building, damp and not quite finished. 'It won't
do, Effi dear,' said Frau von Briest, 'it must be ruled out simply
for health reasons. You don't put in a Geheimrat to dry out
plaster.' [...]

The social season in the city was not yet over when they
started to pay their calls in April, but it was winding down, so
they did not quite manage to enter into it fully. In the second
half of May it dies out completely, and they were even happier
than before to meet in the Tiergarten when Innstetten came
from work in the lunch hour, or to take a stroll in the Charlottenburg Palace gardens in the afternoon. Effi, as they walked up
and down the long frontage between the Palace and the Orang-
erie trees, always looked at the Roman emperors standing there
by the dozen, noting a curious similarity between Nero and
Titus, collected pine-cones that had fallen from the weeping

spruces, and then went with her husband, arm in arm, as far as the distant Belvedere over by the Spree.

Theodor Fontane, *Effie Briest*
translated by Hugh Rorrison and Helen Chambers

✳ ✳ ✳

*At the very end of the nineteenth century well-con-
nected traveller Gertrude Bell found herself in Berlin.
Her letters give a lively insight into the high society
of the time.*

Dearest Elsa,   Berlin, *Jan. 22nd,* 1897

I made my bow to the "Kaiser Paar" on Wednesday. It was a very fine show. We drove to the Schloss in the glass coach and were saluted by the guard when we arrived. We felt very swell! Then we waited for a long time with all the other dips. in a room next to the throne room and at about 8 the doors were thrown open. We all hastily arranged one another's trains and marched in procession while the band played the march out of Lohengrin. The Emperor and Empress were standing on a dais at the end of the room and we walked through a sort of passage made by rows and rows of pages dressed in pink. The "Aller-höcht" looked extremely well in a red uniform – I couldn't look at the Empress much as I was so busy avoiding Aunt Mary's train. She introduced me and then stood aside while I made two curtseys. Then I wondered what the dickens I should do next, but Aunt Mary made me a little sign to go out behind her, so I "enjambéd" her train and fled! [...]

To F.B.   Berlin, *Tuesday,* 1897
... F. and I went to see *Henry IV* last night, the Emperor having invited all the Embassy to come to the royal box. Uncle F. and Aunt M. were dining with the Frederic Leopolds, so they were obliged to decline the box for themselves but the Emperor said that he hoped we should go as we should be

chaperoned by Countess Keller, one of the ladies-in-waiting. Accordingly we went off by ourselves and sat very comfortably with Countess Keller in the second row of chairs – no one might sit in the front row even when the royalties were not in the box. All the Embassy and a lot of the Court people were with us, the Emperor and Empress were in a little box at the side. The play was very well done. The Falstaff excellent and the whole thing beautifully staged. There was no pause till the end of the second act when there was a long entr'acte. Countess Keller bustled away and presently came hurrying back and whispered something to Knesebeck and Egloffstein, two of the Court people, and they came and told F. and me that we were sent for. So off we went rather trembling, under the escort of Countess K. and Egloffstein who conducted us into a little tiny room behind the Emperor's box where we found the "Kaiser Paar" sitting and having tea. We made deep curtseys and kissed the Empress's hand, and then we all sat down, F. next to the Emperor and I next to the Empress and they gave us tea and cakes. It was rather formidable though they were extremely kind. The Emperor talked nearly all the time; he tells us that no plays of Shakespeare were ever acted in London and that we must have heard tell that it was only the Germans who had really studied or really understood Shakespeare. One couldn't contradict an Emperor, so we said we had always been told so. Egloffstein's chair broke in the middle of the party and he came flat on to the ground which created a pleasing diversion – I was so glad it wasn't mine! Countess K. was a dear and started a new subject whenever the conversation languished. After about 20 minutes the Empress got up, we curtseyed to her, shook hands with the Emperor. Florence thanked him very prettily for sending for us and we bowed ourselves out. Wasn't it amusing! Florence said she felt shy but she looked perfectly self-possessed and had the prettiest little air in the world as she sat talking to the Emperor. I felt rather frightened, but I did not mind much as I knew I need do nothing but follow Florence's lead. The Empress sits very upright and is rather alarming. He flashes round from one person to the other and talks as fast as possible and is not alarming at all . [...]

To F.B.   Berlin, *Feb. 12th*, 1897
The Court Ball on Wednesday was much nicer than the first one ... The Emperor wore a gorgeous Austrian uniform in honour of an Austrian Archduke who was there – the brother of the man who is heir to the throne. He will be Emperor himself someday as the heir is sickly and unmarried. The Emperor William is disappointing when one sees him close; he looks puffy and ill and I never saw anyone so jumpy. He is never still a second while he is talking ... .

Uncle Frank is in a great jig about Crete. He thinks there is going to be red war and an intervention of the Powers and all sorts of fine things. I wonder.

Gertrude Bell, *The Letters of Gertrude Bell*

* * *

The Baedeker name has long been synonymous with tourism. This guidebook empire was begun by Karl Baedeker (1801–1859) in Koblenz. This excerpt is from the 1912 edition of his Berlin guide, describing what is clearly a splendid city.

As regards its *General Aspect*, Berlin suffers from the dead level of its site, and also, since three-quarters of its buildings are quite modern, from a certain lack of historical interest. The Church of St. Nicholas, the Church of St. Mary, the Kloster-Kirche, and the Chapel of the Holy Ghost are practically the only buildings remaining of the old town, which consisted of narrow, crooked streets of dwelling-houses, and a few larger cloisters and hospitals grouped round the two Town Halls. With improved means of locomotion the inner town has now gradually become the commercial nucleus of Berlin, like the City in London. Immense and palatial buildings have arisen, occupied from floor to ceiling by business-offices and ware-rooms. The approaches to the old town have been widened, new ones have been built, and the Spree has been cleared of obstructions. The neighbourhood of the *Royal Palace* has been remodelled in harmony with the baroque forms of the palace itself. The Lustgarten, the Opera House Square, and the Linden together form a broad and magnificent thorough-fare of the first rank, such as may possibly be paralleled in Vienna, but certainly not in either London or Paris. The street known as *Unter den Linden* which had hardly lived up to its ancient reputation, has again become one of the chief arteries of traffic. The old houses are disappearing, magnificent hotels and business-premises have sprung up, while the avenues of trees and the footpaths have been altered and modernized. The system on which the *Friedrichstadt*, to the S. of the Linden, is laid out, points to its origin in the mere will of the sovereign. The regular streets crossing each other at right angles have not arisen from the needs of traffic; the few squares, such as the Gendarmen-Markt, have been arbitrarily inserted. Here also, however, the old houses have been replaced by magnificent new buildings, notably in the chief streets. The Behren-Strasse, the chief residence of the diplomats down to 1870, the Mauer-Strasse and the Kanonier-Strasse, all now contain numerous banking-houses and insurance-offices. The Spittel-Markt and the Hausvogtei-Platz are commercial centres, while the inva-sion of the residential quarters by business-premises progresses steadily towards the W. and already extends far up in the neigh-bourhood of the Leipziger-Strasse. [...]

Almost every part of Berlin offers a pleasing picture. Its streets are a model of cleanliness, while a system of main drainage, radiating in twelve directions, carries all of its sewage to distant fields. There are few dark lanes or alleys even in the old part of the city. Nearly all the newer houses have balconies, gay in summer with flowers and foliage. The public squares are embellished with gardens, monuments, and fountains, and the newer churches also are generally surrounded by small pleasure-grounds. Numerous bridges are beautified with sculpture. The centres of traffic, such as the Jannowitz-Brücke, the Trebbiner-Strasse, the Lehrte Station, etc., with their network of railway-lines, and the navigation on the river offer scenes of remarkable animation.

Karl Baedeker, *Guide to Berlin*

✷ ✷ ✷

In the same year as the above edition of Baedeker's guide, the protagonist of Beatrice Collin's novel The Luminous Life of Lilly Aphrodite *catches a glimpse of the Kaiser for the first time, in all the grandeur of Wilhelminian Berlin.*

Lilly saw Kaiser Wilhelm II for the first time on a Thursday in February 1912. A thick fog had been lying across the city all morning, and by mid-afternoon there was the taste of snow in the air. She heard the military procession long before she could see it. Marches played on brass instruments lifted above the rooftops, and drums, the distance throwing them out of beat, boomed along the gutters, sending handfuls of indignant pigeons into the sky. Lilly reached the Unter den Linden just as the kaiser's open-topped automobile was approaching. As the car passed, she glimpsed his face, his huge dark moustache, his withered arm, and the sweep of his pale hair.

Of course, Lilly had seen him before on the cinema screen, walking with the empress and Crown Princess Cecilie in the palace gardens, opening regattas and launching warships. Wilhelm II was so fond of 'film art', as he called it, that he would turn towards the lens, give that famous smile, wave that informal wave, or tousle a child's already tousled hair at the smallest prompt. That afternoon there were no cameras to focus on his smile, but he smiled nevertheless: at his subjects, at the huge crowds, at his city. Beside him, on the soft grey leather seats, sat a dignitary with white whiskers and a slightly morose expression.

'Hooray for the kaiser,' a young man shouted from a lamp-post. 'And hooray for Franz Josef, the Emperor of Austria and King of Hungary.' The applause was spontaneous, the noise almost earsplitting, the emotion palpable, as both men reached up, touched their hats, and set their decorative feathers aquiver.

A few seconds later, there was a small explosion, followed by the skittering somewhere close behind of horses' hooves. The royal car slowed down and stopped. The Kaiser and the emperor both turned and peered back. But it was nothing. A child with a firework, that's all, the whisper went through the crowd. [...]

The brass band began another tune and the royal parade, first the Kaiser in his brand-new Daimler, then the mounted infantry, and finally the goose-stepping cavalry, moved on and headed towards the Brandenburger Tor. As the car approached the stone arch, the processions slowed – this time on purpose – and stopped. On the top of the arch the Goddess of Victory rode in her chariot. Down below, the once king of Prussia, now ruler of Imperial Germany, stood up in his seat. A pair of guns fired. A clutch of swans honked. A horse farted. For a fraction of a second Berlin held its breath. And then Wilhelm cleared his throat twice and saluted. The crowds cheered until they could cheer no more. Dozens of hats were thrown up into the white sky and many were lost forever.

It would be six years before Lilly saw the kaiser again, in a train station at midnight. He missed his chance to meet her gaze at that moment too. His eyes, you see, would be too full of tears.

Beatrice Collin, *The Luminous Life of Lilly Aphrodite*

We all know the story of what happened in those six terrible years between Lilly's two contrasting sightings of Kaiser Wilhelm. The humiliating defeat of Germany and the horrors of the First World War, along with the economically crippling burden of war reparations imposed by the Treaty of Versailles, paved the way for the rise of National Socialism and the disaster of Hitler's influence and ultimate control of the nation. Berlin bore the brunt of the struggle between two opposite world views as both the extreme left and the extreme right – each with their own vision of Germany's future – battled it out on the city's streets.

Berlin was in a state of civil war. Hate exploded suddenly, without warning, out of nowhere; at street corners, in restaurants, cinemas, dance halls, swimming-baths; at midnight, after breakfast, in the middle of the afternoon. Knives were whipped out, blows were dealt with spiked rings, beer-mugs, chair-legs or leaded clubs; bullets slashed the advertisements on the poster-columns, rebounded from the iron roofs of latrines. In the middle of a crowded street a young man would be attacked, stripped, thrashed and left bleeding on the pavement; in fifteen seconds it was all over and the assailants had disappeared. Otto got a gash over the eye with a razor in a battle on a fair-ground near the Cöpernickerstrasse. The doctor put in three stitches and he was in hospital for a week. The newspapers were full of death-bed photographs of rival martyrs, Nazi, Reichsbanner and Communist. My pupils looked at them and shook their heads, apologizing to me for the state of Germany. 'Dear, dear!' they said, 'it's terrible. It can't go on.'

The murder reporters and the jazz-writers had inflated the German language beyond recall. The vocabulary of newspaper invective (traitor, Versailles-lackey, murder-swine, Marx-crook, Hitler-swamp, Red-pest) had come to resemble, through excessive use, the formal phraseology of politeness employed by the

Chinese. The word *Liebe*, soaring from the Goethe standard, was no longer worth a whore's kiss. *Spring, moonlight, youth, roses, girl, darling, heart, May*: such was the miserably devaluated currency dealt in by the authors of all those tangoes, waltzes and fox-trots which advocated the private escape. Find a dear little sweetheart, they advised, and forget the slump, ignore the unemployed. Fly, they urged us, to Hawaii, to Naples, to the Never-Never-Vienna. Hugenberg, behind the Ufa, was serving up nationalism to suit all tastes. He produced battlefield epics, farces of barrack-room life, operettas in which the jinks of a pre-war military aristocracy were reclothed in the fashions of 1932. His brilliant directors and cameramen had to concentrate their talents on cynically beautiful shots of the bubbles in champagne and the sheen of lamplight on silk.

And morning after morning, all over the immense, damp, dreary town and the packing-case colonies of huts in the suburb allotments, young men were waking up to another work-less empty day to be spent as they could best contrive; selling bootlaces, begging, playing draughts in the hall of the Labour Exchange, hanging about urinals, opening the doors of cars, helping with crates in the markets, gossiping, lounging, stealing, overhearing racing tips, sharing stumps of cigarette-ends picked up in the gutter, singing folk-songs for groschen in courtyards and between stations in the carriages of the Underground Railway. After the New Year, the snow fell, but did not lie; there was no money to be earned by sweeping it away. The shopkeepers rang all coins on the counter for fear of the forgers. Frl. Schroeder's astrologer foretold the end of the world. 'Listen,' said Fritz Wendel, between sips of a cocktail in the bar of the Eden Hotel, 'I give a damn if this country goes communist. What I mean, we'd have to alter our ideas a bit. Hell, who cares?'

At the beginning of March, the posters for the Presidential Election began to appear. Hindenburg's portrait, with an inscription in gothic lettering beneath it, struck a frankly religious note: 'He

110

hath kept faith with you; be ye faithful unto Him.' The Nazis managed to evolve a formula which dealt cleverly with this venerable icon and avoided the offence of blasphemy: 'Honour Hindenburg; Vote for Hitler.' Otto and his comrades set out every night, with paint-pots and brushes, on dangerous expeditions. They climbed high walls, scrambled along roofs, squirmed under hoardings; avoiding the police and the S.A. patrols. And next morning, passers-by would see Thälmann's name boldly inscribed in some prominent and inaccessible position. Otto gave me a bunch of little gum-backed labels: Vote for Thälmann, the Workers' Candidate. I carried these about in my pocket and stuck them on shopwindows and doors when nobody was looking.

Brüning spoke in the Sport Palace. We must vote for Hindenburg, he told us, and save Germany. His gestures were sharp and admonitory; his spectacles gleamed emotion in the limelight. His voice quivered with dry academic passion. 'Inflation,' he threatened, and the audience shuddered. 'Tannenberg,' he reverently reminded: there was prolonged applause.

Bayer spoke in the Lustgarten, during a snowstorm, from the roof of a van; a tiny, hatless figure gesticulating above the vast heaving sea of faces and banners. Behind him was the cold façade of the Schloss; and, lining its stone balustrade, the ranks of armed silent police. 'Look at them,' cried Bayer. 'Poor chaps! It seems a shame to make them stand out of doors in weather like this. Never mind; they've got nice thick coats to keep them warm. Who gave them those coats? We did. Wasn't it kind of us? And who's going to give *us* coats? Ask me another.'

Christopher Isherwood, *Mr Norris Changes Trains*

* * *

Early this evening I was in the Bülowstrasse. There had been a big Nazi meeting at the Sportpalast, and groups of men and boys were just coming away from it, in their brown or black uniforms. Walking along the pavement ahead of me were three

111

S.A. men. They all carried Nazi banners on their shoulders, like rifles, rolled tight round the staves – the banner-staves had sharp metal points, shaped into arrow-heads.

All at once, the three S.A. men came face to face with a youth of seventeen or eighteen, dressed in civilian clothes, who was hurrying along in the opposite direction. I heard one of the Nazis shout: 'That's him!' and immediately all three of them flung themselves upon the young man. He uttered a scream, and tried to dodge, but they were too quick for him. In a moment they had jostled him into the shadow of a house entrance, and were standing over him, kicking him and stabbing at him with the sharp metal points of their banners. All this happened with such incredible speed that I could hardly believe my eyes – already, the three S.A. men had left their victim, and were barging their way through the crowd; they made for the stairs which led up to the station of the Overhead Railway.

Another passer-by and myself were the first to reach the doorway where the young man was lying. He lay huddled crookedly in the corner, like an abandoned sack. As they picked him up, I got a sickening glimpse of his face – his left eye was poked half out, and blood poured from the wound. He wasn't dead. Somebody volunteered to take him to the hospital in a taxi.

By this time, dozens of people were looking on. They seemed surprised, but not particularly shocked – this sort of thing happened too often, nowadays. '*Allerhand* … ' they murmured. Twenty yards away, at the Potsdamerstrasse corner, stood a group of heavily armed policemen. With their chests out, and rounds on their revolver belts, they magnificently disregarded the whole affair. […]

Today, January 22nd, the Nazis held a demonstration on the Bülowplatz, in front of the Karl Liebknecht House. For the last week the communists have been trying to get the demonstration forbidden: they say it is simply intended as a provocation – as, of course, it was. I went along to watch it with Frank, the newspaper correspondent.

As Frank himself said afterwards, this wasn't really a Nazi demonstration at all, but a Police demonstration – there were at least two policemen to every Nazi present. Perhaps General Schleicher only allowed the march to take place in order to show who are the real masters of Berlin. Everybody says he's going to proclaim a military dictatorship.

But the real masters of Berlin are not the Police, or the Army, and certainly not the Nazis. The masters of Berlin are the workers – despite all the propaganda I've heard and read, all the demonstrations I've attended, I only realized this, for the first time to-day. Comparatively few of the hundreds of people in the streets round the Bülowplatz can have been organized communists, yet you had the feeling that every single one of them was united against this march. Somebody began to sing the 'International', and, in a moment, everyone had joined in – even the women with their babies, watching from top-storey windows. The Nazis slunk past, marching as fast as they knew how, between their double rows of protectors. Most of them kept their eyes on the ground, or glared glassily ahead: a few attempted sickly, furtive grins. When the procession had passed, an elderly fat little S.A. man, who had somehow got left behind, came panting along at the double, desperately scared at finding himself alone, and trying vainly to catch up with the rest. The whole crowd roared with laughter.

During the demonstration nobody was allowed on the Bülowplatz itself. So the crowd surged uneasily about, and things began to look nasty. The police, brandishing their rifles, ordered us back; some of the less experienced ones, getting rattled, made as if to shoot. Then an armoured car appeared, and started to turn its machine-gun slowly in our direction. There was a stampede into house doorways and cafés; but no sooner had the car moved on, than everybody rushed out into the street again, shouting and singing. It was too much like a naughty schoolboy's game to be seriously alarming. Frank enjoyed himself enormously, grinning from ear to ear, and hopping about, in his flapping overcoat and huge owlish spectacles, like a mocking, ungainly bird.

Only a week since I wrote the above, Schleicher has resigned. The monocles did their stuff. Hitler has formed a cabinet with Hugenberg. Nobody thinks it can last till the spring.

Christopher Isherwood, *Goodbye to Berlin*

✻ ✻ ✻

If you have read Salil Tripathi's article in the 'Out and About' section, you will remember the description of the memorial to the burning of books by the Nazis. The extract below is from a book by Volker Weidermann which portrays each of the authors whose books were on the Nazi blacklist and burned publicly in 1933, shortly after the Reichstag fire (blamed on the Communists, but since thought to be instigated by the Nazis themselves as a ploy to justify repression). We join the late-night crowd gathered around a sinister bonfire.

A fat woman with a ruddy face stands at the edge of the flames, staring after a half-burnt page of a book that has been whirled up in the air by the wind. She keeps a tight hold of her brown-shirted husband's hand and shouts 'Wonderful time! Wonderful time!' over and over into the crowd. She is standing right next to the *Pravda* reporter, set to send his piece to Moscow the next day. It is 10 May 1933, just after midnight. A spectacle is underway on Berlin's Opernplatz. The light of the fire is visible from far and wide. The flames rise ten or twelve metres into the sky; the organisers have hired a pyrotechnics company for the preparations. Eight large piles of metre-long pieces of wood were set up, before that sand was spread on the ground to prevent damage to the cobblestones. It starts to rain at 9.30 in the evening, causing a slight panic among the fire's masters of ceremonies. They keep having to rub the wood dry, as it is supposed to keep the fire burning as long as the objects to be burned today are not yet available. Several thousand people have come, despite the rain. The newspapers have been reporting regularly on the event over the past few days. No one knew quite what was going to happen. But there was a chance that it might be a major rally as uplifting as ten days previously, when Hitler summoned up the new cohesion of the German people on the Tempelhof parade ground with a spectacular lightshow, and even the French ambassador was moved to report: 'Everything gives off a good, happy atmosphere, general joy. Nothing recalls force or constraint.' [… ..]

[Goebbels] stood on a little platform in a pale coat under spotlights with a view of the flames, of the students, the SA men, the expectant audience, and announced the end of the 'age of exaggerated Jewish intellectualism' and the 'breakthrough of the German revolution', which had opened the gates for the German way. He called: 'When the National Socialist movement seized power on 30 January of this year, we could not yet know that things could be cleaned up so fast and so radically in Germany.'

One can well believe him. He himself couldn't believe until the day before the burnings that the Germans had come this far. That they would stand by and willingly watch the books of their best writers being surrendered to the flames.

The night when German literature was driven out for all the world to see, was to be erased from the country's memory, from the past, present and future. This night was like a fracture in the lives of the 131 authors on the list of 'anti-German spirit'. A fracture in their lives and their works. And a fracture in the history of this country.

The Alsatian author René Schickele, whose books were not on the list for that night and were only removed from the country's libraries at a later point, wrote in exile: 'If Goebbels succeeds in wiping our names from the German tablets, we are dead. Ghosts in the diaspora, in the arid provinces. Even the next generation will know nothing more of us.' This was his objective. It was the objective of this fire on that night in May, the objective of all those who threw the books into the flames. They did not succeed.

Volker Weidermann, *Das Buch der verbrannten Bücher*
('The book of burnt books') translated by Katy Derbyshire

❋ ❋ ❋

Hitler decided to use the 1936 Berlin Olympics as a 'showcase' for the success of National Socialism and to reassure the world that rumours of persecution of the Jewish population were unfounded ... that all was simply splendid in the Third Reich. To this end, all public manifestations of anti-Semitism were removed, and the emphasis was on grandeur and efficiency.

This morning, at the corner of Friedrichstrasse and Jägerstrasse, I saw two men. SA men, unscrewing a red *Der Stürmer* showcase from the wall of a building. *Der Stürmer* is the anti-Semitic journal that's run by the Reich's leading Jew-baiter, Julius Streicher. The visual impact of these display cases, with their semi-pornographic line-drawings of Aryan maids in the voluptuous embraces of long-nosed monsters, tends to attract the weaker-minded reader, providing him with cursory titillation. Respectable people have nothing to do with it. Anyway, the two SA men placed the Stürmerkästen in the back of their lorry next to several others. They did their work none too carefully, because there were at least a couple that had broken glass covers.

An hour later I saw the same two men removing another one of these Stürmerkästen from outside a tram-stop in front of the Town Hall. This time I went up to them and asked what they were doing.

'It's for the Olympiad,' said one. 'We're ordered to take them all down so as not to shock the foreign visitors who will be coming to Berlin to see the Games.'

In my experience, such sensitivity on the part of the authorities is unheard of. [...]

In front of the German War memorial a company of Reichswehr were making trade for chiropodists to the accompaniment of a brass band. Sometimes I think there must be more brass bands in Germany than there are motor-cars. This one struck up with *The Great Elector's Cavalry March* and set off at a lick towards the Brandenburger Tor. Everyone who was watching was getting in some arm exercise, so I hung back, pausing in a shop doorway to avoid having to join them.

I walked on, following the parade at a discreet distance and reflecting on the last alterations to the capital's most famous avenue: changes that the Government has deemed to be necessary to make Unter den Linden more suitable for military parades like the one I was watching. Not content with removing most of the lime trees which had given the avenue its name, they had erected white Doric columns on top of which sat German eagles; new lime trees had been planted, but these were not even as tall as the street lamps. The central lane had been widened, so that military columns might march twelve abreast, and was strewn with red sand so that their jackboots did not slip. And tall white flagpoles were being erected for the imminent Olympiad. Unter den Linden had always been flamboyant, without much harmony in its mixture of architectural designs and styles; but that flamboyance was now made brutal.

Philip Kerr, *March Violets*

✳ ✳ ✳

Despite the vast expenditure and huge effort to glorify the Reich through the Games, there came the most famous race in Olympic history – one which was to show Hitler's belief in Aryan supremacy for what it was: bunkum.

It was the season of the great Olympic games, and almost every day George and Else went to the stadium in Berlin. George observed that the organizing genius of the German people, which has been used so often to such noble purpose, was now more thrillingly displayed than he had ever seen it before. The sheer pageantry of the occasion was overwhelming, so much so that he began to feel oppressed by it. There seemed to be something ominous in it. One sensed a stupendous concentration of effort, a tremendous drawing together and ordering in the vast collective power of the whole land. And the thing that made it seem ominous was that it so evidently went beyond what the games themselves demanded. The games were overshadowed, and were no longer merely sporting competitions to which other nations had sent their chosen teams. They became, day after day, an orderly and overwhelming demonstration in which the whole of Germany had been schooled and disciplined. It was as if the games had been chosen as a symbol of the new collective might, a means of showing to the world in concrete terms what this new power had come to be.

With no past experience in such affairs, the Germans had constructed a mighty stadium which was the most beautiful and most perfect in its design that had ever been built. And all the accessories of this monstrous plant – the swimming pools, the enormous halls, the lesser stadia – had been laid out and designed with this same cohesion of beauty and of use. The organization was superb. Not only were the events themselves, down to the minutest detail of each competition, staged and run off like clockwork, but the crowds – such crowds as no other great city has ever had to cope with, and the like of which would certainly have snarled and maddened the traffic of New York beyond hope of untangling – were handled with a quietness, order, and speed that was astounding.

The daily spectacle was breath-taking in its beauty and magnificence. The stadium was a tournament of color that caught the throat; the massed splendor of the banners made the gaudy decoration of America's great parades, presidential inaugurations, and World's Fairs seem like shoddy carnivals in comparison. And for the duration of the Olympics, Berlin itself was transformed into a kind of annex to the stadium. From one end of the city to the other, from the Lustgarten to the Brandenburger Tor, along the whole broad sweet of Unter den Linden, through the vast avenues of the faëry Tiergarten, and out through the western part of Berlin to the very portals of the stadium, the whole town was a thrilling pageantry of royal banners – not merely endless miles of looped-up bunting, but banners fifty feet in height, such as might have graced the battle tent of some great emperor.

And all through the day, from morning on, Berlin became a might Ear, attuned, attentive, focused on the stadium. Everywhere the air was filled with a single voice. The green trees along the Kurfürstendamm began to talk: from loud-speakers concealed in their branches an announcer in the stadium spoke to the whole city – and for George Webber it was a strange experience to hear the familiar terms of track and field translated into the tongue that Goethe used. He would be informed now that the *Vorlauf* was about to be run – and then the *Zwischenlauf* – and at length the *Endlauf* – and the winner:

"Owens – Oo Ess Ah!"

Meanwhile, through those tremendous banner-laden ways, the crowds thronged ceaselessly all day long. The wide promenade of Unter den Linden was solid with patient, tramping German feet. Fathers, mothers, children, young folks, old – the whole material of the nation was there, from every corner of the land. From morn to night they trudged, wide-eyed, full of wonder, past the marvel of those banner-laden ways. And among them one saw the bright stabs of color of Olympic jackets and the glint of foreign faces: the dark features of Frenchmen and Italians, the ivory grimace of the Japanese, the straw hair and blue eyes of the Swedes, and the big Americans, natty in straw hats, white flannels, and blue coats crested with the Olympic seal.

And there were great displays of marching men, sometimes ungunned but rhythmic as regiments of brown shirts went swinging through the streets. By noon each day all the main approaches to the games, the embannered streets and avenues of the route which the Leader would take to the stadium, miles away, were walled in by the troops. They stood at ease, young men, laughing and talking with each other – the Leader's body-guards, the Schutz Staffel units, the Storm Troopers, all the ranks and divisions in their different uniforms – and they stretched in two unbroken lines from the Wilhelm-strasse up to the arches of the Brandeburger Tor. Then, suddenly, the sharp command, and instantly there would be the solid smack of ten thousand leather boots as they came together with the sound of war.

It seemed as if everything had been planned for this moment, shaped to this triumphant purpose. But the people – they had not been planned. Day after day, behind the unbroken wall of soldiers, they stood and waited in a dense and patient throng. These were the masses of the nation, the poor ones of the earth, the humble ones of life, the workers and the wives, the mothers and the children – and day after day they came and stood and waited. They were there because they did not have money enough to buy the little cardboard squares that would have given them places within the magic ring. From noon till night they waited for just two brief and golden moments of the day: the moment when the Leader went out to the stadium, and the moment when he returned.

At last he came – and something like a wind across a field of grass was shaken through that crowd, and from afar the tide rolled up with him, and in it was the voice, the hope, the prayer of the land. The Leader came by slowly in a shining car, a little dark man with a comic-opera moustache, erect and standing, moveless and unsmiling, with his hand upraised, palm outward, not in Nazi-wise salute, but straight up, in a gesture of blessing such as the Buddha or Messiahs use.

Thomas Wolfe, *You Can't Go Home Again*

* * *

At the gun Jesse Owens was away to a good start, and by the first thirty metres he was powering fluently into a clear lead. In the seat next to me the matron was on her feet again. She had been wrong, I thought, to describe Owens as a gazelle. Watching the tall, graceful negro accelerate down the track, making a mockery of crackpot theories of Aryan superiority, I thought that Owens was nothing so much as a Man, for whom other men were simply a painful embarrassment. To run like that was the meaning of the earth, and if ever there was a master-race it what going to exclude someone like Jesse Owens. His victory drew a tremendous cheer from the German crowd, and I found it comforting that the only race they were shouting about was the one they had just seen. Perhaps, I thought, Germany did not want to go to war after all. I looked towards that part of the stadium that was reserved for Hitler and other senior Party officials, to see if they were present to witness the depth of popular sentiment being demonstrated on behalf of the black American. But of the leaders of the Third Reich there was still no sign.

Philip Kerr, *March Violets*

* * *

In 1937, Mussolini visited Berlin – an excuse for one of those highly theatrical events that Hitler liked to stage as a show of power.

At seven in the evening all the lights in Berlin went out, every street sign, every advertising illumination, every traffic light and crossing beacon. They said it was an air-raid drill, a practice blackout. Everyone closed the curtains tight. Some people lit candles and played Puccini. Mussolini was coming on a state visit that very evening.

At nine the citizens were invited by loudspeaker to step outside, and to their delight they found another world. The streets were lit by giant lighting rigs on the backs of lorries. Four rows of painted white columns had been placed along the Unter den Linden, each supporting a massive plaster golden eagle. Banners had been hung over building façades, huge flag-poles erected, pedestals installed, and rows and rows of giant searchlights aimed upwards into the night sky. And then the rumble of a cavalcade could be heard approaching.

Lit by a single spotlight, Mussolini and Hitler in an open-topped car motored slowly through the Brandenburg Gate. Behind them thousands and thousands of soldiers marched in lines that stretched forever. They all carried burning torches or banners or both. The spectators' cheeks flushed, their hands burned from the clapping, their voices grew hoarse, but they didn't care. No, that night was magical, electrifying, epic. Who could not believe at that moment in the heroic vision of our Führer?

Beatrice Collin, *The Luminous Life of Lilly Aphrodite*

✽ ✽ ✽

For any Jews still refusing to believe that they were not safe in Hitler's Germany, the night of 9th – 10th November 1938 could leave them in no doubt. The mass destruction of Jewish property and synagogues that took place that night has come to be known as 'Kristallnacht', or 'Night of the Broken Glass'.

The Schöneberg district is empty this morning. The streets are drenched in a dreamy De Chirico *sfumato*. Neither man nor beast is visible, but a tangible Presence lurks; today's dawn is blood-fingered. Closer to Ku'damm the streets grow more rest-less, the sidewalks are alive with the sweeping of big brooms. A couple of men hunt for cigarettes and dirty magazines in the smoking remnants of a tobacco shop. Stores are being boarded up by old men with shaky hammers; nine-inch nails stick out of their worried mouths. Defiled and decapitated mannequins lean out of broken shop windows. A man complains of a terrible injustice to an empathetic circle of onlookers – apparently his shop has been looted even though he is not Jewish. I race through the streets – riding slowly seems like a provocation, even though nobody ever pays attention to a kid like me. A big pillar of smoke rises out of the golden domes of the Fasanenstraße synagogue. A group of people has gathered in front of the temple; they dance and cheer and shout anti-Semitic slogans. Yes, the crowd is right. The temple does not belong here, its onion-shaped domes are so round and heavenly that they have no place in a city of grey that has its teeth permanently bared. Later in the morning those cupolas will collapse, like so many others in the Reich, dreams of a heaven on earth, carelessly broken. A fire truck is parked in front of the synagogue, but the firemen only keep the neighbouring houses wet, they don't care about G*d's House.

I have seen enough. I have to get to school. And if there was any doubt left: after this night, none of us still considers himself to be German.

Paul Verhaeghen, *Omega Minor*

* * *

The first of these two extracts from German-Israeli Inge Deutschkron's powerful memoir, I Wore the Yellow Star, *also recalls the terrors of Kristallnacht when, according to the New York Times, 195 synagogues were burnt down, 800 stores destroyed and 7,500 looted. The second extract is set in 1943: Inge and her mother were by this time living with a family friend, using forged identity papers. Inge was working at Otto Weidt's Workshop for the Blind on Rosenthaler Straße, now a museum.*

On the morning of that 10 November the news had come flooding in. All hell had broken out on the streets of Berlin. The previous evening, armed with axes, hatchets and clubs, SA men had smashed the windows of the Jewish stores, easily recognised because they were marked *'Jude'*, causing terrible destruction. On Kurfürstendamm stained shop-window dummies lay amidst shards of broken glass. Torn rags fluttered from the empty caverns of the windows. Looters had completed the picture of destruction and violence. In the stores lay ripped-out drawers, scattered clothing, broken furniture, smashed and trampled crockery, misshapen hats. Thick swathes of smoke hung above Fasanenstrasse, where the synagogue was. We didn't dare go any closer. We already knew that all synagogues had been set alight and burnt down by the 'people's spontaneous rage', as they had said on the radio. The police and fire brigade had stood by without intervening and contented themselves with keeping the gaffers away from the fires.

We wanted to see for ourselves what our friends had told us on the telephone, and had gone out onto the street in the early morning. My parents looked upon the disaster that had been wrought, as if turned to stone. Suddenly a barber standing in front of his salon in a white coat, who must have been watching us, called out to my father, using a Hebrew phrase:

'Telech man, you Jew, get lost!' His fat, grinning face showed his schadenfreude. My father spun around and grabbed my mother by the sleeve to get away with us as fast as he could.

But my mother, who wasn't scared of anything, launched into the stunned barber: 'You damned swine!'

My father went white as a sheet for fear. 'For God's sake, stop it!' he remonstrated. But my mother pulled herself free and, walking towards the barber as he retreated into his shop, shouted at him again: 'You damned swine!' Once she had left the barber alone she turned back to my father and said, very quiet and calm now: 'We can't let them get away with everything.' [...]

It must have been around 25 February when Hans called me at the shop.

'For God's sake, don't go to Weidt's tomorrow!' I wanted to know why but he refused to answer my questions. I promised not to leave the house.

The next morning, we saw police vans speeding through the streets of Berlin. Every time they stopped outside a building, officers in plain clothes and uniforms stormed out, ran inside and marched someone off, put him in the van and drove quickly on to the next building. They were collecting the last Jews left in Berlin. The dragged them out of their homes and out of the factories, wherever they found them. And they took them with them just as they were – in pyjamas, in their work clothes, without coats. Watching from the window I saw them, I can still see them now – as if frozen by shock – as they were shoved into the vans by policemen, SS men, plainclothes men.

'Quick, quick!' they hurried them on. The police vans picked them up, drove away, returning again empty. They were everywhere. The people on the streets stopped to stare, whispering to one another. Then they rapidly broke up their groups, going back to the protection of their houses. From behind the curtains, they looked surreptitiously down at the street and watched what was going on.

My mother and I were petrified. Where was Hans? Where were my friends from the workshop for the blind? It was impossible to imagine there were to be no more Jews in Berlin.

'For God's sake, don't leave the house!' Grete told us. We sat in her apartment. I cried. My mother hardly spoke. Grete and Ostrowski were silent. What could they say? Only once did Grete have an outburst.

'Those swine!' she erupted, and ran out of the room.

The 'operation' lasted several days. Then they were all gone. We hadn't heard a single scream, no protests. On Monday I went back to Weidt's workshop. There was no one left there. My steps echoed through the empty rooms. The blind workers were gone, the bookkeeper Werner Basch, the sighted workers.

Only the few non-Jews were sitting at their workplaces. Blind Charlotte was crying; she had been with her Jewish work-mates for so long. Fritz, who had had a 'hat business' – as the Berliners called beggars – before he came to Weidt, kept saying, 'Oh God, oh God, what'll they do to them?'

Inge Deutschkron, *Ich trug den gelben Stern* ('I wore the yellow star') translated by Katy Derbyshire

✳ ✳ ✳

After Kristallnacht, the remaining Jewish families left if they possibly could. Hard decisions were made about who would go and who would stay. Novelist and feminist Eva Figes recreates an anguished childhood memory of leaving Berlin ... and her grandparents.

Just a silent procession of black cars making its way to the airport, winding its way through busy morning traffic. Exit. Another exit. Just a grey cold morning, the northern light of a northern city, and a woman leaning forward, refusing to look out of the window as the familiar housefronts recede for the last time. Just an ordinary family of four struck dumb by this unceremonious expulsion from the city in which they were born and, at the airport, during the hubbub of passengers all trying to make their voices heard by the men behind the high counter handling exit papers, passports, valid tickets, the figure of my grandfather suddenly appearing on the far side of the plate glass running from floor to ceiling, trying – I could see vainly – to catch a last glimpse, but seeing, I think, only his own reflection, or at most a dark mass of people with their backs to him. All of them clamouring to get on the next plane, to get out of this city, to make their voices heard. I, only I, having nothing to do at this particular moment, stood staring out at the grey light and saw him, peering fruitlessly at a point above and beyond my head, and I tugged at my father's coat to tell him, but he just said curtly: Not now. I thought about banging on the window.

When exactly? Then, or afterwards, when it was much too late? Time and memory are a plate glass window, no sound, no sight can go through in the other direction, however much I pound my childish fists on the frozen air and shout his name. Time and the moment have passed. It has begun to hail, the icy stones are falling on his bare head, on the shoulders of his overcoat. Hailstones bounce on the ground, fall out of the bleak March sky into the space between the window and the dark wooden wall two yards further, on to the blades of grass and asphalt between the base of the window and his feet, the no man's land where he has found this window, through which he cannot see us. I see him, for the last time. And then the space is empty.

Eva Figes, *Tales of Innocence and Experience*

✳ ✳ ✳

And the parades and the theatrical shows of power went on. It was more than one's life was worth not to salute along with everyone else.

That evening it seemed as though almost all of Berlin was on its way to Neukölln to witness Goebbels conduct the orchestra of soft, persuasive violins and brittle, sarcastic trumpets that was his voice. But for those unlucky enough not to have sight of the Popular Enlightener, there were a number of facilities provided throughout Berlin to ensure that they could at least have the sound. As well as the radios required by law in restaurants and café, on most streets there were loudspeakers mounted on advertising pillars and lamp-posts; and a force of radio wardens was empowered to knock on doors and enforce the mandatory civic duty to listen to a Party broadcast.

Driving west on Leipzigerstrasse, I met the torchlight parade of Brownshirt legions as is marched south down Wilhelmstrasse, and I was obliged to get out of my car and salute the passing standard. Not to have done so would have been to risk a beating. I guess there were others like me in that crowd, our right arms extended like so many traffic policemen, doing it just to avoid trouble and feeling a bit ridiculous. Who knows? But come to think of it, political parties were always big on salutes in Germany: the Social Democrats had their clenched fist raised high above the head; the Bolshies in the KPD had their clenched fist raised at shoulder level; the Centrists had their two-fingered, pistol-shaped hand signal, with the thumb cocked; and the Nazis had fingernail inspection. I can remember when we used to think it was all rather ridiculous and melodramatic, and maybe that's why none of us took it seriously. And here we all were now, saluting with the best of them. Crazy.

Philip Kerr, *March Violets*

✢ ✢ ✢

At first, things went well for Germany. Any victory over their old enemy, France, was an excuse for dancing in the streets and the inevitable 'parades'. But, as Geert Mak tells us, by the autumn of 1941, a certain unease had set in.

Most people in Berlin lived through summer 1940 in a state of ecstasy. There was singing and dancing in the streets with every victory in France. When the great triumphal parade came goose-stepping by on 18 July, the cheering crowd stood twenty deep along the streets, people climbed into trees and on lamp posts, women ran out and hugged the soldiers, flowers and confetti rained down. 'We, the boys of Berlin, thought the English were fantastic as well. The Battle of Britain was, in our eyes, a jousting match. People talked about the 'campaign against France' and the 'campaign against Holland'. War, no, that wasn't a word we used.'

The first booty began pouring in: furs from Norway, art, tobacco and Bols gin from Holland, wines and perfumes from France, glass from Bohemia, vodka from Poland. In the occupied areas, *Sonderkommandos* began combing the libraries and museums in search of the best European art for the big

Berlin museums, and for Hitler's planned Führer Museum and Göring's Karin-Halle. [...]

It was only in autumn 1941, when the soldiers still had not returned and winter was fast approaching, that the city grew uneasy. The loudspeakers stopped reporting victories. The shop windows were full of empty biscuit boxes and wine bottles filled with water. The enormous map of Russia in front of the Wertheim department store, where the progress of the German troops had been charted each day, was taken down. Gloves, wool caps and fur coats were collected for the front. By the end, at least 100,000 German soldiers literally froze to death there.

Soviet prisoners of war were brought to Berlin to work in the factories, some 300,000 in all. Before the eyes of the townspeople, they were treated like animals. Half of them died of hunger or perished in the bombardments.

Geert Mak, *In Europe*
translated by Sam Garrett

* * *

And then the bombs began to fall on Berlin and the civilian population began a long period of the most terrible suffering.

The first bombs fall on Berlin. A single attack, and for Helmut the novelty is frightening but thrilling. After the deep, distant thumping in the earth subsides, the sky to the south is lit a brilliant orange. Helmut's bed rattles gently with the explosion, but far less than it does when the trains go by. His parents wake him. Berlin burns on the horizon, the fires clearly visible from Helmut's bedroom window. Mutti and Papi sit with him on his bed and watch. Mutti asks if he is afraid, but Helmut shakes his head, glad of the quiet company, the warmth of his father's legs so close to his own cold feet.

Rachel Seiffert, *The Dark Room*

* * *

She said thank you and went to see her dressmaker. But when she reached the premises, she stopped in bewilderment. The house had been bombed overnight; there was nothing but rubble. People hurried past it, some purposely averting their eyes, unwilling to see the devastation or afraid of being unable to conceal their anger. Others went by specially slowly (the police saw to it that no one stopped), either with expressions of curiosity or else frowning at the destruction.

Yes, Berlin was being sent down to bomb cellars more and more often, and more and more bombs were falling on it, among them the feared phosphorous canister bombs. More and more people now quoted Göring's saying that his name would be Meier if an enemy plane showed its face over Berlin. The night before, Hetty had sat in her bomb shelter – alone, alone, because she didn't want Enno to be seen as her official boyfriend and house-mate. She had heard the nerve-racking sound of planes, like mosquitoes droning and whining. She hadn't heard any bombs falling: thus far her part of the city had been spared. People told each other the British didn't want to hurt working people, they just wanted to bomb the rich people out west …

Her dressmaker hadn't been rich, but she had been bombed just the same.

Hans Fallada, *Alone in Berlin*
translated by Michael Hoffman

* * *

Helmut is in bed when the second wave of bombing begins. […]

Without knowing what the low drone is, Helmut lies still and listens to the hundreds of Lancasters carrying their lethal tonnage into the sky above Berlin.

Moments after the siren sounds, the tenement comes to life. Mothers bundle children out of bed and old people pull on their thick socks. The stairwell is full of people. Helmut can hear them rush to the cellar: sharp voices, quick feet. He knows he should go with them, but doesn't want to be near their fear and their hurry, so he stays in bed. He has heard people describing the incendiary bombs, Christmas trees falling from the sky, lighting the bombers' path to their target. He watches from his window but there is nothing to see yet, just a black sky above and a dark Berlin below. [...]

Helmut hears the drone under the siren now. Becoming louder, becoming a roar. He stands with his hand in his pocket, fingers firmly wrapped round the camera, makes his way cautiously down the empty stairs.

The first bombs hit when he gets to the second floor. They are not very close, but the impacts tear into his legs. The building shifts, and Helmut is hurled off balance. Plaster falls on him in chunks and dust, and in his mind's eye a thousand pots and pans tumble down the stairs to cover him as the kitchen cupboards in every flat empty their contents to the floor.

Shock and pain. Everything moves fast now and Helmut can't keep up. He doesn't run to the cellar, instead his legs carry him out on to the street. The first fires are starting in the neighbourhood districts and Helmut runs away from the heat and the light. Not fast enough. He knows he is not fast enough, because now the bombers are here. The roar. Directly overhead. Skimming the tops of the tenements, vast and frighteningly close, they follow Helmut's bare and bobbing head as he runs.

He takes a zig-zag course through the pitch-black streets to escape them, can feel himself screaming, but can hear nothing save the roar of fire and bombs and places.

The impacts resurface from deep underground, kicking into his hips, his spine. It rains tile and brick and glass, and Helmut cannot see where he runs, the flat pounding of anti-aircraft guns in his ears, noise blackening sight. He is blind but not out of breath. His throat is raw and his face is wet, and he runs in the darkness while the street shudders under him, buildings reeling, each footfall as heavy as a bomb.

A body runs in front of him, black shape towards him. Helmut hears the curses, feels the hands on his coat, and the man's breath in his ear. Torn off course, swung off his feet. A bomb. Two arms. The grip. Helmut twists and screams and is pulled underground. From outside dark to dark inside, but just as loud.

He spends the rest of the raid in a cellar full of strangers. They are silent and still while he lies on the floor and cries. The adrenaline makes him shake, involuntary shudders, uncontrollable, and he is afraid and ashamed, feeling the people stare.

After the noise subsides they are all cold. The man who pulled Helmut down with him says this is good. The fires have not reached this part of Berlin at least. After that they are quiet again. Wet eyes, small movements in the black.

Helmut leaves the cellar without saying goodbye. He has come a long way from home in his flight, at least four or five kilometres. He doesn't know where he is, and everything looks different. Bricks where there shouldn't be, gaps where there should be walls. Helmut feels his way down the first street, to the first corner and on, finds his route blocked by chairs, glass and window frames, an empty, unmade bed. Picks his way round the rubble and on to cobblestones again, towards what he hopes is home. It takes him some time to find his way back. The streets are deserted and deathly silent. His eyes get used to the dark, but the quiet is unsettling, and he feels dizzy and sick. Helmut's footsteps echo loud against the tenement walls and he regrets leaving the wordless company of the cellar.

Slowly people emerge, tiny grey shapes against the black walls. More and more, until the streets are swarming. People fleeing from torn buildings, lost and searching through the dark, new mountains of stone. The sky above the roofs is bright with fire, and the streets have become progressively lighter as Helmut nears home. He hears the clattering of the fire-brigade bells, and walks through streets alive with disoriented people, their clothing ripped and sometimes charred, many of them walking barefoot through the rubble. No matter where he turns, Helmut cannot escape the sound of children crying. He is sweating now in his coat and pyjamas; blinking against the hot air and the soot, thinking, Berlin is full again. Full of children.

Rachel Seiffert, *The Dark Room*

✻ ✻ ✻

There was no moon, and there were three air-raids in the three nights that I was in Berlin. The bombs fell indiscriminately on Nazis and anti-Nazis, on women and children and works of art, on dogs and pet canaries. New and more ravaging bombs – block-busters and incendiaries, and phosphorous bombs which burst and glowed green and emptied themselves down the walls and along the streets in flaming rivers of unquenchable flame, seeping down cellar stairs, and sealing the exits to the air-raid shelters. [...].

I learned when I was in Berlin that those wanton, quite impersonal killings, that barrage from the air which mutilated, suffocated, burned and destroyed, did not so much breed fear and a desire to bow before the storm, but rather a certain fatalistic cussedness, a dogged determination to survive and, if possible, help others to survive, whatever their politics, whatever their creed.

Christabel Bielenberg, *The Past is Myself*

✻ ✻ ✻

Hitler committed suicide on 30th April 1945. The war was over, but not the suffering of the civilian population. Berlin was a conquered city, occupied by the Russian army. A young woman takes us to look at its conquered remains.

At 3 p.m. we were ready to set off on our first tour of the conquered city.

Poor words, you do not suffice.

We clambered past the cemetery in the Hasenheide park – long, uniform rows of graves in the yellow sand from the last big air raid in March. The summer sun was scorching. The park itself was desolate. Our own troops had felled all the trees to have a clear field for shooting. The ground was scored with trenches strewn with rags, bottles, cans, wires, ammunition. Two Russians were sitting beside a girl on a bench. It's rare to see one on his own; they probably feel safer in twos. We went on, through what were once heavily populated working-class streets. Now they seem so mute, the houses locked up and shut off from the world – you would think the ten thousand people who lived there had emigrated or were dead. No sound of man or beast, no car, radio or tram. Nothing but an oppressive silence broken only by our footsteps. If there are people inside the buildings watching us, they are doing so in secret. We don't see any faces at the windows.

Onward to the edge of the Schöneberg district. We'll soon find out whether we can continue, whether any of the bridges leading west over the S-Bahn survived intact. Some of the buildings have red flags, the first we've seen. Actually they're more like flaglets, evidently cut from old Nazi flags – here and there you can still make out the line of a circle, where the white field containing the black swastika used to be. The little flags are neatly hemmed, undoubtedly by women's hands. How could it be otherwise in our country? […]

Glaring sun. The bridge is deserted. We pause to look down at the railroad embankment, a jumble of tracks, straw-coloured in the sunlight, pockmarked with craters one yard deep. Pieces of rail wrenched high above the ground, upholstery and scraps of fabric streaming out of bombed sleepers and dining cars. The heat is stifling. The smell of fire hangs over the tracks. All around is desolation, a wasteland, not a breath of life. This is the carcass of Berlin.

On into Schöneberg. Here and there we see people in the doorways – a woman, a girl, their blank eyes staring into space, their features vapid and bloated. I can tell by looking that the war has only recently ended here. They still haven't recovered from the shock; they're still as numb as we were several days back.

We head down Potsdamer Strasse, past blackened offices, empty tenement, heaps of rubble.

A moving sight on one corner: two rickety old women standing in front of a pile of rubble so huge it towers above them. They scratch at the refuse with a small shovel, load it onto a little cart. At that rate it will take them weeks to move the entire mountain. Their hands are knobby and gnarled, but perhaps they'll finish the job. [...]

At around 2 p.m. we heard loud shouting from down on the street outside our house – a kind of official town-crier, exactly like a thousand years ago. He'd planted himself under the maple tree and was rattling off information from a piece of paper: all men and women between fifteen and fifty-five years of age capable of work and currently unemployed should report to the Rathaus at once for labour duty. [...]

The steps outside the Rathaus were filled with women pushing and shoving one another – the men were few and far between. With a great deal of shouting and gesticulating, a youth took down our names. The patch of street outside the town hall looked like an extremely busy construction site. The trench in the middle of the boulevard, which was carved out for mysterious military purposes by a handful of Germans and several Russian girls in quilted jackets – forced labour – is now being filled in again, this time solely by Germans. This has a certain logic for me. Women are pushing the carts loaded with sand, brick rubble and fire-blackened debris up to the edge and tipping the contents into the trench. Bucket brigades have been lined up on all the side streets, and bucket after bucket is being passed up to the carts. I'm supposed to join in tomorrow morning at 8 a.m. I have nothing against that.

Anonymous, *A Woman in Berlin*
translated by Philip Boehm

＊ ＊ ＊

Taking revenge for the terrible suffering inflicted on their own country by the Germans, the invading Russians mercilessly raped the women of Berlin. In Dan Vyleta's novel Pavel and I, *a woman remembers that terrible time.*

Sonia remembered, too, the propaganda flyers outlining what the Russians did to the women along the moving front. She found them posted on advertising pillars and lampposts; tore them off sometimes and took them home to peruse them at her leisure. The flyers were fond of facts: the age, whether the woman had been married or not, and how many times – it all boiled down to numbers. Three in one night for a virgin of sixteen. Seven in an hour for a mother of two, the last one a Mongol who had the daughter next. A war widow endured twenty-three before slitting her own throat, the Führer's name upon her lips. A girl of fourteen, a girl of twelve. A girl of seven. There was, to Sonia, a strange fascination about the flyers; they brought the war home somehow, and mixed it with the mystery of sex. Sonia remembered hunting for them on her city strolls. She read them and broke into goose bumps; blushed at the thought of bodies exposed. […]

She never spoke about the rapes. Who could blame her? It had been a trying time. Her reticence was not caused by a failure of memory, or by what psychiatrists call repression. Her first, in any case, she remembered quite vividly. He took time to close the door, secured the latch with great care, and proceeded to undress before he had so much as laid a hand on her. In this he was different from many others who took their women standing up against some kitchen table, trousers around their ankles. Whole queues formed like this, man standing after man with a loosened belt. Sonia's first scorned such rush, found time even to roll up his socks and stick them into his boots' grease-slick shaft. He had spindly white legs, skinny white buttocks, untouched by the sun, save for the feet which showed signs of some tanning. Out of this meagre carriage grew a solid body the colour of dried earth, sunburned and knotty like a bulbous root. She had never seen anything quite so grotesque.

Afterwards, when he stepped back into his underwear, she looked on in wonder as he carefully pulled away the elastic and reached in to arrange himself to the best of his comfort. Only then did he step into his trousers and pull his soldier's shirt over his head. His face, as she lay there and bled, was serenely peaceful and he rubbed his neck and cheeks with his palms, delighted at his good health.

Dan Vyleta, *Pavel and I*

✳ ✳ ✳

Suffering does not, of course, end when the rape is over. This extract from a short story by Tamsin Walker reminds us that the consequences for many of the women shaped the rest of their lives.

She stands just outside the entrance to a small shop, her spindly legs bowing beneath her shapeless dress of workhouse blue. Raising an elderly hand to her hip and steadying herself thus, she turns her face up towards the buildings which surround her. As her eyes sweep her Berlin street, they push through the parched ivy that dangles neglected from a first-floor balcony, and come to rest on something that doesn't belong here.

They come to rest on me.

And as they take me in, those eyes which water with age rather than emotion, they prise her mouth open in disapproval. The distance between she and I is not great enough to disguise what she sees when she looks at me. She shakes her head and I know why: I see myself through my eyes in her head and I am offended by my presence on her street. I am wearing just the nightdress in which I ventured outside to feed my cat, and that is not enough. It symbolises the brazen ease with which I live on borrowed ground. She does not grant me my foreign ways in this city of told and untold agonies in which every street corner – and most certainly on this one where I have chosen to live and she to stand –has witnessed acts that not even walls should see. [...]

> *She dresses in her father's old clothes and climbs the rotting ladder to her childhood retreat in the chestnut tree in the communal back yard. But she is too young and too female to be safe from the enemy, come cross-country to destroy the relatives of those who crushed their own kin and kith.*
>
> *She hears the demanding clump of their heavy boots on the cobbled yard, and seconds later the guttural resolve of a language she knows to be Russian. She curls into a ball, covers herself head to toe with blankets and again pleads to the skies, begging in fierce silence for safety. But that is not what she gets. Not this time.*
>
> *And when the three men climb the ladder, boots and all, she has neither the courage nor the strength to fight them. Each one dirtier and smellier than the other, she lets them take of her what they have come for. Over and over again. [...]*

Today her memory came, triggered by the sight of me, wearing too little as I bent down to feed my cat on a little balcony just one block from where her tree house once stood.

I am still looking at the entrance to the little shop when the old woman reappears from inside. Again she looks towards me, only this time she smiles and holds something up. I immediately recognise it as a tin of cat food. My fantasy about her life fizzles and dies. Oh dramatic me! So that was what her head-shaking was about. My foreign, unsuitably dressed presence on her street did not offend her, nor did it inflame in her memories of an unchangeable past; it simply reminded her to buy food for her cat. I return her smile and go inside to dress properly. As I take off the nightdress, I realise it is me who feels ill-at-ease living so well in a city where so many millions were made to suffer.

Through my window, I watch the old woman stagger up the street on arthritic legs and I can't help but wonder where she is going. So I follow her home, and I watch as she strokes the cat for which I unwittingly reminded her to buy food. It stands tail high on a sideboard that accommodates an old black and white photograph of her smiling son. I observe the old woman for a moment longer, just long enough to see the pain that passes over her face as she lifts up the image of her boy and ask him for the millionth time which of the three soldiers was his father.

Tamsin Walker, 'Old Woman'

✳ ✳ ✳

Like Eva Figes and her family, the writer and academic W. G. Sebald came to Britain to escape Nazi Germany. In this passage from The Rings of Saturn *he describes a return to Berlin after the war in search of the life he had lost as a result of the escape.*

Michael was nine and a half when, in November 1933, with his siblings, his mother and her parents, he came to England. [...]

How little there has remained in me of my native country, the chronicler observes as he scans the few memories he still possesses, barely enough for an obituary of a lost boyhood. The mane of a Prussian lion, a Prussian nanny, caryatids bearing the globe on their shoulders, the mysterious sounds of traffic and motor horns rising from Lietzenburgstraße to the apartment, the noise made by the central heating pipe behind the wallpaper in the dark corner where one had to stand facing the wall by way of punishment, the nauseating smell of soap-suds in the laundry, a game of marbles in a Charlottenburg park, barley malt coffee, sugar-beet syrup, codliver oil, and the forbidden raspberry sweets from grandmother Antonina's silver bonbonniere – were these not merely phantasms, delusions, that had dissolved into thin air? The leather seats in grandfather's Buick, Hasensprung tramstop in the Grunewald, the Baltic coast, Heringsdorf, a sand dune surrounded by pure nothingness, the sunlight and how it fell ... Whenever a shift in our spiritual life occurs and fragments such as these surface, we believe we can remember. But in reality, of course, memory fails us. Too many buildings have fallen down, too much rubble has been heaped up, the moraines and deposits are insuperable. If I now look back to Berlin, writes Michael, all I see is a darkened background with a grey smudge in it, a slate pencil drawing, some unclear numbers and letters in a gothic script, blurred and half wiped away with a damp rag. Perhaps this blind spot is also a vestigial image of the ruins through which I wandered in 1947 when I returned to my native city for the first time to search for traces of the life I had lost. For a few days I went about like a sleepwalker, past houses of which only the façades were left standing, smoke-blackened brick walls and fields of rubble along the never-ending streets of Charlottenburg, until one afternoon I unexpectedly found myself in front of the Lietzenburgstraße building where we had lived and which had escaped destruction – absurdly, as it seemed to me. I can still feel the cold breath of air that brushed my brow as I entered the hallway, and I recall that the cast-iron balustrade on the stairs, the stucco garlands on the walls, the spot where the perambulator had been parked, and the largely unchanged names on the metal letter boxes, appeared to me like pictures in a rebus that I simply had to puzzle out correctly in order to cancel the monstrous events that had happened since we emigrated. It was as if it were now up to me alone, as if by some trifling exertion I could reverse the entire course of history, as if – if I desired it only – Grandmother Antonina, who had refused to go with us to England, would still be living in Kantrstraße as before; she would not have gone on that journey, of which we had been informed by a Red Cross postcard shortly after the so-called outbreak of War. […]

I left the building with a sick feeling in the pit of my stomach and walked and walked, aimlessly and without being able to grasp even the simplest thought, well past the Westkreuz or the Hallesches Tor or the Tiergarten, I can no longer say where; all I know is that at length I came upon a cleared site where the bricks retrieved from the ruins had been stacked in long, precise rows, ten by ten by ten, a thousand to every stacked cube, or rather nine hundred and ninety-nine, since the thousandth brick of every pile was stood upright on top, be it as a token of expiation or to facilitate the counting. If I now think back to that desolate place, I do not see a single human being, only bricks, millions of bricks, a rigorously perfected system of bricks reaching in serried ranks as far as the horizon, and above them the Berlin November sky from which presently the snow would come swirling down – a deathly silent image of the onset of winter.

W. G. Sebald, *The Rings of Saturn*
translated by Michael Hulse

* * *

No-one who saw the destruction of Berlin could ever forget it.

We raced towards Berlin. The Grunewald woods soon gave way to the city's outskirts, and country road turned into thoroughfare. It never ceased to take my breath: those majestic roads lined by a landscape of rubble. Here and there a wall stood up out of the debris, five storeys high, its windows shattered, the roof collapsed, leaning into the moon like a drunk picking a fight. At the next corner, two lampposts, bent at the waist as though in curtsy. The car hurtled on and came upon a street where buildings stood plentiful; a little chipped, it is true, but defiantly beautiful with their twelve-foot doorways and *Jugendstil* balconies. Drawn curtains at the windows, the streets too cold for foot traffic, and too poor to afford more than a handful of cars. One could drive through Berlin on nights such as this and feel like there was not a living soul beyond those headlights; the city dead and one's every breath a smoke signal, sent into the air in the vain hope of an answer.

Dan Vyleta, *Pavel and I*

❋ ❋ ❋

Mutilated statues lie under mineral sedation: frock-coated marble torsos of bureaucrats fallen pale in the gutters. Yes, hmm, here we are in the heart of downtown Berlin, really, uh, a little, Jesus Christ what's *that* –

"Better watch it," advises Säure, "it's kind of rubbery through here."

"What *is* that?"

Well, what it is – is? what's "is"? – is that King Kong, or some creature closely allied, squatting down, evidently just, taking a shit, right in the street! and everything! a-and being ignored, by truckload after truckload of Russian enlisted men in pisscutter caps and dazed smiles, grinding right on by – "Hey!" Slothrup wants to shout, "hey lookit that giant *ape*! or whatever is it. You guys? Hey … " But he doesn't, luckily. On closer inspection, the crouching monster turns out to be the Reichstag building, shelled out, airbrushed, fire-brushed powdery black on all blastward curves and projections, chalked over its hard-echoing carbon insides with Cyrillic initials, and many names of comrades killed in May.

Thomas Pynchon, *Gravity's Rainbow*

* * *

It wasn't long, however, before Berlin, with a super-human effort, began to rebuild itself. But 'rebuilding' is about more than bricks and mortar: the past is not so easily put behind one. The protagonist of Ian McEwan's The Innocent *overhears talk in a Berlin bar ...*

As far as he could see, the restoration work had been intense. The pavement had been newly laid, and spindly young plane trees had been planted out. Many of the sites had been cleared. The ground had been levelled off and there were tidy stacks of old bricks chipped clear of their mortar. The new buildings, like his own, had a nineteenth-century solidity about them. At the end of the street he heard the voices of English children. An RAF officer and his family were arriving home, satisfying evidence of a conquered city.

He emerged onto Reichskanzlerplatz which was huge and empty. By the ochre gleam of newly erected concrete lampposts he saw a grand public building which had been demolished down to a single wall of ground floor windows. In its centre, a short flight of steps led to a grand doorway with elaborate stonework and pediments. The door, which must have been massive, had been blasted clean away allowing a view of the occasional car headlights in the next street. It was hard not to feel boyish pleasure in the thousand pounders that had lifted roofs off buildings, blown their contents away to leave only façades with gaping windows. Twelve years before he might have spread his arms, made his engine noise and become a bomber for a celebratory minute or two. He turned down a side street and found an Eckkneipe.

The place was loud with the sound of old men's voices. There was no one here under sixty, but he was ignored as he sat down. The yellowing parchment lampshades and a pea souper of cigar smoke guaranteed his privacy. He watched the barman prepare the beer he had ordered with his carefully rehearsed phrase. The glass was filled, the rising froth wiped clear with a spatula, then filed again and left to stand. Then the process was repeated. Almost ten minutes passed before his drink was considered fit to serve. From a short menu in Gothic script he recognized and ordered Bratwurst mit Kartoffelsalat. He tripped over the words. The waiter nodded and walked away at once as though he could not bear to hear his language punished in another attempt.

Leonard was not yet ready to return to the silence of his apartment. He ordered a second beer after his dinner, and then a third. As he drank he became aware of the conversation of three men at a table behind him. It had been rising in volume. He had no choice but to attend to the boom of voices colliding, not in contradiction but, it seemed, in the effort of making the same point more forcefully. At first he heard only the seamless, enfolding intricacies of vowels and syllables, the compelling broken rhythms, the delayed fruition of German sentences. While he was downing his third beer his German began to improve and he was discerning single words whose meanings were apparent after a moment's thought. On his fourth he started to hear random phrases which yielded to instant interpretation. Anticipating the delay in preparation, he ordered another half litre. It was during this fifth that his comprehension of German accelerated. There was no doubt about the word Tod, death, and a little later, Zug, train, and the verb bringen. He heard spoken wearily into a lull, manchmal, sometimes. *Sometimes these things were necessary.*

The conversation gathered pace again. It was clear that it was driven by competitive boasting. To falter was to be swept aside. Interruptions were brutal, each voice was more violently insistent, swaggering with finer instances than its predecessor. Their consciences set free by a beer twice as strong as English ale and served in something not much smaller than pint pots, these men were revealing when they should have been cringing in horror. They were shouting their bloody deeds all over the bar.

Ian McEwan, *The Innocent*

* * *

*The winter of 1946 was a particularly long and harsh
one, but the welcome arrival of 1947's spring brought
worsening relations between occupiers of the city –
the Soviets and the Allies – and still more suffering for
the already ground down Berliners.*

Winter did not break until the fourteenth of March, when the temperature suddenly rose by twenty-five degrees in a matter of hours. There was a moment when the air was already warmer than the frozen ground, and water collected in the streets and hardened into black ice. It cost a few lives, and of all those lost to this winter, they may have been the most tragic, tripped up on the verge of spring. Berlin's streets were full that day, and even more so the next: people staring up into the sun, and breathing air that no longer stung their lungs. All of a sudden the city was alive with the smell of grass and dog shit. By the end of the week, Berlin stood in the fullest of blooms. I am no sentimentalist, but I bought myself a big bunch of flowers as soon as they became available. They gave a little beauty to my poky little room. [...]

I found myself stranded in Berlin without an income, living frugally off my meagre savings. It was from the marginal vantage point of a middle-aged pauper that I watched history unfold. Berlin was in the eye of the world in the spring of 1947.

As the new year got going, the relationship between the western Allies and the Soviets slowly dipped from bad to worse, and it was beginning to smell like another conflict. By March, the Americans had declared the 'Truman Doctrine', vowing to 'contain' the spread of Communism throughout the world. The Soviets reacted by sabotaging Berlin's electricity and water supply at random intervals and by filling the streets with violence. Incidences of murder spiralled out of control, and there was talk of German prisoners of war dying in Russian uranium mines. Scientists and engineers continued to disappear at alarming rates. New rumours made the rounds day after day, growing more outlandish with every passage from tongue to tongue, and feeding a mounting economic panic. Berliners talked food stamps, talked currency, talked glorious Hitler.

Dan Vyleta, *Pavel and I*

❊ ❊ ❊

What to do with such a traumatic and devastating history? One thing Berlin does not do is ignore it: it's as up front about its past as about everything else. When Darky, in Paul Beatty's Slumberland, *goes to Berlin, he finds the past commemorated everywhere.*

Always a clean city, on winter nights Berlin is especially antiseptic. Often, I swear, there's a hint of ammonia in the air. This is not the hermetic sterility of a private Swiss hospital but the damp Mop & Glo slickness of a late-night supermarket aisle that leaves me wondering what historical spills have just been tidied up.

The ubiquitous commemorative plaques, placed with the utmost care as to be somehow noticeable yet unobtrusive, call out these disasters like weary graveyard shift cashiers. *We have a holocaust in aisle two. Broken shop glass in aisle five. Milli Vanilli in frozen foods.* These metallic Post-it notes aren't religious quotes and self-help affirmations like those pasted onto bathroom mirrors and refrigerator doors, but they are reminders to never forget, moral demarcations welded onto pillars, embedded into sidewalks, etched into granite walls, and hopefully burnished onto our minds. WAY BACK WHEN, AND PROBABLY TOMORROW, IN THE EXACT PLACE WHERE YOU NOW STAND, SOMETHING HAPPENED. WHATEVER HAPPENED, AT LEAST ONE PERSON GAVE A FUCK, AND AT LEAST ONE PERSON DIDN'T. WHICH ONE WOULD YOU HAVE BEEN? WHICH ONE WILL YOU BE?

At the Nollendorfplatz U-bahn station we catch ourselves staring blankly at a marble plaque memorialising the homosexual victims of National Socialism. People whom the inscription described as having their bodies beaten to death (*totgeschlagen*) and their stories silenced to death (*totgeschweigen*).

Paul Beatty, *Slumberland*

* * *

In C. S. Richardson's moving The End of the Alphabet, *Ambrose Zephyr and his wife Zipper spend what threatens to be the last month of his life travelling to places he has most loved or wanted to visit, in alphabetical order. His visit to Berlin is an attempt both to remember and cut loose from the past – a suitable place to end this section.*

They sat at an outdoor table on the Unter den Linden. The sky was clear, blue, welcoming. The lime trees showed an early-spring green and offered comfortable shade.

Nearby stood a brooding Brandenburg Gate, all heavy stone and column. Tourists and locals and friends and lovers were enjoying the morning, strolling through the gate as if it wasn't there.

Zipper Ashkenazi's legs stretched from under her, her shoes off. She watched a street entertainer prepare for the day's performance: unfolding a music stand, tuning a battered violin. She had passed a poor night, but on this morning and in this place she was content.

Ambrose stewed. He knew he needed to be here. He knew he needed to get past this. He knew it would make Zipper happy. But still he fussed and squirmed in search of a comfortable place in his chair. He kept an eye on the gate and scowled.

He claimed he was only thinking of his uncle, but Zipper knew there was more to it than that.

At one time or another, Ambrose had spoken of his Uncle Jack. How he had taught an annoyingly inquisitive nephew the subtleties of life. The first gentleman I ever met, Ambrose would say.

Every Remembrance Sunday, Jack came up to the city, wearing the same threadbare jacket and regimental tie he had worn the year before. His shoes always shone, he smelt freshly shaved, he stood whenever Mrs Zephyr entered or left the room. He had an unsure smile that matched his limp.

One particular November young Ambrose asked his uncle about the war. What had he done? Where had he been?

All over, said Jack. France, Holland, Berlin.

That's right. Germany.

Wasn't very nice.

People weren't very nice either.

Didn't like us, I suppose. They didn't like a lot of people.

They did. People they'd no business killing.

Friends? A few.

No. I didn't help my friends. I was away.

A few years later at his uncle's funeral, Ambrose read about someone named Sylvia. She had died when an air raid blew up her house near Spitalfields. Jack had left her a note, apologizing for not being there. For not keeping her safe.

Zipper knew that, with odd exception, Ambrose held a modern view of the world. He kept himself informed well enough, knew there was neither black nor white, believed what the BBC told him. Yet when she reminisced about her younger location-shoot days in Germany, she could watch his view become as black and blind as ash. With an unnerving Berlin at its centre.

In its greyness. The weather always threatening, the streets always wet. The architecture all cold stone: large and hard and lacking in windows.

With its inhabitants. Sour and stiff with permanently furrowed expressions. They spoke a jarring language: phlegmy, incapable of expressions of love. No one smiled. Laughter was faked. There never seemed to be any children.

With its music. Unlistenable. Funereal. Loud.

And its ghosts. Prowling, wearing uniforms, black, brown, grey. Lurking in doorways, dropping bombs on houses, burning Zipper's books. Watching and waiting to steal her away.

That was then, Zipper said. Jack was then.

She pulled Ambrose to his feet and they set off to walk the city she knew.

They made their way through the Reichstag. Once an asylum run by madmen, now through its centre an atrium of glass and mirror poured sky into the building and warmed Ambrose's upturned face.

They visited the zoo, where people had once eaten the animals left behind. On this day it was full of children, laughing at the monkeys, waving at the pandas, having their photographs taken by tired parents.

Along more than one boulevard Ambrose and Zipper jostled past crowded coffee bars and neon dance clubs and persistent gypsy beggars; bored fashion models and charged young lovers and old people with old dogs; graffiti artists and boisterous hawkers and women for sale and men who smiled like cartoon spies and made Ambrose chuckle.

They walked, perhaps a little lost, along Oranienburger-strasse and through an ancient neighbourhood. They asked directions from a young man with a long and unkempt beard. He mumbled through his whiskers and pointed vaguely down the street. Zipper thanked him in the only Yiddish she could recall. The man grinned and shuffled Ambrose and Zipper along their way.

As dusk came, they returned to the avenue under the lime trees. The street performer was calling for last requests. Ambrose watched a woman in tailored red trousers and a black turtleneck approach the violinist. She whispered in his ear. The performer bowed and played the opening notes of the woman's request. She turned to her companion, a reluctant gentleman with greying hair, and offered her hand. The couple danced to

149

a waltz composed by a German whose name Ambrose could not recall.

This is now, Zipper said, as she picked up a small stone and slid it in her pocket. The sky grew dark and the stars came out.

Ambrose smiled and asked if she had said something. If she was safe. If she was happy.

C.S. Richardson, The End of the Alphabet

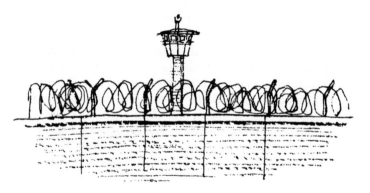

A Tale of Two Cities

The day of Operation Rose was August 13th 1961. Without warning, four hundred trucks headed from the East German countryside at midnight to throw up a ring of barbed wire, formally to divide the city. The border was sealed while the world was on holiday. The Mayor of West Berlin, Willie Brandt, was in Nuremberg. The President of America, John Kennedy, was sunning himself on Cape Cod. And the Prime Minister of Britain, Harold Macmillan, was on the Yorkshire moors, celebrating the first day of the grouse-shooting season. At the news of the construction, Macmillan continued to shoot. The *fait accompli* was achieved with dazzling speed. Protesters gathered at the Brandenburg Gate, making gaps in the wire, and pulling a few people bodily through. But with no Western leader daring to call for insurrection in the East, Berlin was divided. In the following months, seven thousand people would be rounded up and brought to Hohenschönhausen for a programme of sensory deprivation, isolation and secret trial.

David Hare, *Berlin*

❖ ❖ ❖

The divided city of Berlin took on symbolic significance in the Cold War period: the Soviet regime and

Western democracy lived eyeball to eyeball, separated only by the Berlin Wall. The confrontation of two political continents within one country – and even a single city – made Berlin a hotbed of espionage and spawned endless novels that dealt with the subject. Among the most famous is Len Deighton's Funeral in Berlin. *This extract starts with a view from the air, but soon becomes very 'earthbound' (and not for the squeamish …).*

From two thousand feet the Soviet Army War memorial in Treptower Park is the first thing you notice. It's in the Russian sector. In a space like a dozen football pitches a cast of a Red Army soldier makes the Statue of Liberty look like it's standing in a hole. Over Mark-Engels Platz the plane banked steeply south towards Tempelhof and the thin veins of water shone in the bright sunshine. The Spree flows through Berlin as a spilt pail of water flows through a building site. The river and its canals are lean and hungry and they slink furtively under roads that do not acknowledge them by even the smallest hump. Nowhere does a grand bridge and a wide flow of water divide the city into two halves. Instead it is bricked-up buildings and sections of breeze block that bisect the city, ending suddenly and predictably like the lava flow of a cold-water Pompeii. […]

I gave the doorman at the Frühling my bags and stepped out in search of supper. It was late, the animals in the zoo had settled down but next door in the Hilton they were just becoming fully awake. Near by the Kaiser Wilhelm Memorial Church bells clanged gently and around it came a white VW bus, its hoo-haw siren moaning and its blue light flashing a priority. Cars halted as the bus bearing the words 'Military Police US Army' roared past, its fan whining.

Maison de France is on the corner of Uhlandstrasse not far away. I was hungry. It was a good night for walking but the pressure was rising and rain was in the air. The neon signs gloated brightly across the beleaguered city. On the Ku-damm the pavement cafés had closed their glass sides tight and turned on the infra-red heating. In the glass cases diners moved like carnivorous insects. Here the well-dressed *Insulaner* ate, argued, bartered and sat over one coffee for hours until the waiters made their annoyance too evident. Outside, the glittering kiosks sold magazines and hot meat snacks to the strollers, while double-decker cream buses clattered up and down, and nippy VWs roared and whined around the corners past the open-topped Mercedes that drove lazily past, their drivers hailing and shouting to people they recognized and to quite a few that they didn't.

Knots of pedestrians paraded at the traffic crossings and at the given signal marched obediently forward. Young men in dark woollen shirts parked and played jazz on their car radios and waited patiently while their white-haired girl friends adjusted their make-up and decided which club they would like to go to next.

Two men were eating *Shashlik* at a corner kiosk and listening to a football match over a transistor radio. I crossed half of the wide street; down the centre of it, brightly coloured cars were parked in a vast row that reached as far as the Grunewald. High above I could see the lights of the Maison de France restaurant.

I heard footsteps behind. It was one of the men from the kiosk. I was between two parked cars. I turned and let the weight of my back fall upon the nearest car, flattening the palms of my hands against the cold metal. He was a bald-headed man in a short overcoat. He was so close behind me that he almost collided with me when I stopped. I leaned well back and kicked at him as hard as I could. He screamed. I smelled the rich meaty *Shashlik* as he stumbled forward out of balance. I groped towards the scream and felt the wooden *Shashlik* skewer drive into the side of my left hand. The man's bald head smashed against the window of the other car. The safety glass shattered into milky opacity and I read the words 'Protected by Pinkertons – Chicago Motor Club' on a bright paper transfer.

He held his head in his hand and began lowering it to the ground like a slow-motion film of a touchdown. He whimpered softly.

From the kiosk the second man came running, shouting a torrent of German in the ever-comical accent of Saxony. As he began to cross the roadway towards me there was another 'hoo-haw' of police sirens and a VW saloon with blue flasher and spotlight full on came roaring down the wide street. The Saxon stepped back onto the pavement, but when the police car had flashed past he ran towards me. I drew out the 9-mm FN automatic pistol that the War Office Armoury had made such a fuss about and used my left hand to slam the slide back and put a cartridge into the breech. An edge of pain travelled along my palm and I felt the sticky wetness of blood. I was crouched very low by the time the Saxon got to the rear of the car. Just inches to the left of my elbow, the whimpering man said, 'But we have a message for you.' He rocked gently with the pain and blood ran down the bald head like earphones.

'Bist du verrückt, Engländer?'

I wasn't mad I told him as long as he kept his distance. The Saxon called again from the rear of the Buick. They had a message for me 'from the Colonel'. In that town I knew several colonels but it was easy to guess who they meant.

The man sitting on the ground whimpered and, as a car's headlights rolled past, I saw his face was very white. The blood moved down the side of his head. It glued his fingers together and moved slowly to form new patterns like a kaleidoscope. Little puddles of it formed in the wrinkles of his shiny ears and splashed on his knitted tie like tomato soup.

I took the written address from the Saxon with apologies. These were no B-picture heavies, just two elderly messengers.

I left them there in the middle of the Ku-damm, the Saxon and his half-conscious friend. They would never find a taxi on a Saturday night, especially now that rain had begun.

Len Deighton, *Funeral in Berlin*

* * *

Well-known television reporter John Simpson has some positive thoughts about East Berlin.

Everything seemed utterly different this side. Instead of the brightness of the West, the lights on the Eastern side were weak and yellowish-brown. There were no taxis and no one to ask directions of, and on my first visit it took me forty minutes of stumbling round in the semi-darkness before I found my antique, inconvenient, heavily bugged hotel. And yet I found East Germany a more sympathetic society than West Germany, in some respects: much less pleased with itself, and (for a Marxist-Leninist society) relatively open: even though unpleasant things certainly went on there, and people were regarded as state property for the authorities to do what they liked with.

Yet they thought of themselves as being freer than the rest of the Soviet bloc. Here, working with an East German television crew and an East German minder, you entered into a conspiracy to see what you could get away with.

John Simpson, *Strange Places, Questionable People*

* * *

East Berlin may have been a little behind the times, but so what? – the ice-cream was excellent!

The ice-cream parlour was at the corner of Prenzlauer Allee and Sredzkistrasse. The two servers wore red and white frilly frocks with matching caps. One of the servers was in her forties, her dyed blonde hair stacked in a bouffant, a style from the same period as the décor: the net curtains, the stainless-steel counter, the five orange lights encased in black buds. Outside, teenage couples licked their ices astride motorbikes parked on the cobblestone street.

'Brilliant, this commie ice cream,' I said to Johnny. Johnny agreed. Ice cream in East Berlin was still made from traditional recipes. […]

A wooden caravan of the kind gypsies once lived in had been abandoned near Käthe Kollwitz Platz. On its side Pink Floyd was written in drippy white paint.

'Pink Floyd,' mused Wolfgang. 'The east is always ten years behind the west, right?'

I nodded without enthusiasm, but it was true: journeying east was like retracing your steps. You remembered as a child drawing cars like these with curved roofs, bulbous bonnets, enamel radiator grilles like jagged smiles.

These Trabants and Wartburgs were luxury items in the GDR. Only people who were well connected, or who had access to western money, could purchase cars as and when they wished. Most East Germans spent years on the waiting lists. Of the 200,000 motor vehicles registered in East Berlin half were motorcycles or mopeds. West Berlin, with twice the number of people, had more than four times as many cars.

Ian Walker, *Zoo Station*

✽ ✽ ✽

Philip Hensher paints a less than rosy picture of the East in Pleasured. *But even here we see that it has its attractions.*

It was true that each half of Berlin thought of itself as being Berlin and accorded a geographical description only to the other half. But always, emerging into Friedrichstrasse, it was impossible to understand how such a city could maintain any illusion that this was where things really happened, where excitement was perpetually in the air. Nothing was in the air here except the surprisingly sudden smell of brown coal, mysteriously ubiquitous in East Berlin, mysteriously imperceptible even two metres from the Wall on the other side, and the constant sound and smell of building works, the floating damp smell of concrete dust. Astonishing how much time was spent in building work in East Berlin; astonishing how the building, once finished, immediately had the tired and crumpled look of everything else in this half-town, the look of a decade-old pair of underpants.

Everything seemed to move in a denser atmosphere here, more slowly. Friedrichstrasse was, in theory, the tip-top shopping and business street of East Berlin, but, emerging from the train station, all one saw was a very old lady in a moth-eaten coat and a very old man with a vulgarly chirpy little dog, each with two blue-and-white checked woven plastic bags, approaching each other massively, like a slow-motion film of two trains about to collide. God knew what the rest of the country was like; for himself, Friedrich found himself thinking, on his occasional trips to the East, that the whole place had had a collective lobotomy in 1964, after which nobody had felt any urge to behave in any way distinguishable from their parents. Mostly this seemed rather creepy, though Friedrich always had to admit, when proposing this view to a scoffing friend, full of tales of riotous clubs in Prenzlauer Berg, saucy bars wedged between civil-servant apartment blocks in Pankow, that actually, he almost never stayed long enough even to speak to anyone. What he never admitted was that once in a while it seemed not lobotomized but peaceful, innocent, correct, not wrecked like Kreuzberg, but rational, as if it had seen what the future would hold, and turned away, collectively, from the exhausted delights of the Oranienstrasse, seen that there was nothing much to be got in the way of pleasure or goodness or satisfaction out of a neon sign for Mercedes-Benz, and decided, all in all, not to bother. If Friedrich had ever said any of this he, no doubt, would have added that, of course, he didn't have to live there, and settled back on his stool to ignore the arguments of others.

It was always striking how the rambling anecdotal grey of most of East Berlin's streets was occasionally felt to be in need of some kind of spectacular punchline; so, every so often, the long rows of sober palaces and heavy blocks, many still alarmingly marked, forty years on, with the bullet marks of the advancing Russian army, gave way to some inept piazza, lined with buildings constructed out of plastic and pre-stained concrete, some moon-lovely wind-swept motorway, lined with the colossal brick-glazed palaces of correctitude. But more impressive were the periodic statements of unimaginable expense and grandeur; all memorials of some imagined glorious past, all looking forward, unavoidably, towards the tawdry present. It was to one of these memorials that Friedrich now felt like going. He wanted, somehow, to go further into the East, to a famous blank space, to the Soviet Memorial; and not, just yet, to wonder or inquire into or understand quite why.

The Soviet Memorial was set down with brutal massiveness in the Treptower Park. The perfect immaculate blankness of the space, set around with thirty great thick blank sheets of white stone, recording the triumph of the Soviet armies, had its own beauty; the double fold of stone opening, like a vast voluptuous hard velvet curtain, before the theatre of the space, had its own pressing overpowering beauty; and the two kneeling heavily cloaked steel soldiers, the colossal steel blond striding forward from his pedestal into his colossal blond future had a loveliness it was hard, quite, to look at. The glittering confidence of the place made you quail. Only the real, unsatisfactory boys in their neat grey felt uniforms, trembling slightly, as if with nerves, at the weight of the weapons they held before them, not quite letting themselves look at anything, just stomping rhythmically, under the base of their fifteen-metre comrade betrayed the excess of the claims being made in this quiet wooden place.

The memorial had the sober glittering beauty of Berlin; not a picturesque beauty, not a yellow perfumed Tuscan town, sinking into a lavender hill, not the bulging sunset behind a palm-tree, and some double-starred tourist attraction, and a half-smiling blonde bikini'd girl with an umbrella-shaded drink; not a *postcard* in short, but an adult sober city, with solid surfaces and handsome great enduring spaces, grey and brown and white, not seeking to entertain or flirt, but only to stamp its weight and sorrow, its past, its knowledge, on the patient waiting unmarked crust of the earth. There was no one there except the Russian soldiers; the sun was beginning to set.

Philip Hensher, *Pleasured*

* * *

As was common for many Berliners, the young narrator's family in Michael Wildenhain's Russisch Brot *('Russian Bread') is separated by the Wall. He lives in the West with his parents, while their relatives are in the East. A year after the Wall was built, West Germans were finally allowed to visit the East.*

Winter. The birches opposite our flat were bare.

It looked as if the branches, which reached up to the third floor of the school building, had grown up the red bricks of the façade and clung onto the cracks. They imprinted the decorative rosette above the entrance portal with a constantly changing pattern.

A few weeks before Christmas and for the first time since the Wall had been built, an office issuing passes for the East had been opened up behind the high windows. Everyone who had placed an application to travel to East Berlin to visit relatives over the holidays had to return to this office a second time a few days later, where the applicant was handed either a white or a green card. Green meant: You are permitted entry. White meant: Your application has been rejected, with no reason stated.

The moment the West Berlin issuing offices were announced on the radio one evening, the waiters turned up outside the school building. My parents had had another row because my mother had demanded that my father should take a day off work to take her place in the queue outside the school. My father had replied that he couldn't possibly take time off and that it was too late to apply for leave.

'Go then,' said my mother, and I could tell she wanted to make my father feel guilty.

The queue outside the school building grew during the night. It snowed. Some of the people waiting swapped places with friends or relatives. Others stood in the snow in front of the red bricks and the birches until the morning.

I was often off sick from school and was at home again this time. The next day I watched from my bedroom window as my mother pushed her way past the waiting people and entered the school building. I had been given a small pair of binoculars for my birthday, which my father had referred to as an opera glass and with which I could effortlessly follow all that went on opposite.

My mother pushed Frau Blümel, our neighbour from the ground floor, to the entrance portal of the school building in a borrowed wheelchair, claiming to have to help the old woman make her application. Although they complained, the people in the queue let my mother and Frau Blümel pass. [...]

When my mother came back from making her application I pointed across the road and said: 'There's another one fallen over.'

In the fresh snow on the pavement lay a young woman. The brick wall glowed red. The people formed a circle and took a step aside.

No one from the queue quite dared to step over the prone woman yet. At the same time, no one wanted to bend over the woman to help her up or ask her if they should call an ambulance.

The people standing around her hesitated. The young woman looked up at the snow-hung sky. She seemed to be wondering whether it was worth getting up again.

In the end she turned over onto her front like a child making a last exhausted movement at the end of a tantrum, pushed herself up on her hands, got onto her knees and crawled over to a fence, where she stayed sitting.

As the woman crawled through the snow on all fours the spectators moved back. The moment she was leaning against the fence, the gap in the queue closed and the people took no more notice of the young woman crouching in the snow.

My mother looked out of the window and shook her head. I drew a line on the piece of paper in front of me on the window-sill, the fifth line in blue crayon. There was enough space on the paper for almost all the people waiting outside the red-brick school.

Michael Wildenhain, *Russisch Brot* ('Russian Bread')
translated by Katy Derbyshire

✳ ✳ ✳

In her autobiography, The Kindness of Strangers, *veteran reporter Kate Adie recalls visiting the divided Berlin in the mid sixties.*

We did the sights, walking everywhere – we had little money. Berlin looked as if it had only just seen the dust settle on the war. Once-grand buildings sat around in ruins near the Tiergarten. But in the centre, a concrete monster of a shopping centre had just arisen, all modern walkways and ugliness. The city had an energy peculiar to it – or was it that I had read too much Isherwood, and was sniffing a raffishness that had not really survived? Even so, there was an odd excitement in the air. And literally in the air, as we headed past the shiny shops on the Ku'damm. Soviet MiGs overflew at frighteningly low level, part of the regular confrontation and 'show of strength' game – I later learned – that went on at that time. I'd only seen warplanes in films before; not only were these the real thing, they weren't Ours. I wondered if we should fling ourselves into a convenient ditch, only there weren't any ditches in the Ku'damm, and no one else seemed to be taking evasive action. The jets boomed through the sound barrier for good measure. I began to be fascinated. Berlin, to my delight, was not like Newcastle at all, give or take the odd bomb site.

Berlin ladies sat at pavement café tables and shook their fur-cuffed fists at the MiGs. They appeared to be dressed as if ready for church in England ten years previously: neat, buttoned-up, hat-wearing and solemn. And there seemed so many of them. I couldn't understand why the city was peopled with middle-aged females. *Die Witwe* – the widows. I hadn't realised the war had left different marks here. [...]

I'd given the city maps a cursory glance in the student home, and had worked out that there was something funny about them. Berlin was a divided city. So what happened, I'd wondered, when the underground line headed for the Wall? Just an idle bit of wondering, for the very notion of East Berlin was terrifying. This was the era of hideous events on the Berlin Wall; of regular attempts at escape, often with dreadful consequences. By 1964, it had matured as a barrier. It had been heightened and land on the east side laid waste, to give Ossies – Ostdeutsche, East Germans – less chance of making it through the wire and past the dogs and guards. That afternoon we'd paid the statutory visit to Checkpoint Charlie, one of the official crossing-points manned by the Americans. It was on the tourist trail, and a small room nearby was plastered with photographs of escape attempts – some full of cheering people surrounding a wild-eyed winner who'd made it to the West, others showing a dark hump of clothing flopped among the concrete and weeds in the East. It hardly seemed real as we stepped outside the room, for on an ordinary day there was traffic over the checkpoint – the four allies, Britain, France, the United States and the Soviet Union, maintaining the military agreement almost as if the Wall were invisible. Yet there it was, and half a city existed the other side, in another world. [...]

As we alighted at Friedrichstrasse station, I stared up at the huge semi-circle of glass arching over the tracks. There was pinkish soft evening light cross-crossed with the impressive railway ironwork. Suddenly, a figure walked along the narrow catwalk at the base of the semi-circle, a silhouette – a man with a rifle. I couldn't believe my eyes. Walking, in public? Just like that, with people getting off trains below him, and him carrying a dangerous weapon?

I was so shocked. Neither then nor since have I ever accepted the idea that such weapons should form part of normal, everyday life.

An hour later, we were stuffing ourselves with *Wurst* the size of industrial tubing, paid for out of a bag of Ossie cash received in exchange for a few West German deutschmarks. Clearly, the West might feed our minds, but the East did a terrific job on the body. So began weeks of crossing the best-guarded border in Europe, in order to consume mounds of (to us) cheap food. The madness of a divided city had its roots in the war, which had given it its structure. Every day, there were ritual military patrols involving the occupying four powers, 'the allies', crossing the city as if the barbed wire and free-fire zone of unofficial no-man's-land did not exist. Presentation of a British passport in East Berlin produced a strangulated mutter about *Die Alliierten* – but it meant a privileged passage for me, one of the allied citizens; I – or my French and American friends – could travel in minutes via S-Bahn over the strip of land which citizens of the People's Republic saw as a firing range.

I began to cross during the day in order to poke around the gingerbread architecture and the war ruins. I was riveted. Naïve and rather accepting, I'd never had to teach myself about a different system. I sat in bars and met students from the Karl Marx University. They were none too keen on the off-duty Russian soldiers who drank gloomily in corners, but I wanted to meet real Reds with snow on their boots, and happily bought beers, courtesy of the ludicrous exchange rate, with my Ostmarks obtained at the obligatory currency swap at the station (a kind of entrance fee to the People's Republic). Before long, I had a very quirky acquaintance with life in Russia, oiled with honours of alcohol and song.

I walked marathons through the dowdy streets, rewarded one day with a squeaking whine from an alley of tatty lock-up garages and small workshops. Out from a garage crawled a tank. I gaped – another horrible first – and learned that the first instinct is not to cheer such things, as in all those war movies of liberation, but to leg it; even then I could not escape its persistent growling whine, like a monster in a nightmare.

There seemed to be almost no shops, only a few dusty windows full of ugly kitchen equipment and clothes which should only be bought at gunpoint. I unloaded my Ossie cash in the bookshop selling German classics. The Reclam editions were standard, and I acquired two centuries of writing printed in tiny paperbacks for a trifle. Unloading Ossie marks was a bit of a chore each day. You could only eat so much and carry so many books, and the remainder was literally shaken out of you at the railway station by stone-faced old trouts carrying inverted umbrellas into which to scatter your unused money.

Never mind; I was entranced. Each journey was an adventure. Conversations were curious, punctuated by sudden and frequent gaps. There were glaring no-go areas – in politics, in criticism, in opinion. The Karl Marx students wanted to know if we were paid a lot of money by our governments to go on demonstrations. When I explained the reality, they pondered on why we hadn't been shot by our army. I learned to avoid comparisons of societies: some students were Marxist speaking clocks of doctrinal drivel. Music, beer and food were safe bets. Still, the students – and the Russians – threw up little nuggets of information. How the authorities interfered with access to pop music. How short supplies were of certain basic foodstuffs – much of the Soviet Union's food appeared to spend its life either crossing Tajikistan in a railway wagon until it had gone off, or lurking 'under the counter'.

Here, the war seemed only an eye-blink ago. Whereas West Berlin echoed to construction work and rows about dealing with the decayed embassies in the Tiergarten, the East showed no embarrassment at the ghastly scarecrow of the Berliner Dom, the cathedral. I stood under its skeletal dome one morning, taking pictures of a shaft of sunlight in which a continuous stream of fine dust fell from the wrecked roof.

Kate Adie, *The Kindness of Strangers*

* * *

There are many accounts – fictional and non-fictional – of crossing between the two sectors of Berlin. And after a night's clubbing in the East, it was always a nail-biting rush to make it back to the border before the midnight deadline …

I proceeded towards the sign which said in black capitals EINREISE IN DIE DDR. I didn't need the sign, I knew the way. I walked down the stone steps, along a pedestrian underpass and up some more steps into Friedrichstrasse checkpoint. […]

The queues shuffled patiently towards the kiosks. Old women with relatives in the east hauled their loads of food and drink a foot at a time. Transit travellers dragged suitcases and rucksacks. A couple of Mohicans sat glumly on a bench while a policeman explained that they had been denied entry to the GDR. He didn't have to give a reason, but everyone knew that part-shaved heads and torn leather jackets were ill-received at the border. East Berlin had its own community of nihilists and the authorities seemed reluctant to encourage fraternal relations with their counterparts in the west. Western punks with a serious reason to spend the day in East Berlin knew all about this and took the necessary measures, borrowed a dress or jacket, wore a hat, whatever. [...]

I slapped a DM 5 coin down on the Formica next to my passport. This was the entrance fee, the price of a one-day visa. The border guard flicked a bead of sweat from his forehead. His green shirtsleeves were rolled up. Angled above head height in the narrow passageway was a mirrored strip facing the guard. Having glanced at the mirror to establish I was not concealing anything behind my back, he addressed my eyes.

The long hard stare from the guards had ceased to bother me. I had found it unnerving the first time, a uniformed stranger searching my eyes for a full ten seconds, but anything becomes normal in time. [...]

He stamped my visa and pressed a button which made a dull ring signifying the grey metal door could be shoved open. I walked along the corridor to another kiosk where a woman sat behind glass exchanging western money for eastern money. [...]

The final chore was to walk the twelve-yard gauntlet to the exit, past two guards picking on people at random to search and question. I had six records for Tommy I had bought in a record shop on the Kurfürstendamm. I carried them in a plastic bag. There was no point trying to conceal these things.

Shlepping pop music through the border, I had in the past been stopped and questioned. [...]

At 11.45 Astrid tapped me on the shoulder. Standing behind her, Johnny was examining his watch.

'Time to go,' she said. 'Vera's going to drive us to Friedrichstrasse.' [...]

I felt sick in my stomach, as I always did on these Cinderella chases back to Friedrichstrasse for midnight, having to leave one part of the city for another at a particular time for no particularly good reason, having to flee friends, leaving drink and conversation unfinished. [...]

Flat out at 65, the car bumped down the hill towards the Tele-Tower, its mighty concrete pillar lit up like a shaft of sunlight through a break in the clouds.

Winding down the window, I shut my eyes and tasted the cool breeze. It was two minutes past midnight.

'Don't worry,' Vera said. 'The guards don't fuss over the odd minute.'

I wasn't worried. I knew day-trippers from the other side had to be at least thirty minutes late before they were interrogated, asked to supply the names and addresses of those with whom they had been socialising. I wound up the window so Astrid and I could light our cigarettes.

On the pavement outside Friedrichstrasse checkpoint, a steel-and-glass construction known locally as the glasshouse, two grandparents were giving their small grandson a last kiss goodbye. As the old couple took their place in the queue at passport control the mother grasped her son's arm and waved it up and down like a flag. Turning round, the grandparents smiled and waved back. Lovers embraced. Friends solemnly shook hands. Hugs and tears and see you soon. The routine pathos of Sunday night at the border.

Ian Walker, *Zoo Station*

✳ ✳ ✳

A couple of 'crossing the border' snippets from two of the most famous novels set in Cold War Berlin.

There was only one light in the checkpoint, a reading lamp with a green shade, but the glow of the arclights, like artificial moonlight, filled the cabin. Darkness had fallen, and with it silence. They spoke as if they were afraid of being overheard. Leamas went to the window and waited, in front of him the road and to either side the Wall, a dirty, ugly thing of breeze blocks and strands of barbed wire, lit with cheap yellow lights, like the backdrop for a concentration camp. East and west of the Wall lay the unrestored part of Berlin, a half-world of ruin, drawn in two dimensions, crags of war.

John le Carré, *The Spy Who Came In From The Cold*

❋ ❋ ❋

There was plenty of activity at Checkpoint Charlie. Photoflashes sliced instants from eternity. The pavement shone with water and detergent under the pressmen's feet. Way down towards Halle-sches Tor a US military ambulance flasher sped towards the emergency ward and was all set to change direction to the morgue.

One by one the reporters gunned their VWs and began composing tomorrow's headlines in their minds. 'Young Berliner killed in wall crossing' or 'Vopos Gun Down Wall-Hopper' or 'Bloody Sidewalk Slaying at the Wall'. Or maybe he wouldn't die.

Len Deighton, *Funeral in Berlin*

❋ ❋ ❋

Ian Walker can't help wondering just how many photos have been taken by tourists visiting Check-point Charlie, the most famous 'crossing' point between East and West Berlin.

Tourists went to Potsdamer Platz to stand on the viewing platforms overlooking the Wall. Roughly fashioned from wood and scaffolding, like tree-houses made by children, these viewing platforms had served another purpose during the twenty-eight months after 13 August 1961 when West Berliners had been unable to visit their relatives in East Berlin. At pre-arranged times newly-weds would mount the platforms and their relatives would wave flowers and greetings from the other side. New-born babies, too, would be held aloft on the platforms. The parents would cup their hands round their mouths and

168

shout out the names of their babies to the grandparents who would shout the names back and smile and weep and sometimes try and take photographs with a telefoto lens. Now the platforms were mounted daily by tourists armed with Japanese cameras taking shots of the Wall to pass around the neighbours in Phoenix or Florence, Nantes or Nagasaki. [...]

I began to wonder how many photographs had been taken from the scaffolding at Checkpoint Charlie. Of the four million visitors per year maybe half had a camera and of those maybe another half, a conservative estimate, would take pictures on the scaffold. One million cameras a year, therefore, each taking about six standard shots.

1. The wide-angle taking in a section of the Wall, graffiti-spattered in many languages on the western side, and showing the blue-and-white apartment blocks built high on the other side to block out the view of the west.

2. The close-up of the East German guard behind glass in the broad concrete tower that looks like the bridge of a ship. (Often the guard will be training his binoculars right back at the lens, adding an appropriately threatening ambience to the composition.)

3. The art-shot of the *Neue Zeit* sign, faded black on an oblong of sludgy green, with a barred window up above. Best in colour.

4. The landscape shot north along the Wall to the West Berlin HQ of the Axel Springer newspaper empire, a high-rise coated in gold symbolising opulence. Also best in colour.

5. The upright-shot of the Kochstrasse street-scene: western flags, the sign for the Wall Museum, tourist coaches, men in white coats dispensing soft drinks under brightly-coloured canopies, the blue U-Bahn sign in the distance.

6. The head-shot of one's loved one or relative or oneself)if travelling alone one can usually prevail upon a sympathetic fellow tourist to take this) sometimes smiling but often staring moodily against a background of candy-striped road barriers and GDR flags.

Assuming an average of six shots per camera meant six million photographs a year for the last twenty-three years, making 138 million checkpoint Charlie scaffold pictures as the current rough world total.

Ian Walker, *Zoo Station*

＊ ＊ ＊

When the city was divided, the underground stations along that part of West Berlin's U-Bahn stranded beneath East Berlin were closed. The trains sped through these well-guarded 'ghost stations' which were left moldering in a time-warp.

Each ghost station had its own sombre mood and idiosyncrasies, walled-up exits and entrances, and sealed corridors (as if life itself could be immured), but there were a few common features: rampant dilapidation (mountains of bricks, dripping ceilings, peeling plaster), fluorescent bulbs that cast a meagre light, and the ubiquitous presence of armed men, greenclothed sentinels watching over a place no one wanted to enter but most wanted to leave.

When shortly after the fall of the Wall, in November 1989, researchers and city planners and other curious folk descended into this land of spirits they found ads, signs, ticket counters and snack bars waiting where they had been left twenty-eight years earlier. The underground Imbiß at the Oranienburger Straße station was a compendium of abandonment: overturned bottles, crushed cans, stained paper cups, counters thick with dust, rusty racks where small bags of peanuts and potato chips once hung, a mouldy refrigerator that had been unplugged, severed, like everything else, from its life current in 1961. Faded posters advertising obsolete products, their edges peeling away from the walls to which they clung, their sticking power nothing but sheer obstinacy. Crinkled aluminum foil and soiled wax paper that had wrapped sandwiches digested long ago, a sink choking on fallen plaster, power cords and light fixtures protruding from walls like dangling guts.

The ticket counters, Weiss said, were also trapped in time. One service area, near the Russian embassy, boasted five centimetres of dust and half a dozen brittle rolls of red paper tickets for rides on a defunct transport system. Everything had lain for decades in penumbra and neglect, relics of former days buried under the weight of the Communist regime.

As for the men guarding these stations, in photographs they too seemed like relics of the past. Their faces exuding a subterranean pallor, they were spectral, phantasmal, as if nourished by the weak light of the fluorescent lamps, fed by snatches of passing trains and feeble volts of electricity. They had mutated into a new, strange species, these guards, caged in time like the signs on the walls. Semidarkness, semiconsciousness, semibeing. Theirs was a world of dead silence and dead stillness, blitzed, every now and then, by trains from the West hurtling through their muffled realm. The guards in green watched these trains through narrow glass slits. They spent hours and hours down there, amidst walls pockmarked with age, chairs with soiled cushions and thermoses of watery coffee.

Many of the signs in these stations, Weiss went on to say, were in an old typeface resembling Gothic script: bold black letters, angular and curling upwards like pointed arches or flying buttresses. The signs for Potsdamer Platz and Unter den Linden, perfect examples. As for the peeling advertisements, these showed Teutonic families with cartoonish smiles promoting soap, technical apparatuses or concerts long ago heard, discussed and forgotten. Yet down in the depths of the ghost stations these happy families were only there to tease: no one would have needed soap or music or electrical gadgets, nor would they have been smiling had they brushed against the high voltage rails from which the protective shields had been removed or if they had landed on the metal spikes bristling along the tracks.

As for the West Berliners passing through in their trains, many of them, over time, became desensitised and stopped looking out. Others felt like Orpheus crossing the Underworld, forced to continue on a path without looking back. It was an eerie experience, Weiss said, to travel through this hushed realm where even the lights had been muted to a whisper.

Chloe Aridjis, *Book of Clouds*

❋ ❋ ❋

In the next extract, set in 1988, the young narrator is summoned to one of the most feared places in East Berlin – the Stasi headquarters (now a job centre and museum).

In Magdalenenstrasse, the Stasi headquarters, there were above all doors; doors before doors and doors behind doors, doors around doors, for the sole reason that no one was ever to see anyone or, as it was called in secret service jargon, declassify anyone. The corridors here were virtually sprinkled with doors and double-doors every few yards. No other building in the world had as many doors. It may well have been the Stasi's exorbitant demand for doors that brought the GDR to its knees.

By means of a cleverly designed system, only one person was allowed to be in the intersection of two doors, so that you waited between the doors until other doors had opened or closed. It's hard to imagine how early a Stasi officer had to get up from his desk when he set out to heed the call of nature, as he had to open and close hundreds of doors along the way.

The plain-clothes Stasi man who had met me at the entrance of the colossally over-built and over-complicated modern building complex on Magdalenenstrasse called himself Schnatz, First Lieutenant Schnatz. No idea if that was his real name or just one of fifty cover names he kept in a garage of identities. He was around forty at a guess, tall, athletic and alert, and wore a ring of closely shorn hair beneath a bald pate. He worked his way along the obstacle course with me. Whenever we had crossed a threshold he first of all reached around me to close the door behind us, turned back forwards again, opened the other door a crack, poked his head through to see whether there was anyone in the next section, then pushed the door right open and gave me a sign to follow him. Not seeing and not being seen was the motto here. After a considerable distance and several changes of course at double and triple door junctions, we finally reached the darkened, panelled meeting room.

We sat down. He crossed his legs and I did likewise only in the other direction, to indicate my willingness both to cooperate and to resist. The suspicions racing through my head were unpleasant in every respect. What did they want from me? Did they want to recruit me? Or expatriate me? There wasn't much in between the two.

Rayk Wieland, *Ich schlage vor, dass wir uns küssen*
('I suggest we kiss') translated by Katy Derbyshire

✳ ✳ ✳

As it became increasingly difficult for East Berliners to move to the West, the most desperate or foolhardy risked their lives – and many lost them – in an attempt to cross. In fiction, one of the most celebrated attempts comes near the end of John le Carré's The Spy Who Came in from the Cold.

They walked quickly, Leamas glancing over his shoulder from time to time to make sure she was following. As he reached the end of the alley, he stopped, drew into the shadow of a doorway and looked at his watch.

'Two minutes,' he whispered.

She said nothing. She was staring straight ahead towards the wall, and the black ruins rising behind it.

'Two minutes,' Leamas repeated.

Before them was a strip of thirty yards. It followed the wall in both directions. Perhaps seventy yards to their right was a watch tower; the beam of its searchlight played along the strip. The thin rain hung in the air, so that the light from the arclamps was sallow and chalky, screening the world beyond. There was no one to be seen; not a sound. An empty stage.

The watch tower's searchlight began feeling its way along the wall towards them, hesitant; each time it rested they could see the separate bricks and the careless lines of mortar hastily put on. As they watched the beam stopped immediately in front of them. Leamas looked at his watch.

'Ready?' he asked.

She nodded.

Taking her arm he began walking deliberately across the strip. Liz wanted to run, but he held her so tightly that she could not. They were half-way towards the wall now, the brilliant semi-circle of light drawing them forward, the beam directly above them. Leamas was determined to keep Liz very close to him, as if he were afraid that Mundt would not keep his word and somehow snatch her away at the last moment.

They were almost at the wall when the beam darted to the north leaving them momentarily in total darkness. Still holding Liz's arm, Leamas guided her forward blindly, his left hand reaching ahead of him until suddenly he felt the coarse, sharp contact of the cinder brick. Now he could discern the wall and, looking upwards, the triple strand of wire and the cruel hooks which held it. Metal wedges, like climbers' pitons, had been driven into the brick. Seizing the highest one, Leamas pulled himself quickly upwards until he had reached the top of the wall. He tugged sharply at the lower strand of wire and it came towards him, already cut.

'Come on,' he whispered urgently, 'start climbing.'

Laying himself flat he reached down, grasped her upstretched hand and began drawing her slowly upwards as her foot found the first metal rung.

Suddenly the whole world seemed to break into flame; from everywhere, from above and beside them, massive lights converged, bursting upon them with savage accuracy.

Leamas was blinded, he turned his head away, wrenching wildly at Liz's arm. Now she was swinging free; he thought she had slipped and he called frantically, still drawing her upwards. He could see nothing – only a mad confusion of colour dancing in his eyes.

Then came the hysterical wail of sirens, orders frantically shouted. Half kneeling astride the wall he grasped both her arms in his, and began dragging her to him inch by inch, himself on the verge of falling.

Then they fired …

John le Carré, *The Spy Who Came In From The Cold*

✳ ✳ ✳

Monika Maron suggests a different mode of escape. In Animal Triste, *the narrator looks back on her life as a palaeontologist at the Natural History Museum in East Berlin, which displays the world's largest dinosaur skeleton.*

Some thirty metres away from our museum was the Wall, which they had built around the West European enclave in the middle of East Germany, around the western part of Berlin. During the decades of its existence, I found it of secondary importance that it separated me from the larger part of my city, though it always surprised me that this gangster coup had succeeded and the four million inhabitants of the city put up with the stony piece of insolence like the Californians would have to put up with it if the San Andreas Fault were to finally break open. But what made me dizzy as soon as I thought of it, like the attempt to imagine infinity, was the inconceivable idea that this ugly, three-metre-high concrete wall not only separated me from the rest of the world, but also from its entire prehistory. It robbed me of the Palaeozoic, the Mesozoic, the chalk cliffs and Jura Mountains, it robbed me of everything to which I had intended to devote my life. I remember a young man who worked in the dinosaur department like myself and dreamed for years of using the glass roof above the brachiosaurus' head as a launching place for a balloon flight across the three hundred metres to the other side of the Wall. Only he would have needed an East wind, which was rare and almost impossible to predict. On the other hand, the plan required conspicuous preparation. A hot-air balloon was out of the question because of the burner flame, which would have shone out for miles at night, as of course the young man could only have flown at night. For a hydrogen balloon, though, he would have had to lug at least ten heavy steel bottles, each a metre and a half long, onto the glass roof, where they might have had to be stored for weeks, until the next East wind came along, without being discovered. Nevertheless, one day the young man had disappeared, like my daughter. He wrote us a postcard from Rome. I remember him well because at the time I often imagined standing in the dark hall at night next to the brachiosaurus and watching through the glass roof as the balloon gradually filled up, until its skin was taut and it lifted the young man off the roof. I really lived in a strange time.

Monika Maron, *Animale Triste*
translated by Katy Derbyshire

❋ ❋ ❋

And to round off the section, Philip Hensher describes the move from the endless repressive Berlin winter to the relief of spring with a suggestive metaphor for the end of the Wall.

Those Berlin winters; how they went on, lightlessly. In November, the clouds rolled over, hanging low above the divided city, sheltering, oppressive, blanketing; there was a palpable proximity to them, sense that the thick layer of cloud would reach down at any time and envelop the city. From November onwards, that was how the winter days were; the narrow strip of hours filtered through the thick cloud, a weak grey day extending from mid-morning to mid-afternoon, and the rest was darkness and night.

The winter seemed so lightless and heartless only afterwards in Berlin. Only, really, when the clouds broke in March – April – or even, that year, in May – and the sun was quite abruptly there did anyone think that they had been living under zinc-black skies with no sign of any break, any sun, for months. The fretted city, snapping at itself in queues, in trains, put up with the dark days without knowing, entirely, the simple thing they were putting up with; finding causes for rage in ticket machines, in telephone bills, in anything except the sky, because against the skies, there was no point, none at all, in raging.

By May there was a sense of layer upon layer, thick cloud upon thick cloud, built up slowly and impermeably over the months. If you flew out of Berlin, it was almost a surprise how quickly the machine broke through the thudding grey, broke through into something which was as one imagined, the vast plains, valleys and rearing hills of cloud below, and, above, the clear winter's blue, sunlit, unbounded, unbordered. There was something wrong about the skies over Berlin; they took no account of Berlin's borders, took no interest in where lines on earth were drawn. No circular ray of sunshine pierced the clouds to outline the circular walled city in the West, no beneficent parting of the clouds conferred any blessing on one system or another, and West Berlin – deprived of the saccharine benediction which the sun, like a torch held steady and pointing into unfathomable black waters, would, surely, if it had known, conferred on it – made up for its deprivation with electricity and neon and the constant roaring generators. It was a diamond on black velvet; a colossal beautiful cheap artificial jewel. And every year with the spring breaking of the clouds it was as if a great blank wall had been punched, and shown to be only great grey paper. And quite abruptly, people found they could breathe, without knowing they hadn't been able to; they only knew that, now, they could begin.

Philip Hensher, *Pleasured*

And the Wall came tumbling down

That night, as we followed Kohl's party back to Warsaw, I saw a group of his officials whispering to one another, and over-heard the word '*Mauer*'.

'Something seems to have happened at the Berlin Wall,' I said to one of my colleagues. It proved to be an understatement.

Over the next few weeks all sorts of weird stories went the rounds about the way in which the Wall had been breached that evening, 9 November. Everyone who watched the live television broadcast at which the general secretary of the East German Communist Party, Günther Schabowski, had announced that the Wall was open, seemed to have a different version. Some people said an East German radio correspondent had handed him a piece of paper. A West German tabloid newspaper reported that the message had been delivered by someone nobody recognized. 'The Finger Of God', announced another. If you looked at the video, you could see that after making a series of announcements Schabowski had paused, whispered something to his neighbour, and shuffled his papers.

The man next to him leant over, and a piece of paper appeared in Schabowski's hand. He read it out, slowly and hesitantly:

Transcript of press conference by Günther Schabowski,
East Berlin, 9.11.89
GS: This will be interesting for you. Today the decision was taken to make it possible for all citizens to leave the country through the official border crossing-points. All citizens of the GDR can now be issued with visas for the purposes of travel or visiting relatives in the West.
This order is to take effect at once.

It was the signal for tens of thousands of people to rush to the crossing-points at the Wall and head into the forbidden land of West Berlin, without being shot or controlled or even stopped. The nights of 9 and 10 November were two of the most exciting in modern history: the bloodless crash of an entire system, the simple joy of being free. The party continued all night, all day, all night again; and it still didn't stop, even then.

A few months later, when the fuss had died down and the two parts of Germany were coming together, I went to see Günther Schabowski. He lived in a nice flat which overlooked the Wall he had personally breached, but he clearly didn't have much money. He was writing his memoirs, and at first he didn't want to give away the key part of them: what happened on the night of 9 November. In the end, though, he agreed to tell me.

Transcript of interview with Günther Schabowski,
11.2.90
Speakers: Günther Schabowski (non-staff). John Simpson (staff)
GS: I finished giving my information about the Central Committee business, and then I turned to the next item on the agenda.
JS: But it wasn't as simple as that, was it? I mean, you had to lean over and speak to someone, and there was a long pause.
GS: All right. [Laughs] I'll tell you. The Politburo decision

about opening the borders was the first thing I had planned to
announce. But as I was walking into the room I somehow got
my papers mixed up. I thought I would find it as I went, so I
just started reading out the other things first. At the end I still
couldn't find it, but it turned out to be underneath everything.
JS: And that was it? No miracle? No finger of God?
GS: No. [Laughs] Just the finger of Schabowski.

It should have been easy enough for me to get from Warsaw to
Berlin the next morning. It was only 320 miles away. But it meant
travelling from one part of a still-divided Europe to the other; and
the crowds fighting to get on the flights from West Germany to
Berlin that evening were huge. In the end, though, I managed to
get a seat on the last flight to get me there in time for the *Nine
O'Clock News*. Not for the first or last time in my life, I sat down
and fastened my seat-belt with a feeling of profound relief.

My colleague Richard Sambrook picked me up at the airport
and drove me to the makeshift BBC studio, in a caravan in
front of the Brandenburg Gate. There were Trabants everywhere, hooting their tinny horns, pumping out clouds of bluish
smoke, breaking down and being pushed. People crowded
round them, shaking hands and kissing everyone inside. We
nearly hit another car as we went, but the driver just waved at
Richard and grinned.

June 17 Street, which led to the Brandenburg Gate, was
crammed with vehicles and people: a solid mass, the breath
of the people rising in clouds. Above was the Gate, and the
Quadriga, Victory's chariot, was green in the floodlights as it
faced the Unter Den Linden. Only the day before, that had
been hostile territory; now it was all Germany once again. Even
at that moment of joy – and it was one of the happiest nights
it has ever been my good fortune to see – it occurred to me to
wonder what Germany, which had been so modest and quiet
for so long, would be like when it had the pompous grandeur
of Berlin as its capital again: a city built for victory marches.

We abandoned our car by the roadside and hurried on. I had more time than I had expected, so I wandered around talking to everyone and getting a sense of what was happening. And it was then that I caught sight of the great miracle of my time: hundreds of people standing and dancing on the top of the Berlin Wall, waving sparklers, kissing, jumping up and down, singing. It took me some time to make out the words:

Geh'n wir mal rüber, die Mauer ist weg
(We're going over, the Wall's gone)

It was time to stand in for my live interview with John Humphrys for the *Nine O'Clock News*. I stood there with the Brandenburg Gate behind me and the continual shouting and honking of horns in my ears, while someone clipped a microphone on me and put an earpiece in my ear so that I could hear John's voice.

'You look happy,' said the soundman. I was.

But it was a disaster, all the same. In the middle of an answer, in front of the biggest audience ever recorded at that stage for a British television news bulletin, someone from an American network pulled the plug on us, just in case New York might want the line at some stage. I fizzled out on the screen. In my ear I could hear John saying the most depressing words in live broadcasting:

'Well, we seem to have lost John Simpson there, but … '

I felt deeply humiliated as I unclipped the microphone and wandered away from the interview point.

But it wasn't a night to be gloomy. Someone suggested we should all go for a walk along the Wall towards the Potsdamerplatz. It took us along a little dirt path, through the woods which had grown up over the ruins of what had once been Hitler's seat of government. The division of the city had turned this area into a wasteland, and it had become overgrown, the haunt of wild animals, like the Forum in Rome. Once, near here but on the other side of the Wall, I had been filming the site of Hitler's bunker when a patrol of

East German border-guards came running up with their dogs, which cornered us, barking and slavering.

Well, that wouldn't happen again, for better or worse. The little dirt path was crowded with rejoicing people, and it seemed perverse to think there could be any reason for worry, now that the two parts of Germany were being reunited.

The reunification was going on all along the Wall. There was the sound of hammering on both sides. People were beating at the Wall with pick-axes and hammers and chisels. The candles they worked by cast a golden light on the Wall itself, and threw the shadows of their picks onto the bushes, onto the other faces, onto the Wall itself. This was a very sweet revenge indeed. They worked away at the joins between the slabs of concrete, making little loopholes which were slowly getting bigger; when the crowds parted you could sometimes get a glimpse through to the no man's landscape beyond.

And there was a strange echo, which turned out not to be an echo. When the men with the pick-axes paused, the hammering continued. There was a sudden upsurge of shouting and cheering, as we realized that someone was trying to break through from the other side. At last, by alternate strokes from East and West, another wound appeared in the Wall. In the candlelight a hand came through the little gap, and waved about; and the man with the pick-axe on our side grasped it and shook it. I had never thought anything of the kind was possible. This wasn't a phoney miracle, like Schabowski's announcement. It was the real thing.

John Simpson, *Strange Places, Questionable People*

✳ ✳ ✳

As John Simpson observes, "all sorts of weird stories went the rounds about the way in which the Wall had been breached", but I wonder if any of them came close to the version of events in Thomas Brussig's ferociously funny satire on the times in Heroes Like Us?

Just then the proceedings were interrupted by the sort of person who always intervenes on such occasions: the circumspect rebel whose opening words are "I'd like to speak to whoever's in charge!" A man of around thirty, he looked like an experienced moderate who had learned his trade in countless debates on grass-roots democracy. He was also run to earth by the media, but long before me. "*Someone* must be on charge here!" cried Aram Radomski, for such was his name. And, turning to the crowd: "Surely there must be someone in charge!" Eager to know how his quest for someone in charge would end, the crowd waited. Someone did, eventually, admit to being that someone. "Are you the person in charge?" asked Radomski, and proceeded to try to persuade the person in charge to open the gate at once.

That was when I had an idea, a kind of inspiration: the border guards might also be sons of mothers of the *Have-you-been-playing-with-it?*" type. It *was* an inspiration, there's no other word for it. Slowly and deliberately, I unbuttoned my coat, undid my belt, and unzipped my trousers, looking the border guards full in the face as I did so. They'd paid particular attention to me ever since my cry of "Give it all you've got!" – in fact they hadn't taken their eyes off me. So much the better. Grinning, because I'd known that grinning was *de rigueur* ever since encountering the flasher on the tram, I lowered my under-pants. And, while Aram Radomski continued to argue with the man in charge in lucid and committed language, unaware of what I was doing beside him, the border guards stared spell-bound at my display. When all of them were standing at the gate, transfixed, I turned to face the man in charge. His flow of counter-argument ceased abruptly. "Then you can let us across!" said Radomski, still unwitting, and the man was too bereft of energy to contradict him – too flabbergasted even to invoke some regulation or other. He simply stared at me with ever widening eyes. [...]

I gazed at each man in turn until one of them, as if mesmerised, unbolted the gate. Before they could have any second thoughts – Radomski was still arguing, still *reasoning* with them – I gripped the bars of the gate and pushed it open. "There," I cried, loudly enough to be heard by the crowd behind me but reluctant to turn and face them with my flies open, "the rest is up to you!"

Thomas Brussig, *Heroes Like Us*
translated by John Brownjohn

* * *

But maybe the version told in Philip Hensher's Pleasured *is nearer the truth ...*

And behind her and in front of her and around her come dozens, then hundreds, then thousands of people, running towards the Wall; and on the other side of the Wall, there are the same numbers, all running towards her. Two great waves of people, all running as fast as they can to see this unthought of amazing thing, this banal demolition which resembles something which happens, somewhere, every day, and which will only happen once; two floods of different peoples, two floods of different crowds of Germans, running to meet each other this rainy November night, and not quite knowing what they are going to find. Each one of them with a different feeling; each one of them with different thoughts, about the Wall, about their own lives, about what they have lost and what they will never find again; and, for some reason none of them will ever be able, quite, to explain, in may of them, a feeling of dread and wrongness and of catastrophe about to happen. What is happening is what was always meant to happen, that is clear; but they cannot for the moment rid themselves of the sensation that such an overturning of what has always been, what, for many of them, was always going to be the same, cannot be right. And yet they run, and, like the blue clean wall of a wave, the crowd – the crowds, multiplying at every point, until there is no one in Berlin left inside, no one who can still walk who is not at the Wall, shouting and screaming at the Brandenburg Gate – the crowd batters up against this temporary barrier, and with unarguable innocent rightness, breaks through.

Philip Hensher, *Pleasured*

❊ ❊ ❊

However it happened, it was a night no-one who was there would ever forget. In Mein 9 November, *editors Hans-Hermann Hertle and Kathrin Elsner have gathered recollections of the event from many different people. Here are just two – one an ordinary, unknown Berliner, the other a world-famous cellist.*

STEFFI BADEL, assistant at the Humboldt University, East Berlin

At some point someone called out of the window of a tower block bordering on the Sonnenallee crossing point: 'Come up here and watch TV! Bornholmer is open!' The border guards were on the phone the whole time in their hut. Then the first people wanted out in their Trabis and showed the guards their exit applications. The guards replied: 'It's not that simple!' and handed out forms to fill in. We all laughed because then the border guards said the things had to be filled out in duplicate but they couldn't hand out enough of them. Not much later, the barrier was raised and several soldiers dismantled the road block.

All of a sudden the border was open, just like that. Then we all walked slowly through the checkpoint past the guard, with no visas and nobody checking our ID. Only the Trabis were checked. The whole of the border setup looked rather primitive. On the West side, a couple of locals from Neukölln were standing around and welcoming everyone who arrived with sparkling wine. Then the apparently endless, empty, dark Sonnenallee lay ahead of us. Despite our euphoria at the border opening, it was disappointing – this wasn't how I'd imagined my first visit to the West. The familiar sight of concrete blocks, the street almost empty, no advertising, no cars, nothing. A good way along came a couple of bars, but there wasn't much life in them. Now and then we saw couples and groups of people wandering around like us, chirpy and aimless. I got the impression no one had really heard the news in Neukölln. At least we knew now where the smell of burnt cocoa in Treptow had always come from.

We walked on and on until we came close to where we lived in the East, only on the West Berlin side. Then suddenly we thought: 'What shall we do if they won't let us back in, if this was a one-off?' Our children were at home all alone. Then we took to our heels and walked back. We were home again at around two. The children were asleep when we got back; they hadn't noticed anything.

Mstislav Rostropovich, cellist

I saw pictures of the fall of the Wall in my Paris flat in the evening. Seized with joy, I immediately booked a flight to and flew to Berlin the next morning with an old friend. We took a taxi at Tegel airport and said: 'Take us to the Berlin Wall please.' The driver asked, 'Whereabouts?' 'Wherever you like,' I said. We ended up near the Springer Building. I said to my friend: 'I want to play and say a prayer of gratitude to God, just me on my own.' Well, my whole life I've always gone to concerts with just my cello, not a chair. But now I saw there was obviously no chair on the street. But I have to play sitting down. So I said to my friend, 'We've got to get hold of a chair.'

We went into the Springer Building and I said to the doorman on reception: 'Excuse me, I need a chair for half an hour. I promise to bring it back.' He was a very nice doorman; he recognised me and shouted out: 'Ah, you're Rostropovich, of course you can have a chair!'

We left the Springer Building with about 20 people following us. I sat down not far away next to the Wall; I can still remember there was a picture of Mickey Mouse painted on it. I played a Bach Sarabande Suite, a serious memorial piece. There weren't many people there, thank God. A young man was standing next to me, with tears running down his face. I was very happy. After a while we got another taxi and drove to the airport. Then we drank a bottle of champagne and flew back to Paris.

Mein 9 November: Der Tag an dem die Mauer fiel
('My 9 November: the day the Wall came down')
translated by Katy Derbyshire

✳ ✳ ✳

When Hasan, a young Turkish-German, hears the Berlin Wall has fallen he heads straight back home from Istanbul. He starts to discover the East – at the now world-famous Tacheles bar.

At some point late at night, we took Kazim's taxi to East Berlin. Live music sounded out from a squat on Oranienburger Strasse. The whole of the outer façade was missing from one part of the building, like a ruin after the war. Kazim wanted to meet a few people here. The place was bursting at the seams. Grey smoke hung below the high ceiling and the sweet smell of joints wafted through the crowd. Wessis in black leather jackets and PLO scarves stood back to back, rocking to the music. The band was good. A mixture of free jazz, soul, funk and rock with all the trimmings.

I checked out the crowd, trying to tell the Easterners from the Westerners. My secret game. The majority were Westerners who couldn't resist the place's dilapidated charm. East Berlin was like a whole different era. Dark streets, bullet-ridden facades, cobblestones; rusty signs reading 'Lehmann's Laundry' or 'Potato Erna' hung on blackened buildings. It was as if time had stood still here. It was a bit like postwar Germany, like in the black-and-white films from the weekly news.

Yadé Kara, *Selam Berlin* ('Salaam Berlin')
translated by Katy Derbyshire

* * *

Not surprisingly, the fall of the Wall caused panic at the Stasi headquarters ...

At the Normannenstrasse headquarters, there was panic. Stasi officers were instructed to destroy files, starting with the most incriminating – those naming westerners who spied for them, and those that concerned deaths. They shredded the files until the shredders collapsed. Among other shortages in the east, there was a shredder shortage, so they had to send agents out under cover to West Berlin to buy more. In Building 8 alone, members of the citizens' movement found over one hundred burnt-out shredders. When the Stasi couldn't get any more machines, they started destroying the files by hand, ripping up documents and putting them into sacks. But this was done in such an orderly fashion – whole drawers of documents put into the same bag – that now, in Nuremberg, it is possible for the puzzle women to piece them back together.

Anna Funder, *Stasiland*

* * *

Travel writer Jan Morris enjoys the festive atmosphere in the days immediately following the Wall coming down.

The top end of the Kurfürstendamm, the showiest boulevard of West Berlin, offers the liveliest and least inhibited street scenes in Europe. Beneath the glare of the neon signs, past the crowded pavement cafés, flooding through the tumultuous traffic, an endlessly vivacious young populace laughs, struts, sits around, eats, plays music, kisses, and shows off from the break of afternoon to the end of dawn. It is like a perpetual fair, or perhaps a bazaar, the genteel with the rapscallion, the indigent with the well-heeled: gypsy beggars with babies, bourgeois ladies with dogs on leads, lovers embracing at restaurant tables, unshaven money-changers in dark doorways, an elegant wind trio playing Scarlatti outside a brightly lit shoe shop, a not very skilful acrobat treading a rope between two trees, tireless drummers, tedious mimes, unpredictable skateboarders, portrait sketchers, hang-dog youths with ghetto blasters squatting among their own rubbish, smells of coffee and fresh rolls, double-decker buses sliding by, fountains splashing, sidewalk show-cases of leathers and jewels – and presiding over it all, incongruously preserved there as a reminder of old horrors, the ugly tombed hulk of the Kaiser Wilhelm I Memorial Church, defiantly floodlit.

Berliners have always been famous for their irrepressible disrespect and hedonism, maintained through all oppressions and apparent even when I first came here to find a city half in ruins. Even on the east side, where the equivalent of Kurfürsten-damm is the loveless Stalinist Alexanderplatz, even there, now that the dictatorship has gone, flashes of high spirit often show through the authoritarian grumps (fostered not only by forty years of communism, but by a decade of National Socialism before that). A waiter winks and bypasses the management ruling that we are too late for a cup of coffee. A young man dashingly V-turns his car, with a glorious screeching of brakes and skidding of tyres, across Karl-Marx-Allee to pick up his laughing girl. A stretch of the hitherto sacrosanct Wall – the wrong side of the Wall – has been covered with murals and called the East Side Gallery.

Liberty is in the very air of Berlin now. It is good to be alive here, and to be young must be heaven. Everything is in flux, everything is changing, new horizons open, and nothing demands unqualified respect or allegiance. Although half of Berlin is the theoretical headquarters of the about-to-be-dis-banded and thoroughly discredited People's Republic of East Germany, the city is not really the headquarters of anything much, and this gives it a stimulating sense of irresponsibility. Tokens of fun abound, indeed, and none are more endearing than the preposterous little Trabant cars, like goblin cars, that swarm out of East Berlin for a night out or some shopping in the West, with hilarious clankings and wheezings of their primitive engines, and faces smiling from every window.

Jan Morris, *A Writer's World: Travels 1950–2000*

* * *

It didn't take long for Berlin's divided past to be turned into tourist attractions. Anna Funder goes on a tour and is shown a microcosm of the mentality that brought about the original dividing of the city.

Today I walk from my place up Brunnenstrasse, past Frau Paul's tunnel to Bernauer Strasse where the Wall is. There is a new museum here. Its greatest exhibit is opposite: a full-size reconstructed section of the Wall, complete with freshly built and neatly raked death strip, for tourists. Right alongside it in Bernauer Strasse there are still some pieces of the real Wall, covered, as they always were on the western side, with bright graffiti. These remnants are behind bushes though, scrappy and crumbling. In some places the steel reinforcements in the concrete are bare as bones.

The new Wall, however, is pristine. It is utterly without graffiti. I can understand why the original has all but disappeared, and why, as Frau Paul and Torsten said, people wanted it to. But this new one is a sanitised Disney version; it is history, airbrushed for effect.

Inside the museum there are displays and touch-screen presentations showing how the Wall was built, recordings of Kennedy's '*Ick bin ein Berliner*' speech, and dramatisations of various escape attempts. 'Yes, yes, yes,' a man with his back to me is saying to another man behind the counter, 'I'll take them from here and bring them back here. I think it'll take about two hours. That's what I'm going to check now.'

'Right then,' the other man says, then he looks over at me. He is wearing fancy eyeglasses that appear to be held together by a row of miniature, multicoloured clothes pegs, 'Can I help you?'

The man standing at the counter turns around to have a look at me. 'Frau Funder!' he cries. It is Hagen Koch. 'Well, well, well! How are you? Yes! You might like to come with me!' He speaks in exclamation marks. It is as if I have hardly been away. For him the past is the Wall, and I am part of the present, whether three years ago or now. His hair has turned white, but his eyes are the same bright and smiley brown.

'Herr Koch, I'm well, thank you. Come where?'

'I'm taking a busload of tourists tomorrow along the route where the Wall was, because you can hardly tell any more. I'm off now to check how long it will take.'

'I'd love to come.' [...]

We drive along Zimmerstrasse away from the centre to Bethaniendamm. It is a scrawny part of town. There are more new brightly painted apartments on one side, and grey cement buildings on the other. In between there's what looks at first like an empty lot, fenced in with wire mesh and boards and sticks. Behind the fence someone has planted potatoes and eggplants in neat rows, and tomatoes on stakes. But I'm still not sure what we're looking at. 'These,' Herr Koch says, 'are the Turkish onions.'

He takes me around the fenced area, a small triangle of land. There is an elaborate three-storey shack at one end made of pieces of fibroboard, crates and a ladder, with a grapevine climbing over it. Outside it there's an old couch and chairs, and at the other end of the plot a child's wooden swing hangs from a tree, painted red and yellow.

Herr Koch says that this land was, strictly speaking, in the eastern zone, but that it was too hard to build a bend in the Wall to include it, so the Wall went straight along the nearest street, leaving this island of land out in the west. No-one in West Berlin knew what to do with it; it could not be resumed for any purpose without antagonising the eastern regime. It was, literally, no-man's land. Eventually, a Turkish family simply fenced it off and planted vegetables. When the Wall came down, no-one seemed to have a claim, so they are gardening here still. I gaze through the fence. There's an apricot tree, and a large oak at the end. I imagine great family working bees; grandma on the couch, the kids on the swing and the smell of coffee from the summer palace at the end.

'But you know what happened,' Koch says. I turn back to him. 'The family eventually fought – it was two brothers, I think. They fought so badly that in the end all they could do was to put a fence down the middle of the garden and split it into two separate zones!' His face is alive with the irony of it. 'Come here, look.' We walk to the middle where a two-metre-high cyclone fence runs right through the little field, separating the part with the hut from the part with the swing, and no way of going between.

Anna Funder, *Stasiland*

* * *

As journalist and blogger Simon Cole goes about the city, he reflects on how Berlin's iconic and inescapable television tower – the Fernsehturm – reflects the changes in the city since reunification, while reminding us of its more sinister past.

The Fernsehturm looks pretty now, this 1,200ft long futuristic rocket to the stars. It welcomes you to an ultra-modern city where individuality is welcomed and self-expression encouraged. But spend a few days in Berlin, and read your Stasi history, and you start seeing it in a different light.

There it is again, as you cross the street. And over your shoulder as you drink a coffee outside. It's like being shadowed by an impassive silvery spy. Outwardly symbolic of communist construction skills – and a giant "Up yours" to West Berlin – it would also have jammed TV pictures and Radio Free Europe, just like its Prague counterpart.

And that mirrored glass; maybe a too little like the windows in an interrogation room or the shades on the guy who always happens to turn up when you do in the café. The tower once served – like all communist architecture – to dwarf those below it; to remind you that you were nothing compared to the collective, namely the state and its many tentacles. There is a reason why dictators build big, just like they did at the imposing Tempelhof under a different – but equally totalitarian – regime. Always there. Always watching. Always bigger.

Little could they know they would be building one of the city's top tourist attractions, bringing the enemy from all over the globe to spend their ill-gotten capitalist gains. It is now the drab socialist showpiece of Karl-Marx-Allee that shrinks beneath the tower. And at night, looking up from Rosa-Luxemburg-Platz, this trophy of the former anti-fun state resembles a glitter ball in a decadent disco. The Spartacists must be turning in their spartan coffins.

Simon Cole, Berlin Blog at Bookpacking.com

✳ ✳ ✳

Just as the television tower turned from a threat to a major tourist attraction, so even the dreaded Stasi headquarters rapidly turned into a museum. Anna Funder again ...

Outside the cold is bitter and soggy. There's no wind; it is as if we have all been refrigerated. In the stillness people trail comets of breath. I catch the underground to the national Stasi Headquarters at Normannenstrasse in the suburb of Lichtenberg. The brochure I picked up at the Runde Ecke shows a vast acreage of multi-storey buildings covering the space of several city blocks.

The picture is taken from the air, and because the buildings fold in at right angles to one another the complex looks like a gigantic computer chip. From here the whole seamless, sorry apparatus was run: Stasi HQ. And, deep inside this citadel was the office of Ertich Mielke, the Minister for State Security.

On 7 November 1990, only months after the citizens of Berlin barricaded this complex, Mielke's rooms, including his private quarters, were opened to the public as a museum. The 'Federal Commissioner for the Files of the State Security Service of the Former GDR' (the Stasi File Authority) has taken control of the files. People come here to read their unauthorised biographies.

I see through a window into a room where several men and a woman sit each at their own small table. They look at pink and dun-coloured manila folders and take notes. What mysteries are being solved? Why they didn't get into university, or why they couldn't find a job, or which friend told Them about the forbidden Solzhenitsyn in their bookcase? The names of third parties mentioned in the files are crossed out with fat black markers so other people's secrets are not revealed (that Uncle Frank was unfaithful to his wife, that a neighbour was a lush). But you are entitled to know the real names of the Stasi officers and the informers who spied on you. For the moments that I stand there at least, no-one is crying or punching the wall. […]

After the Wall fell the German media called East Germany 'the most perfected surveillance state of all time'. At the end, the Stasi had 97,000 employees – more than enough to oversee a country of seventeen million people. But it also had over 173,000 informers among the population. In Hitler's Third Reich it is estimated that there was one Gestapo agent for every 2000 citizens, and in Stalin's USSR there was one KGB agent for every 5830 people. In the GDR, there was one Stasi officer or informant for every sixty-three people. If part-time informers are included, some estimates have the ratio as high as one informer for every 6.5 citizens. Everywhere Mielke found opposition he found enemies, and the more enemies he found the more staff and informers he hired to quell them. [...]

The foyer of Stasi HQ is a large atrium. Soupy light comes through the windows behind a staircase that zigzags up to the offices. A small woman who reminds me of a hospital orderly – neat hair, sensible white shoes – is showing a tour group around. The visitors are chatty, elderly people, who have just got off a bus with Bonn numberplates. They wear bright colours and expensive fabrics, and have come to have a look at what would have happened to them had they been born, or stayed, further east.

The group is standing around a model of the complex, as the guide tells them what the demonstrators found here on the evening of 15 January 1990 when they finally got inside. She says there was an internal supermarket with delicacies unavailable anywhere else in the country. There was a hairdresser with rows of orange helmet-like dryers, 'for all those bristle-cuts'. There was a shoemaker and, of course, a locksmith. The guide crinkles her nose in order to push her glasses up its bridge; a reflex which doubles as a gesture of distaste. She explains that the neighbouring building – the archive – was invisible from outside the complex, and a copper-lined room had been planned for it, to keep information safe from satellite surveillance. There was a munitions depot here, and a bunker underneath for Mielke and select few in the event of a nuclear catastrophe. She says Berliners used to refer to this place as the 'House of One Thousand Eyes'.

I start to look about the atrium. An arrow points toward a library, another up the stairs to an exhibition room. It smells of dust and old air. [...]

When Mikhail Gorbachev came to power in the Soviet Union in 1985 he implemented the policies of *perestroika* (economic reform) and *glasnost* ('openness' of speech). In June 1988 he declared a principle of freedom of choice for governments within the Eastern Bloc and renounced the use of Soviet military force to prop them up. Without Soviet backup to quash popular dissent, as there had been at the workers' uprising in Berlin in 1953, in Hungary in 1956, and in Prague in 1968, the GDR regime could not survive. The options were change, or civil war.

By comparison with other Eastern Bloc countries, East Germany never had much of a culture of opposition. Perhaps this was in part due to the better standard of living, perhaps to the thoroughness of the Stasi – or, as some put it, to the willingness of Germans to subject themselves to authority. But mostly it was because, alone of all Eastern Bloc countries, East Germany had somewhere to dump people who spoke out: West Germany. It imprisoned them and then sold them to the west for hard currency. The numbers of dissidents could not reach a critical mass until 1989 when the changes in the Soviet Union gave ordinary people courage and they took to the streets.

Anna Funder, *Stasiland*

* * *

With the Wall down and the Iron Curtain melting away, where does Europe now end and the rest of the world begin? This is the question travel writer Rory MacLean has in mind to investigate as he sets out on a trip from the Baltic to the Black Sea – until the trip is high-jacked by a recently-widowed aunt and he recounts, in Stalin's Nose, *a journey made with the eccentric aunt and her pet pig on board. Here's how it begins …*

Winston the pig fell into Zita's life when he dropped onto my uncle's head and killed him dead. The news reached me in Rostock, drab, damp and winter grey, where my trip had begun. I had planned to travel from the Baltic to the Black Sea, across the continent's waist, along the line of the old Iron

Curtain, but a telephone call changed everything.

'It's your uncle,' she shouted. The line was bad. I couldn't hear. Was it his legs? 'He's finally kicked buckets.' My aunt had learnt her English after the war, while the Allies remained allied, from the British military attaché in Budapest. It hadn't improved with age.

I caught the train to Berlin and changed for Potsdam. The lost corner of the West had regained its central position and Europe had reclaimed its east. The Wall, which had been open for only a few weeks, was breached in places, like a sandbank by the current, and rivers of people streamed across the false divide. They gathered in pools on no man's land, lapped against the barrier and wore it away with hammers then pocketed the detritus as mementos. The late great division of the world, between a capitalist West and a communist East, passed away as an historical aberration. Where then, if no longer down this line, was the real end of Europe?

Rory MacLean, *Stalin's Nose*

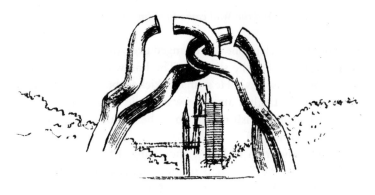

Berlin: Weltstadt

'Construction of the Arch of Triumph was commenced in 1946 and work was completed in time for the Day of National Reawakening in 1950. The inspiration for the design came from the Führer and is based upon original drawings made by him during the Years of Struggle.'

The passengers on the bus tour – at least those who could understand – digested this information. They raised themselves out of their seats or leaned into the aisle to get a better view. Xavier March, half-way down the bus, lifted his son on to his lap. Their guide, a middle-aged woman clad in the dark green of the Reich Tourist Ministry, stood at the front, feet planted wide apart, back to the windscreen. Her voice over the address system was thick with cold.

'The Arch is constructed of granite and has a capacity of two million, three hundred and sixty-five thousand, six hundred and eighty-five cubic metres.' She sneezed. 'The Arc de Triomphe in Paris would fit into it forty-nine times.'

For a moment, the Arch loomed over them. Then, suddenly, they were passing through it – an immense, stone-ribbed tunnel, longer than a football pitch, high than a fifteen-storey building, with the vaulted, shadowed roof of a cathedral. The headlights and tail-lights of eight lanes of traffic danced in the afternoon gloom.

'The Arch has a height of one hundred and eighteen metres. It is one hundred and sixty-eight metres wide and has a depth of one hundred and nineteen metres. On the inner walls are carved the names of the three million soldiers who fell in defence of the Fatherland in the wars of 1914 to 1918 and 1939 to 1946.'

She sneezed again. The passengers dutifully craned their necks to peer at the Roll of the Fallen. They were a mixed party. A group of Japanese, draped with cameras; an American couple with a little girl Pili's age; some German settlers, from Ostland or the Ukraine, in Berlin for the Führetag. March looked away as they passed the Roll of the Fallen. Somewhere on it were the names of his father and both his grandfathers. He kept his eyes on the guide. When she thought no one was looking, she turned away and quickly wiped her nose on her sleeve. The coach re-emerged into the drizzle.

'Leaving the Arch we enter the central section of the Avenue of Victory. The Avenue was designed by Reich Minister Albert Speer and was completed in 1957. It is one hundred and twenty-three metres wide and five point six kilometres in length. It is both wider, and two and a half times longer, than the Champs Elysées in Paris.'

Higher, longer, bigger, wider, more expensive ... Even in victory, thought March, Germany has a parvenu's inferiority complex. Nothing stands on its own. Everything has to be compared with what foreigners have ...

'The view from this point northwards along the Avenue of Victory is considered one of the wonders of the world.'

'One of the wonders of the world,' repeated Pili in a whisper.

And it was, even on a day like this. Dense with traffic, the Avenue stretched before them, flanked on either side by the glass and granite walls of Speer's new buildings: ministries, offices, big stores, cinemas, apartment blocks. At the far end of this river of light, rising as grey as a battleship through the spray, was the great Hall of the Reich, its dome half hidden in the low cloud.

There were appreciative murmurs from the settlers. [...]

'The Great Hall of the Reich is the largest building in the world. It rises to a height of more than a quarter of a kilometre, and on certain days – observe today – the top of its dome is lost from view. The dome itself is one hundred and forty metres in diameter and St. Peter's in Rome will fit into it sixteen times.'

They had reached the top of the Avenue of Victory, and were entering Adolf Hitler Platz. To the left, the square was bounded by the headquarters of the Wehrmacht High Command, to the right by the new Reich Chancellery and Palace of the Führer. Ahead was the hall. Its greyness had dissolved as their distance from it had diminished. Now they could see what the guide was telling them: that the pillars supporting the frontage were of red granite, mined in Sweden, flanked at either end by golden statues of Atlas and Tellus, bearing on their shoulders spheres depicting the heavens and the earth.

The building was as crystal-white as a wedding cake, its dome of beaten copper a dull green. Pili was still at the front of the coach.

'The Great Hall is used only for the most solemn ceremonies of the German Reich and has a capacity of one hundred and eighty thousand people. One interesting and unforeseen phenomenon: the breath from this number of humans rises into the cupola and forms clouds, which condense and fall as light rain. The great Hall is the only building in the world which generates its own climate ... ' [...]

'On the right is the Reich Chancellery and residence of the Führer. Its total façade measures exactly seven hundred metres, exceeding by one hundred metres the façade of Louis XIV's palace at Versailles.'

The Chancellery slowly uncoiled as the bus drove by marble pillars and red mosaics, bronze lions, gilded silhouettes, gothic script – a Chinese dragon of a building, asleep at the side of the square. A four-man SS honour guard stood at attention beneath a billowing swastika banner. There were no windows, but set into the wall, five storeys above the ground, was the balcony on which the Führer showed himself on those occasions when a million people gathered in the Platz. There were a few dozen sightseers even now, gazing up at the tightly drawn shutters, faces pale with expectation, hoping ...

Robert Harris, *Fatherland*

❋ ❋ ❋

Happily, Robert Harris's Fatherland *is a work of fantasy, imagining what might have happened had Hitler won the war and been able to carry out Albert Speer's vast architectural plans for turning Berlin into 'Germania', capital of a 'thousand-year Reich'. Maybe Speer's extraordinary vision of what it might be like reflects the fact that, even from its earliest days, Berlin had been anxious for recognition as a world-class city – a 'Weldstadt'. Its identity crisis seems to have come partly from the distrust of other German cities towards it, and partly from suspecting that it couldn't quite compete with other top European cities like Paris and London. Iain Bamforth tracks a self-doubting Berlin's journey towards becoming a world-class city ... in a modern sense.*

Haupstadt Berlin: One of the figures that haunts the history of the city on the Spree from its 1871 promotion as Reichshauptstadt through to the year 2000 is a ghost: self-doubt. [...] Bismarck, like his sovereign, distrusted the new capital's bombast and swagger: it was a sump of liberalism, sucking in new people from the eastern marches. Thousands of enterprising Jews from the marches were drawn there, and many poorer Jews too: the Scheunenviertel ('barn district') north of the Alexanderplatz became a haven for refugees from Russia and Poland. [...]The rest of Germany found Berlin alien, both parvenu and preposterous–an attitude that has never entirely disappeared. It is akin to the shudder some Americans used to get at the sight of Chicago, though they never had to live with it as their capital. Seafaring Hamburgers mocked Berlin as an outpost on the pampas; ecclesiastically conservative Bavarians loathed it for being northern and Protestant. Berliners replied with their famous blunt cheek, the Berliner Schnauze.

Wilhelmine Berlin: Within a few decades of its inauguration in 1871, Berlin had become an urban laboratory: it was the world's newspaper capital and home to its first fast-food chain (Aschinger's). It stood at the cutting edge of scientific progress: Koch, Ehrlich, Planck and Einstein made some of the most important advances in modern science in the city, despite their misgivings about the grip of the Prussian military on the academy. Indeed Elektropolis, as it was known in the early years of the twentieth century, heralded the ascension of the empirical sciences over the older humanistic disciplines and the new international image of Germany as the 'machine nation'; even the Kaiser, who presided over Berlin's odd blend of uniform worship and urban modernity, exhorted his subjects to participate in the game of power. Knowledge was power for those who wanted to achieve more than truth. Tradition always had a caricatural quality in Berlin, such was the city's thralldom to hard facts, to the lure of efficiency and Technik. This very modern amalgam of feudal attitudes–no other European industrial power was so dominated by the landed aristocracy and traditional military figures–and an almost unquenchable belief in the power of machines was to prove the undoing of the Kaiser, and Germany itself, in the longer run.

Weimar Berlin: Long before the wild twenties, Berlin was renowned for its strenuous hedonism and armies of prostitutes: it was the great Babylon of the East. The collapse of civil order that followed the end of the Great War, with violent street battles between the Spartacists and government troops culminating in the murder of Rosa Luxemburg and Karl Lieb-knecht, convinced the rest of Germany that its capital was not just corrupt, but dangerous. The novelist Alfred Döblin, working as a doctor in the working class Lichtenberg district, wrote in disgust at the indifference in the better heeled parts of the city to the bloodshed around him. The First International Dada Fair, in 1920, took art more seriously than anyone had hitherto thought possible, and instructed dilettantes to rise up against it. Overthrow art, and society would be easy game. Social conditions in Berlin were not helped by the draconian terms imposed on Germany by the treaty of Versailles, which led to the hyperinflation of 1922–23; in November 1922, the mint was printing 100 trillion mark notes. Their value depreci-ated before the printer's ink was dry: in what became known as the Great Disorder a loaf of bread cost 80 billion. Doctors began to talk about 'zero stroke' or 'cypher stroke', a kind of nervous breakdown induced by contemplation of the spiralling currency figures. Berlin's streets began to dominate the screen in Fritz Lang's films, the stage in Brecht's dramas of the 'jungle of the cities', and the newspapers in the articles of Egon Erwin Kisch, the first journalist to turn the reporter into a recognis-able figure: the entertaining crusader. The cynic was no longer a socially critical thinker living outside the city: his mindset was inextricably part of the social substance. Tucholsky, Roth, Kafka and–perhaps most surprisingly of all–Nabokov (whose father was shot at a political meeting when he tried to protect the speaker, one of Kerensky's ill-fated Russian cabinet of 1917) all lived and wrote there during the twenties. In fact, Berlin was the first cultural capital of the Russian émigré commu-nity: it had Russian theatres, bookshops, hairdressers, grocers and even a football team (with Nabokov in goal). At the end of the decade Berlin could claim to be the most progressive city in the world: Stresemann, Germany's conciliatory foreign minister, son of a Berlin innkeeper, was perhaps the first prominent politician to be genuinely fond of the capital: his death in 1929 deprived the Weimar Republic of the one person who might have held it through the terrible year of the Wall Street crash, which allowed the Nazis to make their bid for power. What are often thought of as Nazi projects, such as Berlin's new airport at Tempelhof, and its elevated trains, roads and egalitarian housing were all launched during the Weimar years. Weimar Berlin was modernity's advance post.

Hitler's Berlin: Following Bismarck's adroit military campaigns against Denmark, Austria and France, the city was laid out, its roads diverging like Ixion's axles, on a scale to rival Vienna, Paris and London. 'Hyperthyroid neoclassicism' is its default style. Hitler didn't like Berlin, but he needed its bigness. With the help of Albert Speer, his general inspector of buildings, he intended to transform it into a cultic city which, by 1950, would contain the crowds whose arousal was the secret of his power. The whole thing was to look like a vast, militarised Ufa premiere. Germania would have a new north-south axis, a triumphal arch four times bigger than the one at the top of the Champs-Elysées and a central dome, the Kuppelberg, sixteen times bigger than St Peter's. Other European cities would be lilliputian by comparison. In fact, he was planning for a mausoleum on the largest possible scale, a Piranesi doom-machine made with an eye for its own sublime destitution. Hitler wanted to see what his Rome would look like once its thousand years of glory had passed. Visiting the ruins of the Chancellery in late 1945, Stephen Spender noted the reams of building manuals above the Führer's bed. Hitler didn't believe in much, but he believed in architecture.

Rubble Berlin: While every European city offers the historian a biography (the history of Europe is, in large part, the history of its cities), Berlin, since 1870, has acquired an archaeology, too. Some of its layers are made of compressed nightmare, deposits of sordid misery and not just the eerie atmospheres of the "weird tales" that made E.T.A. Hoffmann famous in the days when Berlin was a most respectably enlightened regional capital. A couple of weeks ago I stood with my son flying a kite on the top of a large sandy hill in the Grunewald area, between Berlin and Potsdam. The hill is called Teufelsberg. The only incline for miles, it offers a superb vantage point across the city from Spandau and Reinickendorf in the north to Tempelhof and Kopenick in the south. In winter it becomes a ski resort. But Devil's Mountain is no ordinary hill: pipes, bricks, tiles and other detritus can be seen poking out from beneath its sand and scrub. This 120-metre-high heap is the derelict body of prewar Berlin; this is the city carted away brick by brick at war's end by the famous 'rubble women'.

West Berlin: After a collapse so total it ended up as a hill, half of its population dead or dispersed, Berlin became extraterritorial. [...] While the rest of the world moved into the era of mutually assured destruction (MAD), Berlin became a kind of conservatory for espionage and counter-espionage. The visit of the young Augustus of the new American age ('I am a doughnut' Kennedy told the packed crowds, though nobody seemed to mind), and the overnight construction in 1961 of the thirteen-foot high 'anti-fascist protection barrier', as they called it in the DDR. Berlin never regained the array of industries that had made it the nerve-centre of the Nazi military-industrial complex, but it became the vitrine of the free world. It was a city on the take. The communist half of it was drab, virtuous and uninspiring, the other heavily subsidised by Bonn and rather self-conscious about its decadence. Draft-dodgers flocked there, and it seethed with anti-establishment sentiment and student provocation. Bohemians dressed in black.

Stoned out of their minds, Iggy Pop and his friend David Bowie sang about having plans for everyone. Here was all the dark glamour of the twentieth-century, pretty much risk-free. For others, Berlin was a hope of heightened sentience.

Berlin Redux: Now the Wall is gone and Berlin has, for the first time in its recent history, the chance to grow bit by bit as a national capital, rather than an international showcase–as a 'capital-redux'. The fact that unity ultimately came about not through anything like Bismarck's 'blood and iron' but through the implosion of an ideology and that singular event in modern history–the peaceful withdrawal of an undefeated army–offers grounds for some confidence in the future. Germany's place in the world is quite different from what it was in 1870, or is it? The common European home seems to be extending eastwards, and Berlin is bound to dominate it.

Iain BAMFORTH, 'Believing in Architecture' in
The Good European: Essays and Arguments

✳ ✳ ✳

Of course, there had been times in its past when Berlin seemed to have become 'the' European city par excellence, but the disasters of two world wars beat the city down each time. Some reflections on this situation by Geert Mak and Paul Verhaegen.

And in that same ragbag of a town, a miracle took place: Berlin became, for Europe, the city of the modern day. Perhaps it had to do with the way Wilhelm's Berlin had suddenly deflated like a balloon in 1918, leaving an enormous vacuum behind and the accompanying demand for new content, radically different forms and ideas. A cursory glance at the names of those who fled the city in the 1930s shows us something of the talent that had gathered in Berlin: Albert Einstein, Arnold Schönberg, Alfred Döblin, Joseph Roth, Heinrich Mann and his two children Klaus and Erika, Arthur Koestler, Marlene Dietrich, Hermann Ullstein.

In the eyes of many, Berlin was a man-eating monster of machines, factories, anonymous housing blocks and speeding trains and cars. It served as the model for *Metropolis*, the masterpiece by Viennese-born cineaste Fritz Lang. But at the same time it was the world in which Bertolt Brecht and Kurt Weill created their *Threepenny Opera*. It was there that Yehudi Menuhin gave his first concert, at the age of thirteen.[...]

The epicentre of this movement of modernity was Café des Westens. This was where the literary magazines were passed around, hot off the presses. This is where the captains of the avant-garde granted audience to their followers, the expressionists associated with *Der Sturm*, with artists like Oskar Kokoschka, Paul Klee, Vassily Kandinsky, the young Marc Chagall and countless Futurists, constructivists and Dadaists. One of the café's focal points was the Dadaist painter George Grosz, famous for his unflattering prints of whores, beggars, paraplegic war invalids on rollers and fat-necked real-estate speculators, street scenes often not at all far removed from reality.

When the owner of Café des Westens boosted his prices in 1920, they all moved to the Romanisches Café, a huge, ugly space across from the Kaiser-Wilhelm-Gedächtniskirche. In Paris the tone was set by the *esprit du salon*, but the Romanisches Café had the atmosphere of a popular uprising. Everyone shouted, everyone wanted to be right. Beside the revolving doors sat the old, bearded expressionist painters. Up on the balcony people played chess. There was a sculptors' table, a philosophers' table, a newspaper table, a sociologists' table. Pulling up a chair at a table to which one did not belong gave immediate cause for uproar. George Grosz would come storming in, dressed as an American cowboy, complete with boots and spurs. The Dutch poet Hendrik Marsman made 'calligrams' there ('*Gertrude. Gertrude. GERTRUDE. Slut.*'), and spoke of city life that had run amok into 'randiness, opium, madness and anarchy'. 'Berlin,' he wrote, 'hung from the sky on a silken thread, a ponderous, colossal behemoth dangling above a roiling inferno.'

Geert Mak, In Europe
translated by Sam Garrett

* * *

When we arrived here, Berlin was the most amazing city in the world. Even I, a small child, got drunk on the fabled *Berliner Luft*, the Berlin air – it poured down the canyons between the tall stone office colossi; it fermented in the half-dark of the *Filmpalasten*; it clouded up the theatres and the *Kaffeehäuser*. Within walking distance of our house I counted more than a handful of those coffee shops: Café Trump, Café Stefanie, the Romanische Café – on a good day, you could see *le tout Berlin* there, the whole Berlin art scene: Kokoschka, Döblin, Brecht, Lenya, Weil, Tucholsky, Nußbaum, Pritzel, Grosz, etcetera – and then there's Café Wien, and let's not forget Café Kempinski and the wonderful Schicksaal, and the most famous of all *Konditoreien*, Café Kranzler. Kranzler was the place my father used to take me on Sunday mornings. He would study the breakfast menu for a full fifteen minutes, in complete silence, as if the right choice of pastry was a matter of life or death – is *Baumkuchen* rolled in chocolate an acceptable choice so early in the morning, or should we order something else and take some in complete silence, as if the right choice of pastry was a matter of life or death – is *Baumkuchen* home for later, for afternoon tea?

Paul Verhaegen, Omega Minor

* * *

In this campaign for glory, Kaiser Wilhelm himself set the tone. The whole city was permeated with his romanticised view of history. Wilhelm's hand could be seen everywhere: in the countless statues of winged deities, in the many museums, in the thirty-five neo-Gothic churches – one of the empress' hobbies – in the thousands of oak leaves, laurel wreaths and other 'national' symbols, in the copper statue of the city's pudgy pseudo-goddess, Berolina, at Alexanderplatz, in the Siegfrieds with their imperial swords, in the Germanias with their triumphal chariots. London and Paris had long histories, but Berlin lacked continuity; these instant monuments served to fill the historical vacuum.

Wilhelm was deeply impressed by his arch rival England and copied whatever he could: Kew Gardens at Lichterfelde, Oxford at Dahlem, the famous Round Reading Room of the British Museum in his own Kaiserliche Bibliothek. But everything, of course, had to be bigger than its counterpart in England. At the Tiergarten, as an eternal tribute to his ancestors – but above all to himself – he had built the 700-metre-long Siegesallee, lined with marble statuary. That eternity, by the way, did not last long: the marble statues of the Electors (which Wilhelm felt looked 'as though made by Michelangelo') were tossed into the Landwehrkanal not long after the Second World War; today, a few of them have been dredged up and brought back to the Siegesallee and the Tiergarten.

Geert Mak, *In Europe*
translated by Sam Garrett

✳ ✳ ✳

The Communist east also had its grand architectural visions for Berlin, nowhere more obvious than in the building of the television tower and the Palace of the Republic – both remarkable for their time. With the fall of the regime, the Palace no longer had its former function. The protagonist of Fridolin Schley's story, 'The Heart of the Republic', visits this extraordinary building – his father was largely responsible for its design – given over to all kinds of entertainment.

Fabian had the feeling that it was only a caprice of his poor sense of direction that had led him there. On one of his evening strolls through the city centre, which, despite the spaciousness of the streets seemed to close in on him threateningly particularly as darkness fell, he had soon lost his way in the Scheunenviertel and, to stem his rising panic, had fixed his gaze on the flashing coloured lights of the TV tower on Alexanderplatz, hurrying towards them as if drawn by a spell, without paying any attention to the traffic or the lively bustle in the side streets. As a child he must once have known these streets inside out, something which seemed to him now like an opaque trick played by his memory.

The sight of the dark expanse of the Lustgarten and the baroque grandeur of the Berliner Dom finally calmed him so he was able to stand still for a second, look around and recognize that the Palace of the Republic on the other side of the street was not, as he assumed, lurking in the darkness like a long-abandoned factory building but rather that light was shining through some of the windows onto the former Schlossplatz, and that in front of the entrance a large cluster of people had formed, which at that very moment started to move and surged into the building.

Of course the Palace had been Fabian's destination from the outset. In a childish way he felt quite daring, when he reached the end of the queue and joined in line without knowing what awaited him and he heightened this pleasant sense of risk even more by nodding in friendly fashion to the couple in front of him who were elegantly dressed, and wished them 'a pleasant evening'. The man returned the greeting and said, 'Wagner à la GDR, that could be interesting', and Fabian even acknowledged the attendant checking the tickets on the door with a knowing smile, and then walked without being detained into the entrance hall. The public was already spreading out; some people were milling around by a temporary metal railing and were watching the musicians tuning up their instruments on the other side, who had gathered at the foot of a grand stone staircase, others like him made their way further into the room and into a dimly lit corridor, whose dimensions he couldn't make out.

Fabian remembered that this catacomb-like storey had originally not been open to the visitors to the Palace, but had instead been used as storage and cloakroom space with its many small rooms. The ceiling above the main corridor was suspended only just above head height, he felt his way along the cold damp walls, with the old gas pipes which ran on the left and right like veins, putting each foot down cautiously and didn't let the man in front of him get more than three metres ahead. Whatever you do, don't get left behind down here, he thought, no-one said a word any more, behind him only the scraping sound of footsteps, the increasingly distant discord of the instruments and them, the visitors, like prisoners, escaping together. They reached the first floor via a staircase which opened up out of nowhere on the right hand side, and relieved, entered a broad room which they could hardly take in at a glance, which seemed to have corners on all sides that opened out into other rooms and the room's height stood in opposition to the constrictive narrowness of the entrance area. From here, Fabian reckoned he knew, stairs and lifts had once led to all floors, and linked the Great Room with the People's Chamber. For some minutes he stood on the spot, simply turning his head to look all around. The walls had for the most part been torn down, the whole room was a fleshless skeleton, crossed by weight-bearing steel girders and metal poles; of the more than a thousand globe lights which had once lit up the room only rusting iron fittings remained, marked with yellow symbols and numbers at regular intervals. Fabian wasn't able to take in the whole room, in the distance the contours became too fluid. The pattern of collapsed brick walls, individual columns sticking up, the sills and panes of the high-set windows at the side, in addition to the faint, diffuse light in which silhouettes of visitors occasionally appeared briefly and disappeared again, created an impression of great indistinctness. In the distance even bigger rooms seemed to loom in a blur, there were rows of pillars and brickwork arches, which supported the upper level. In the warped floor he could make out patches of the black and white marble mosaic that at one time must have added to the effect of splendour – balls, conventions, and concerts had all taken place here – and all of a sudden, after Fabian had torn himself away and was wandering round aimlessly, it seemed incomprehensible to him that this building could have succumbed to the destruction so completely in such a short space of time, that it could stand here in the middle of a growing, constantly evolving city and at the same time continue to disintegrate from the inside out, and he thought about many memories of this place, its stories, which, given it had no memory of its own, were being consumed together with its interior without ever having been heard or recorded.

The music must have started a while ago, for the visitors now came rushing out of the mist from all around the room towards the balustrade, from where they could see into the lobby. That was where the majority of the orchestra and the conductor had taken up their places. But after a few minutes Fabian could hear, between the strings and brass, growing clearer, a scratchy drone, which sounded like an old record player arm had come out of the groove, and the dull thud of electronic bass. He looked around and spotted more musicians on other floors; a DJ wearing headphones on a ledge on the third floor was actually using a record player. The music seemed to do what Fabian himself had failed to shortly before, it seemed to be able to reach into the whole building, into every corner and moreover to fill the space.

Gradually some of the listeners broke away from the crowd, by the balustrade and continued their tour. The movement of the visitors, their wandering, must have been an integral part of the concept for the evening, because Fabian couldn't see any seating anywhere, apparently people were meant to walk around freely on the different levels during the concert, as if they were acting out in slow motion the proceedings of a ball from bygone parties in the Palace.

Fabian too had moved on, but soon stopped with a few others in front of a blown up photograph displayed on an easel, which he stared at for a long time before he recognized on it that very room, that is, the main foyer in which he was currently standing. [...]

Fabian must have raised and lowered his head for a while, to compare the photo of the former splendour with the state of dilapidation, with the effect that afterwards he had no memory of the concert itself, and he could only assume that there had been a constant stream of visitors who walked past him, stood next to him for a moment, glanced at the photograph and then went on their way, while he stood there almost motionless. The *Glass Flower*, his father had said, was nearly five metres tall and like so much had simply disappeared after the Palace was closed; works of art had also been stolen from the gallery, large oil-paintings by Willi Sitte and Arno Mohr, which had been put on display in the very first exhibition, the now famous, 'Are Communists allowed to dream?'

Fabian had gone on a bit further and ended up on the second floor via a staircase, from where you entered the former Great Hall, which surpassed even the lobby in height and length.

Eighteen metres high, 67 metres long, his father had explained over and over again, conventions and political gatherings had been the main events here, but thanks to the technical construction and fittings the hall had also been used for balls, banquets, and all sorts of orchestra concerts. The seating capacity which could be changed at the touch of a button, indeed, the completely flexible functionality and aesthetics of the space had been the only one of its kind in the world; at conventions 5,000 people could be seated at a writing desk, for dance competitions on the other hand they had raised the six swivel-mounted seating levels to sixty degrees and lowered by nearly six metres 24 ceiling plates which had built-in lighting bridges. The mechanism was still intact, so too the moving stages in the old theatre in the fourth floor, but to maintain technical functioning permanently these needed to be moved at least once a week, and the last official use had been some (and here Fabian's father looked shocked every time) twelve years ago. [...]

For Fabian's father had designed the Palace and built it, not on his own of course, but he had been part of the collective of architects who had been commissioned after the ministerial decision in 1973 to build a house for the people, the topping out ceremony had taken place as early as the end of 1974, and the official opening of the Palace had been in April 1976 [...]

At the time it was said to be the most modern edifice for culture in Europe (and that despite the fact that the GDR state was practically broke), at least as far as the interior design was concerned, the world had never seen such cleverly designed multifunctionality before. His father recalled the details of the development ever more precisely, and nearly every day, if he wasn't too weak to speak, he would explain to his family once again that they had taken their direction from Schinkel's idea of the house of the people, parliamentary debates and restaurants for the public under one roof, plus bowling alley, theatre, and art galleries. No-one had ever dared to do something like that before.

Fridolin Schley, 'The Heart of the Republic', in *Berlin Tales*
translated by Lyn Marven

❋ ❋ ❋

One of the indicators of being a world-class city today – perhaps even more so than in the past – is having an international population. Berlin's largest group of residents of non-German origin are Turkish. In this next passage, Turkish writer Emine Sevgi Özdamar talks about her relationship with and experiences of Berlin, at the same time giving us a portrait of the city.

In 1975 I returned to Berlin after nine years. After the military putsch in Turkey I had ended up in the hands of the police. My friends Theo and Kati in Berlin had mobilized Amnesty International to fetch me to Berlin. They lived in the first floor of a villa in Steglitz. Kati's mother lived below them. Kati said, 'You can stay in her flat for a week. She's at a health farm.' The flat was cold, there was no central heating, just a Kachelofen.[1] 'My mother hasn't had proper heating installed,' Kati said, 'she thinks the Russians will come anyway, why should I have heating put in for the Russians.' Kati and Theo were Young Socialists.

Between 1965 and 1967 I had already lived in Berlin and had returned to Istanbul with two records of Brecht's Songs by Lotte Lenya and Ernst Busch. Then in Istanbul I attended the Drama School and listened to these songs over and over again for years. My grandmother would listen with me and ask, 'What are they singing?' I translated 'Und der Haifisch / der hat Zähne / und die trägt er im Gesicht'[2] – 'I hope the shark doesn't get into paradise,' she said. She was expecting to go to paradise herself you see, because eight of her children had died. 'On the Day of Judgement I will stand on the bridge between heaven and hell. This bridge is as thin as a hair and as sharp as a sabre. If the sins were too great, the bridge cuts the sinner in half, and he falls down into hell. But because my eight sons and daughters died when they were just children, they hadn't yet sinned and now they are angels. They will come flying and lift me off the bridge onto their backs and take me to heaven.'

When I left this time, Grandmother said to me 'You will come back in a few days won't you? When I'm dirty you'll wash me again won't you?'

---

1 A tiled stove.
2 The first lines of Mack the Knife, 'Oh the shark has pretty teeth dear / And he shows them pearly white' (in the 1954 Marc Blitzstein translation).

'Grandmother, don't cry, don't cry!'

'Look, I'm not crying, but please come back again in two days!'

When my grandmother next needed a bath I was sitting in the train to Berlin. I had left behind many friends who had been killed. For one young man who had been hanged there would be no more evenings, no cat, no cigarettes.

At Zoo Station I waved to all the buses going past. I was in freedom and was pleased about the rain. I thought, Berlin has waited for me for nine years. It was as if back then when I had gone back to Istanbul Berlin had frozen like a photo, to wait for me – with the long, tall trees, with the Gedächtniskirche, with the double-decker buses, with the corner pubs. Berliner Kindl beer, the crosses on the beer mats. Walls. Checkpoint Charlie. U-Bahn. S-Bahn. Cinema on Steinplatz. *Abschied von gestern* (Yesterday Girl). Alexander Kluge. Bockwurst sausages. The Brecht theatre Berliner Ensemble. *Arturo Ui.* Canals. The Peacock Island. Tramps in the stations. Pea soup. Lonely women in Café Kranzler. Black Forest gateau. Workers from different countries. Spaghetti. Greeks. Cumin-Turks. Café Käse. Telephone dances. Bullet holes in house walls. Cobblestones. Curried sausage. White bodies waiting for the sun at lake Wannsee. Police dogs. East German police searchlights. Dead train tracks, grass growing between them. House notices: 'In the interests of all residents children are forbidden to play games'. Stations left behind in East Berlin which the West Berlin underground trains pass through without stopping. A solitary East-policeman on the platform. Soljanka soup. Stuyvesand cigarettes. Rothhändle cigarettes. Signs: 'Achtung Sie verlassen den Amerikanischen Sektor / Warning you are leaving the American sector'. Jewish cemetery in East Berlin. Ducks on Lake Wannsee. A bar with music from the 1940s, old women dancing with women. Broilers. [...]

Before I moved to East Berlin I walked through West Berlin once more and read the writing on the house and the Wall:

Why are you all so desperate ... Everything we have forgotten screams for help in our dreams ... God is dead, the executioners aren't ... We don't need tear gas, we already have plenty of reasons to cry ... GDR: German Dross ... Attention! You are entering the Axel Springer sector ... Reds for the gas chambers ... Time to live – got to go to work first ... USA-Army go home ... Shame concrete doesn't burn ... Die Deutschland ... People wake up – better shake up the state ... Death to mediocrity ... Women strike back ... No riots without demolition ... I loves ya ... Being a cop, that's top ... Fire & flames for this state ... Learn peace ... Germany shut up ... [...]

Sometimes on a Saturday or Sunday I went to Friedrichstraße station. That's where the trains stopped in which West Germans sat, and then they carried on to West Berlin. Here even I really began to long for the West. I called Kati. 'Is it snowing where you are too?' When the trains had departed, the people went back into the station bar, but they came up again immediately the next train came which was going to the West with its doors that had to stay shut. Down below in the station there was a cigarette kiosk. One of the brands was called 'Speechless'.

In the theatre canteen an actor told stories about getting out. Once a man had tried to flee to the West as a swan. He made himself a swan's head, put it on and swam through the Spree. The real swans came over to him, pecked at his fake swan head and swam with him to the West.

I walked from the station to the cemetery in Chausseestraße. There some of the gravestones lay like giant books on the ground. I always went to Bertolt Brecht's gravestone. He had made specifications for his gravestone himself. It was to be a simple stone, 'which every dog wants to piss on'.

On his grave had grown the same flowers that my grandmother always used to plant in Turkey. KÜPELI (with earrings). On the gravestone was written: 'He made suggestions and they were carried out'. Near Brecht was the grave of Heinrich Mann, on which I often saw an East Berlin cat sitting. In the evening I had a dream. I found myself in a large, crooked room. Brecht was lying in a bed. I said to his wife Helene Weigel, 'I want to speak to him' – 'but he is dead' – 'no, he is not dead, he is just sleeping. Please, give me something of his. His tie or his pillowcase.' Weigel gave me Brecht's pillowcase.

Then suddenly I found myself on the steps of a moving ship.

Behind me were standing fascists from Turkey.

And Hegel lay there, his gravestone was red granite. One time I came across an eight- or nine-year-old boy at his grave. He said to me, 'Georg Wilhelm Friedrich Hegel wanted to be buried next to Johann Gottlieb Fichte. Fichte died of typhus, Hegel died of cholera.' From Hegel's grave I went to Brecht's, the boy came too and I sang quietly' … Und der Haifisch, der hat Zähne … ' Then I said to him, 'My grandmother was scared that the shark might get into paradise.' – 'Where do you come from?' – 'From Turkey.' – 'Where is Turkey?' – 'Near Bulgaria.'

We sat a while by Brecht's grave. Then the boy wanted to accompany me to my flat. When we were standing in front of the house, he said to me,

'My father has an atlas. When I'm home I will ask him to show me where Turkey is.' – 'Perhaps we'll see each other again.' – 'Yes, I come to the cemetery at 2 o'clock on Saturdays.' – 'See you on Saturday.'

Emine Sevgi Özdamar, 'My Berlin', in *Berlin Tales*
translated by Lyn Marven

✳ ✳ ✳

Ian Walker also reminds us of the many cultures existing side-by-side in post-war Berlin.

There were 6,000 Jews still living in the west and 400 in the east. The Jewish community centre in the west was on Fasanenstrasse, the site of the synagogue burned down by Nazi mobs in 1938. Turk, Arab and Pakistani Moslems had between them built twenty mosques in West Berlin. In East Berlin there were no guest workers and no mosques. In West Berlin there was a Buddhist temple in Frohnau and a Russian Orthodox cathedral at Hohenzollerndamm. Tai Chi, Hari Krishna, Holistic Masseurs, Hypnotherapists, Mongolian and Tibetan Overture Chanters (with Mantra and Sonic Meditations), astrologists, Bhagwan, Re-birthers, Tarot and Psychic Counsellors, Primal Screamers, these people all had buildings in West Berlin too, advertising their spiritual services in the classifieds of *Tip* and *Zitty*, supermarkets for lost souls.

In the east Christ had been re-born as Marx and Engels. In the west Christ had been re-packaged as a capitalist hero waging holy war against communism (the Antichrist). Never had the Second Coming been more badly needed, I said to Al and Mark and there were predictable jokes.

Ian Walker, Zoo Station

✳ ✳ ✳

In his fascinating Berlin blog, Rory MacLean asks whether Berlin really has become a world city again …

Cities are enriched by diversity and my excitement in moving to Berlin springs in part from its cultural and ethnic mix: Ossie and Wessie, German and Turk, Russians and Americans. Last night a London academic, with Bengali roots and a Masters from McGill in Montreal, came by for supper. At the Goethe-Institut a spiky-haired student from Seoul is teaching me about Korean hip-hop. On Saturday mornings a Syrian named Nora is tutoring our son in German. Tonight I'm due to meet a Moscow filmmaker at Café Sopranos on Ku'damm.

So is Berlin once again a world city? For all its international gloss, the capital of Europe sometimes feels like a provincial backwater. Take our local supermarket for example. Above its bright open door flashes a large neon sign which declares

'Always Open'. A couple of Sundays ago – as the Bialetti espresso pot hissed on the stovetop and blueberry pancakes warmed in the oven – I strode down to buy a litre of milk. But beneath the flashing 'Always Open' sign the door was firmly locked. A passing dog-walker looked at me as if I'd just arrived from Mars. 'Of course it's shut,' she barked at me. 'Everything is shut on Sunday.'

Berliners may work and party six days a week but, on Sunday mornings, the Haupstadt becomes a village. Apart from the odd Turkish baker, and tourist industry workers, everyone stays firmly under the duvet. In residential areas the streets feel all but deserted. In Berlin 24/7 actually means 24/6.

Rory MacLean, Rory's Berlin Blog

❊ ❊ ❊

To be a destination that all the world loves to visit, a city has to have more than grand monuments to offer. Nitasha Kaul writes a letter urging the protagonists of her novel Residue – *Leon Ali and Keya Raina – not to be content with the version of Berlin they experience in their narrative but to freely explore the non-monumental delights of Berlin in the future.*

Dear Leon and Keya,

Both of you travelled to Berlin because of me. Though you found each other there, that city was, for you, a museum of divided, conflicted and often traumatic histories.

But there were sides of Berlin you never encountered! I write now to take you on a short journey to the lighter side of the city, the way I often experienced it myself.

You never met the happy young crowd at Alex (Alexanderplatz) on the U2 line or learnt that the bars never close in Berlin. You can find cafes in Friedrichshain where the owner makes you a coffee, chats about art and there is no price list; you can pay what you like. You should have defied my instructions to visit ex-prisons and gone aboard the big bright balloon at Potsdamer Platz or the mirrored heights of the Parliament building for a view of the glittering city below.

You should go Goth and strum a guitar at the S-bahn station, have strangers listen to it. Get into the underground and softly murmur Bayleen, Bayleen, Bayleen, trying to copy the voice on the announcement system. Let the edgy spirit of Bairleen get into you.

I'm glad that you cavorted near the fountain of the four rivers by Begas where the gleaming polished metal skins of the large feminine statues arouses desires that can be indulged on the grassy Spree riverside. You should have followed it with a luxuriating dalliance at the palace Schloss Charlottenburg.

It's good that you visited the Kunsthaus Tacheles, the abode of artists of all kinds who have inhabited this building which stands at one end of the bustling and hip Oranienburger Strasse. Next time, in lively Kreuzberg, enjoy the savouries at midnight. In Prenzlauerberg, find a music mecca.

When you walk by the Lutzowufer canal in beautiful leafy Tiergarten, choose the side densely lined with trees. Don't miss the boats anchored near the metallic arches of small red bridges. Under the greening trees, you may see a family of swans gliding on the waters – two adults and three young ones __sssSS__ a bright white troupe. A galaxy of petals scattered where an extravagantly flowering bush weighs spring's soul on its tender arms. A bird might drop diagonally from a branch in front of you, chirping. The tiniest cygnet may open its beak for an instant ...

I've never told anyone this, but let me confess to you some of the eccentric things I did in Berlin. I stepped into the underground at Zoologischer Garten and spent an entire day going from one end of Berlin to another on the different U-bahns and S-bahns. For the price of a day pass (handful of euros) you become an anthropologist of the city. You see what the different suburbs feel like, you learn what's cool where (and what's not!), and you certainly get an eyeful of everything from ornate graffiti to fabulous handbags. If you decide to do this, carry water, rush like mad for the corner seat with side support panels in the train, be prepared for ticket inspectors, and keep change for buskers. A cheerful outlook will be especially essential when, at the end of the day, you get out at a station with a triple-barrelled name (e.g., Oskar-Helen-Heim) and feel urban suffocation from circulating in the city innards for what feels like millennia!

What is more, in the course of my subterranean wandering, I found a station named Kaulsdorf. My surname 'Kaul', from Kashmir, is shared by Germans for reasons that no one has worked out. In addition, a special Kashmiri vegetable, the Kohl Rabi (called Monj in Kashmiri) is ubiquitous in Germany. With ideas like this, I stepped out at Kaulsdorf station one night and rambled about the quiet suburb looking for clues about the origin of the name 'Kaulsdorf'. Was it literally the 'village of the Kauls'? I found a pub where I made diligent enquiries, the amused and helpful publican and his customers dug out history books but could not find anything definite as to how the place got its name. I was referred to a bookshop that had closed. Someone speculated that the name Kaulsdorf might have come from: 'village of the tadpoles', the tadpole being a 'Kaulquappe'. We laughed. Perhaps the origin led to being Caul-born. It was funny and rather crazy to be there at that hour and discussing intercontinental commonalities!

My dear characters Keya and Leon, Berlin is a city of friendly surprises. There are so many free internet areas; you must go there undirected by my pen and email me back the details of your visit.

With love,
Nitasha

Nitasha Kaul, 'Letter'

Goodbye to Berlin

*And finally, three superb writers on the city recreate
the feelings of leaving a city one has grown to love,
for all its complexities and difficulties, as they say
'Goodbye' to Berlin ...*

Once you decide to leave, you view a city through an entirely
different lens. The simplest of actions, actions you have repeated
one hundred, maybe a thousand, times, swell in significance since
each time may now be the last: the last time you buy bread at the
bakery, the last time you ride on the U-Bahn Line 2, the last time
you get your boots fixed at the cobbler, the last time you go to
the newsagent's for a travel pass or a pack of gum. There were
so many things I would miss, I realized, even things I hadn't seen
in a while, like the stone-faced museum guards from the days
when I still went to museums and the scenester kids plowing
through the flea markets in search of the holy vintage grail and
the stern women from the bank and the post office with their
eighties hairdos and the ice-cream place on Stargarder Straße,
where there was always a line, even in winter, and that German
punctuality, which made you miss your bus by seven seconds
but also ensured you arrived at your appointments on time, and

of course the voice of the S-Bahn announcer as he rolled off the stations and Alexanderplatz with its ever-changing face and the yellow streetcars, napping or in motion.

In a similar way, streets acquired a new sheen, as if I were discovering them for the first time, especially my own street, where I began noticing many details I'd failed to notice before, like the way the crests of the two trees on the corner seemed to interlock, and the graffiti on the streetlamp with the broken bulb, and the blue curtains with embroidered yellow stars hanging in the second floor window of the house three doors down. The apartment had been my home for only half a year but now that I was leaving it came to embody every Berlin home I'd ever had, each its own repository of reverie and melancholy and downtrodden expectation, a little cave of solitude I'd both shunned and withdrawn to depending on mood.

But in the midst of all this I felt like the city had given up on me, that the moment I handed in my notice and had my ticket to Mexico, Berlin turned its back on a former inhabitant. Even the people with whom I crossed paths on the street seemed to harden in attitude as if no longer heeding the impulse to be civil since soon I would be gone, or else they were extra aggressive in reproach for my having decided to leave when they were staying put and sticking it out, and I almost felt like grabbing the impatient bus conductor by the shoulders and saying, Look, I'm not from here and as it is I have given five years of my life to this country and am now ready to return to my own, with its own cauldron of problems.

I also found I had more patience for some things, now that I knew I would soon never have to deal with them again, and yet less patience for others. I could finally stop making an effort and actually let myself act out the irritation I had smothered all this time, so when a jogger seized the last supermarket cart I snapped at her, and when my upstairs neighbor, Felix the accountant, played the Scorpions at four in the morning I didn't think twice about going up to complain and even looked over his shoulder at the dark outline on the wall, which for some inexplicable reason he had yet to cover up. All the shyness and inhibition I'd felt during my years in Berlin fell away and in the last weeks and days my spoken German flowed more smoothly than ever as I found myself being assertive in a way I'd never dared to before, a final battle cry before heading back to the New World.

At moments I felt a huge wave of relief, and at others a pang of incipient nostalgia, knowing that soon all this would belong firmly and squarely to the past, to a phase in my life, "the Berlin years" perhaps, and that once I reached Mexico and succeeded in resuscitating my life there I would probably feel a reluctance to return for realistically, the only way to move on is to avoid sentimentality about the past, especially the recent past, which will always try to reclaim you.

Chloe Aridjis, *Book of Clouds*

✳ ✳ ✳

I walked out the unlocked door, borrowed Uschi's bicycle for the last time and rode to the wide-open dereliction of Potsdamer Platz. I had a cup of coffee in the orange corrugated Imbiss and browsed among the stalls selling cuddly toys, painted mirrors of Elvis and Marilyn and James Dean, postcards of the Wall. A gruff-voiced drunk drew my attention to his watercolours of Berlin street-scenes. I said I was skint, I was just looking. He asked why I was writing things down in my notebook.

'For a book,' I said.

'About Berlin?' he said.

I nodded.

'That's beautiful,' he said, his purple face erupting in forced laughter. 'A book about Berlin! That's a good one!'

He slapped his thigh and shared the joke with the neighbouring stall-holder. Their jeers faded as I cycled away, parallel to the Wall, along Bellevuestrasse. I cycled past the ruins of the ballroom called Esplanade, its gold thirties lettering mellowed through the years to weak brown. It was just before five, a hot grey afternoon. I needed some breakfast, I decided. I knew a good café at the top of the Kurfürstendamm, one of those places frequented by older women with hats.

The café had Louis XIV chairs upholstered in crushed velvet the colour of wet roses. The tables were gold-leafed, the carpet grey. I ate my boiled eggs and toast. Tom Jones was playing softly across the PA.

> *And they'll all come to meet me.*
> *In the shade of that old oak tree.*
> *As they lay me, in the green green grass of home.*

There was no escape. The Welsh miner went to Las Vegas and his voice went round the world. I finished breakfast quickly and jumped back on the bicycle. I had gone about 200 yards back down the Kurfürstendamm when a sudden gale, the storm's messenger, whipped up all the trash from the street. Panicked pigeons wheeled in the sky. Pages of newsprint clung to human legs. Men and women chased bouncing hats. Dogs slunk scared, tails between their legs. Glasses, cups and bottles flew from the café tables and shattered on the paving stones, where cigarette butts and sweet wrappings were trapped in manic little whirlwinds. Everyone hurried, hands shielding eyes against the stinging dust, their ears full of the wind's fierce music; the lowing of a million beasts and the singing of the sea.

The sky was rent with electric yellow and some people screamed.

The wind was banished by the thunder.

God turned off the lights and flung down the cleansing rain.

I got off my bicycle at the corner of Cicerostrasse and the Kurfürstendamm, seeking refuge beneath the blue canopy of a Peugeot showroom, together with a group of motorcy-

226

clists. The green C on the neon sign of a restaurant called Ciao sparked out.

Those already ensconced in the pavement cafés, dry and comfortable beneath the canvas, turned their chairs round to get a better view of the mayhem: the drenched and running people, skidding cars, fallen cyclists, wrecked umbrellas. They sipped their drinks and said nothing, like they were watching a rather boring disaster film which had the saving grace of some unintentionally amusing moments.

Wearing a lace shawl, seamed stockings and a black pencil skirt, one young woman was striding up the Kurfürstendamm as though nothing had happened. She must have been half-blinded by the torrential rain, but she had decided to disobey the general edict to run and hid. Why should she be scared of rain? Rain was the least of her problems. She let it beat uselessly against her pale face. She laughed and the rain beat even harder, filling up her eyes which ran with black tears. The rain did its best. It glued the cloth to her skin, tried to make her shiver. It filled up her laughing mouth. She was ankle-deep in the flood but she didn't once check her stride, her swaggering heroic procession up the main drag. Her skirt shone like fresh coal. I wondered who she was. She loved the rain. The rain had cleared the fucking streets. The rain was her friend. The rain had rescued the day, mocked the fragile city, washed the day into her memory, clear bright things that would not be forgotten.

Ian Walker, *Zoo Station*

* * *

The porter was already there. He had the baggage on the curb. A taxi was just drawing up, and he stowed the baggage in. George tipped him and shook hands. He also tipped the enormous doorman, a smiling, simple, friendly fellow who had always patted him upon the back as he went in and out. Then he got into the taxi, sat down by Heilig, and gave the driver the address – Bahnhof Am Zoo.

The taxi wheeled about and started up along the other side of the Kurfürstendamm, turned and crossed into the Joachimtaler-strasse, and, three minutes later, drew in before the station. They still had some minutes to wait before the train, which was coming from the Friedrich-strasse, would be there. They gave the baggage to a porter, who said he would meet them on the platform. Then Heilig thrust a coin into the machine and bought a platform ticket. They passed by the ticket inspectors and went up the stairs.

A considerable crowd of travelers was already waiting on the platform. A train was just pulling in out of the west, from the direction of Hanover and Bremen. A number of people got off. On other tracks the littering trains of the Stadtbahn were moving in and out; their beautiful, shining cars – deep maroon, red, and golden yellow – going from east to west, from west to east, and to all the quarters of the city's compass, were heavily loaded with morning workers. George looked down the tracks towards the east, in the direction from which his train must come, and saw the semaphores, the lean design of tracks, the tops of houses, and the massed greens of the Zoologic Garden. The Stadt-bahn trains kept sliding in and out, swiftly, almost noiselessly, discharging streams of hurrying people, taking in others. It was all so familiar, so pleasant, and so full of morning. It seemed that he had known it forever, and he felt as he always did when he left a city – a sense of sorrow and regret, of poignant unfulfillment, a sense that here were people he could have known, friends he could have had, all lost now, fading, slipping from his grasp, as the inexorable moment of the departing hour drew near. [...]

There was a flurry of excitement in the crowd. A light flashed, the porters moved along the platform. George looked up the tracks. The train was coming. It bore down swiftly, sweeping in around the edges of the Zoologic Garden. The huge snout of the locomotive, its fenders touched with trimmings of bright red, advanced bluntly, steamed hotly past, and came to a stop. The dull line of the coaches was broken vividly in the middle with the glittering red of the Mitropa dining car.

Everybody swung into action. George's porter, heaving up his heavy baggage, clambered quickly up the steps and found a compartment for him. There was a blur of voices all around, an excited tumult of farewell. […]

He climbed into the train. The guard slammed the door. Even as he made his way down the narrow corridor towards his compartment, the train started. […]

The train gathered speed, the streets and buildings in the western part of the city slipped past– those solid, ugly streets, those massive, ugly buildings in the Victorian German style, which yet, with all the pleasant green of trees, the window boxes bright with red geraniums, the air of order, of substance, and of comfort, had always seemed as familiar and as pleasant to George as the quiet streets and houses of a little town. Already they were sweeping through Charlottenburg. They passed the station without halting, and on the platforms George saw, with the old and poignant feeling of regret and loss, the people waiting for the Stadtbahn trains. Upon its elevated track the great train swept on smoothly toward the west, gathering momentum steadily. They passed the Funkturm. Almost before he knew it they were rushing through the outskirts of the city towards the open country. They passed an aviation field. He saw the hangars and a flock of shining planes. And as he looked, a great silver-bodied plane moved out, sped along the runway, lifted its tail, broke slowly from the earth, and vanished.

And now the city was left behind. Those familiar faces, forms, and voices of just six minutes past now seemed as remote as dreams, imprisoned there as in another world – a world of massive brick and stone and pavements, a world hived of four million lives, of hope and fear and hatred, of anguish and despair, of love, of cruelty and devotion, that was called Berlin.

Thomas Wolfe, *You Can't Go Home Again*

Selective Index

*after name indicates a writer whose work is excerpted in this book

A

Adie, Kate*   161, 165
Alex, the (see also
  Alexanderplatz)   44–5, 46,
  220
Alexanderplatz (see also 'Alex,
  the')   28, 37, 44–5, 46, 49,
  56, 96, 189, 201, 209–10,
  220, 224
Anarchists   57
Andersen, Hans
  Christian   73–4, 76
Anonymous*   136
Aridjis, Chloe*   37–8, 40–1,
  46, 92, 96–7, 172, 225

B

Baader, Andreas   77–8
Badel Steffi *   185
Baedeker, Karl*   105, 107
Bamforth, Iain *   201, 206
Beatty, Paul *   146–7
Bebelplatz   41, 43–4
Beckmann, Max   13
Bell, Gertrude*   103, 105
Berghain (club)   21–4
Berlin Wall, the (see also 'Wall,
  the')   56–7, 72, 77, 152, 162,
  178, 181, 186
Berliner Dom   165, 210
Berliner Ensemble (theatre)   81,
  216
Berliner Schnauze   202
Berliners   2–3, 6, 23, 57, 58,
  59, 61, 64, 81, 89, 96, 126,
  145–6, 159, 168, 172, 173,
  189, 195, 202, 220
Bielenberg, Christabel*   6, 85,
  87, 133

Bismarck, Otto von   201, 204,
  206
Blue Angel, The (film)   2, 71–2
Bornholmer Strasse   57, 185
Bowie, David   1, 18, 78–81, 206
Brandenburg Gate   28, 40, 122,
  147, 151, 180–1, 185
Brandenburg Gate /
  Brandenburger Tor   108, 117,
  119
Brandt, Willie   151
Brecht, Bertolt   3, 13, 26, 67,
  69, 81, 203, 207–8, 215, 217
Brussig, Thomas*   4, 61, 63,
  182–4
Bülowstrasse   111

C

Cabaret   2, 5–30, 70
Cabaret (the musical/film)   8,
  18, 26, 27
Café des Westens   207
Café Kempinski   208
Café Kranzler   208, 216
Café Sopranos   219
Café Wien   208
Canetti, Elias*   6–7, 67–9
Chagall, Marc   207
Charlottenburg   140, 229
Charlottenburg Palace   38, 102,
  221
Checkpoint Charlie   18, 28, 81,
  162, 168–70, 216
Christmas markets   46–7
Cold War   34, 79, 151, 167
Cole, Simon*   25, 56–7, 97–8,
  192–3
Collin, Beatrice*   67, 83, 87–9,
  107–8, 122

Collins, Ian* 70, 73
Communism/Communist 3, 10, 16, 27, 29, 42, 49, 55, 96, 98, 109–10, 112–13, 114, 145, 171, 178, 189, 192–3, 197, 205, 209, 213, 219

D

Dadaists 207
Dahlem 6, 77, 85, 209
DDR 165, 205
DDR Museum 29
Deighton, Len* 152, 155, 168
Demnig, Gunter (sculptor) 43–4
Der Sturm 116, 207
Deutschkron, Inge* 123–6
Dietrich, Marlene 1, 2, 18, 70–3, 79, 206
Döblin, Alfred* 3, 44–5, 203, 206, 208

E

East Berlin 21, 27, 29, 49, 56, 65, 81, 93, 151, 155–9, 162–3, 165–6, 168, 170, 172, 175, 179, 185, 187, 190, 216, 218–19
East Side Gallery 189
Einstein, Albert 3, 202, 206
Eisenman, Peter (architect of the Holocaust Memorial) 39
Eugenides, Jeffrey* 4, 63–4
Europa Center 47

F

Fallada, Hans* 130
Fasanenstrasse synagogue 124, 218
Fassbinder, Rainer Werner 44, 56
Fernsehturm (see also 'Television Tower') 55, 192
Fichte, Johann Gottlieb 218

Figes, Eva* 126–7, 139
Fink, Werner 15
First World War 2, 28, 109
Fontane, Theodor* 102–3
Franz Josef 108
Friedrichshain 18, 25, 55, 220
Friedrichstadtpalast 94
Friedrichstrasse 28, 36, 55, 61, 65, 116, 156–7, 163, 165–7, 228
Friedrichstrasse Station 35, 38, 102, 217
Funder Anna* 49–50, 188, 190–3, 196
Futurists 207

G

Gastarbeiter 64
Gay, Peter* 1, 12–14
GDR 49, 156, 165, 169, 172, 179, 194, 196, 210, 214, 217
Gennat, Detective Ernst 64
Gendarmen-Markt 106
Germania 3, 201, 204, 209
Goebbels, Joseph 3, 79, 115, 127
Goethe, Johann Wolfgang von 2, 43, 110, 119
Goethe Institute, the/Goethe-Institut 219
Gorbachev, Mikhail 195
Grass, Günter 3, 25, 26
Grosz, George 1, 68–9, 207, 208
Grunewald 140, 141, 153, 205

H

Hackescher Markt 61
Haffner, Sebastian* 14–16
Hansa Studios 78–9
Hare, David* 39–40, 151
Harris, Robert* 201
Haugaard, Mikka* 73–6
Hegel, Georg Wilhelm Friedrich 43, 218

Hein, Jakob* 59–61
Heine, Heinrich 42
Hensher, Philip* 53–4, 156, 159, 176–7, 184–5
Himmler, Heinrich 57, 66
Hindenburg, Paul von 110–11
Hitler, Adolf 2–3, 17, 42, 72, 86, 90, 109, 111, 114–15, 116, 117, 121–2, 129, 133, 146, 181, 194, 201, 204
Hitler's Bunker 49, 181
Hohenschönhausen 151
Holocaust Memorial, the (see also Memorial to the Murdered Jews of Europe) 4, 40
Holocaust, the 26, 29–30, 43
Humboldt University 92, 185
Humboldt, Alexander von 99–101

I
Isherwood, Christopher* 2, 8–10, 25, 27, 30, 80–1, 83–5, 111, 114, 161

J
Jewish 10, 12, 28, 42–3, 65–7, 89, 94, 115–16, 122–4, 126, 216, 218
Jewish conspiracy 66–7
Jews 3–4, 11–12, 29, 39, 40, 65, 125–6, 201, 218

K
KaDeWe (Kaufhaus des Westens, department store) 28, 95
Kaiser 103, 104, 107–8, 202
Kaiser Wilhelm II 107, 109, 208
Kaiser-Wilhelm-Gedächtniskirche (see also Kaiser Wilhelm Memorial Church) 207

Kaiser Wilhelm Memorial Church (see also Kaiser-Wilhelm-Gedächtniskirche) 4, 152, 189
Kaminer, Vladimir* 92–3
Kandinsky, Vassily 207
Kant, Immanuel 43
Kara, Yadé* 187
Karl Marx Allee 25, 189, 193
Karl Marx University 164
Kästner, Erich 13
Kaufhaus des Westens (KaDeWe, department store) 95
Kaul, Nitasha* 220
Kehlmann, Daniel* 99–101
Kennedy, (John F.) 64, 151, 190, 205
Kerr, Philip* 6, 59, 117, 121, 128
Klee, Paul 207
Koestler, Arthur 206
Kokoschka, Oskar 207
Köpenick 55, 205
Kreuzberg 18, 21, 53–5, 81, 157, 221
Ku'damm (see also 'Kurfürstendamm') 122, 161–2, 219
Kurfürstendamm (see also 'Ku'damm') 4, 14, 28, 31, 65, 81, 119, 124, 166, 188–9, 226–8

L
Landwehr Canal 79
Lang, Fritz 2–3, 203, 207
Lange-Müller, Katja* 53
le Carré, John* 1, 168, 173, 175
Lenya, Lotte 208, 215
Lessing, Gotthold Ephraim 65
Lichtenberg 55, 193, 203

Liebknecht, Karl   54, 112, 203
Love Parade   21
Lustgarten   106, 111, 119, 210
Luxemburg, Rosa   54, 193, 203
Lyon, Wenonah*   25, 30

M
MacLean, Rory*   1–4, 196–7
Mak, Geert*   64, 128–9, 206–8, 209
Mann, Heinrich   2
Mann, Thomas   12
Maron, Monika*   175–6
Marx, Karl   25, 42, 77, 164, 189, 193
Marx-Engels Platz   152
Mauer   178, 181, 187
Mauer(wall) park   56–7
Mauersound   17
McEwan, Ian*   143–4
Meinhof, Ulrike   76–8
Memorial to the Murdered Jews of Europe (see also Holocaust Memorial)   39, 40
Mendelssohn, Felix   76
Mendelssohn, Moses   65
Menuhin, Yehudi   207
Mies van der Rohe's New National Gallery   79
Mitte   50, 52, 55, 61, 93
Moabit   52, 54
Morris, Jan*   188, 190
Mussolini, Benito   121–2

N
National Socialism   8, 58, 70, 109, 116, 147, 189
Nazi/Nazis/Nazism   1, 3, 4, 10, 14, 15, 40, 41–3, 49, 62, 66, 72, 76, 79, 81, 83, 109, 111–13, 114, 120, 128, 133, 134, 139, 204–5, 218
Nazi youth   42–3
Neo-Nazi   49, 72

Neukölln   18, 127, 185–6
Nietzsche, Friedrich   43
Nollendorfplatz   83, 146
Nooteboom, Cees*   3, 31–3, 38–9
Normannenstrasse   188, 193

O
Olympic Games / Olympiad (1936)   116–17
Operation Rose   151
Opernplatz   89, 114
Oranienburger/Strasse/Tor   61–2, 149, 170, 187, 221
Oranienstrasse   53, 157
Ossis (East Berliners)   57, 173
Owens, Jesse   121
Özdamar, Emine Sevgi*   214, 218

P
Palace of the Prussian Kings   49
Palast der Republik/Palace of the Republic   49–50, 209–10
Pankow   157
Parei, Inka*   94
Plattenbau(s)   96
Potsdamerplatz   4, 78, 79, 168, 171, 181, 221, 225
Potsdamerstrasse   70, 78, 112, 135
Prenzlauer Berg/Prenzlauerberg   18, 55, 56, 97–8, 155, 157, 221
Pynchon, Thomas*   142

Q
Quadriga, the (on top of the Brandenburg Gate)   180

R
Radio Free Europe   193
Rapp, Tobias*   21, 25
Rathenau, Walter   66

Red Army   76, 152
Red Army Fraction (RAF)   76
Reichstag   28, 45, 66, 114,
    142, 149
Remarque, Erich Maria   42
Richardson, C. S.*   147, 150
Romanisches Café   207
Rosa-Luxemburg-Platz   193
Rösinger, Christiane*   50–1
Rostropovich, Mtislav*   186
Roth, Joseph*   10, 12, 203, 206
Rothmann, Ralf*   48
Rüther, Tobias*   78, 81

S

Savignyplatz   31–2
S-Bahn   37–8, 56, 96, 134, 163,
    216, 221, 224
Schabowski, Günther   178–80,
    182
Schickele, René   115
Schicksaal   208
Schley, Fridolin*   209, 214
Schneider, Rolf*   18, 20
Schoeller's Bookstore   31
Schönberg, Arnold   206
Schöneberg   55, 63, 81, 90,
    122, 134–5
Schopenhauer, Arthur   43
Sebald, W. G.*   139, 141
Seiffert, Rachel*   129, 133
Simpson, John*   155, 179,
    181–2
Socialism   8, 29, 58, 70, 81,
    109, 116, 147, 189
Soviet Army War
    memorial   152
Spandau   55, 205
Spartacists, the   193, 203
Speer, Albert   1, 199, 201, 204
Sportpalast   79, 111
Spree (river)   25, 54, 103, 106,
    152, 201, 217, 221
Springer Building, the   186

SS   4, 125
Stasi   4, 172, 188, 194, 194, 196
Stasi HQ/Headquarters   172,
    188, 193–5
Storm Troopers   120

T

Tacheles bar   187
Tegel airport   186
Television Tower/Tele-
    Tower/TV Tower (see also
    'Fernsehturm')   37, 46, 49,
    55, 167, 192–3, 209–10
Tempelhof   115, 152, 193, 204–5
Teufelsberg (Devil's
    Mountain)   205
Third Reich   15, 116, 121, 194
Tiergarten   52, 54, 102, 119,
    141, 161, 165, 209, 221
Trabant(s)/Trabis   156, 180,
    185, 190
Treptower Park   152, 158
Tripathi, Salil*   41, 114
Tucholsky, Kurt   203, 208
Turks   63, 216
Turmstrasse   52–3

U

U-Bahn   26, 33–4, 82, 146,
    169, 170, 216, 221, 223
Unter den Linden   28, 40, 41,
    65, 74, 89, 106, 107, 117,
    119, 122, 147, 171, 180

V

Verhaeghen, Paul*   5, 55, 61,
    90, 123
Vyleta, Dan*   90–1, 136–7,
    142, 146

W

Wagner, Bernd and Luise*   96
Walker Ian*   16–18, 66, 76, 78,
    156, 167, 168, 170, 218–9, 227

Walker, Tamsin* 137, 139
Wall Museum, the 169
Wall, the (see also 'Berlin
  Wall') 1–4, 18, 21, 28, 56,
  57, 72, 73, 77, 79, 81, 152,
  157, 159–63, 168–70, 173–6,
  178–97, 206, 216, 225–6
Walser, Martin 39
Wannsee Lake 81
Wedding 18, 55, 60, 90
Weidermann, Volker* 114, 116
Weill, Kurt 207
Weimar/Weimar Republic 8,
  12, 14, 37, 76, 82, 202, 204
Wessis (West Berliners) 56, 187
West Berlin 3, 17, 21, 28, 65,
  77–8, 95, 151, 156, 160, 165,
  168–70, 172, 177, 179, 186,
  188, 191, 192, 205, 216–17, 219
Wieland, Rayk* 173

Wildenhain, Michael* 159,
  161
Wilhelminian architecture 6,
  21, 107
Wilmersdorf cemetery 72
Winger, Anna* 33, 37, 47
Wolfe, Thomas* 120, 229
World War II 34, 43

Z
Zehlendorf 55
Zionskirche 57
Zoo/Zoogarten/Zoologischer
  Garten/Zoologic Garden 10,
  89, 90, 94, 102, 149, 152,
  221, 228
Zoo Station/Bahnhof Am
  Zoo 18, 59, 66, 78, 156 167,
  170, 216, 219, 227, 228
Zweig, Stefan 4

Acknowledgements

Oxygen Books would like to thank the many people who have supported *city-lit BERLIN* with their enthusiasm, professional help, ideas for texts to include, and generosity. Among them we would like to mention particularly the staff of the Marga Schoeller bookshop in Berlin, the permissions personnel in the many publishers and agencies we have dealt with, along with Elisabeth Pyroth of the London Goethe Institute, Rebecca Morrison of *New Books in German*, Rory MacLean, Steph Morris, Graham Main, Mikka Haugaard, and above all our wonderful Berlin-based co-editor and translator, Katy Derbyshire.

Bamforth, Iain 'Believing in Architecture', *The Good European: Essays and Arguments*, published by Carcanet Press, Manchester, 2006. (An edited version appears in *city-lit BERLIN* with the permission of the author and publisher.) Reprinted by permission of Carcanet Press.

Beatty, Paul *Slumberland*, published by Bloomsbury USA, 2008. Copyright © 2008 by Paul Beatty. Reprinted by permission of The Wylie Agency on behalf of the author.

Bielenberg, Christabel *The Past is Myself*, published by Corgi Books, 1984. Copyright © Christabel Bielenberg 1970. Reprinted by permission of The Random House Group Ltd. and by kind permission of Katharina Bielenberg.

Brussig, Thomas *Berliner Orgie* copyright © Piper Verlag GmbH, Munich 200X, 1995. Translation © Katy Derbyshire 2009. Reprinted by kind permission of Piper Verlag GmbH.

Brussig, Thomas *Heroes Like Us* first published in Germany as *helden wie wir* by Verlag Volk und Welt GmbH, Berlin, 1995. Published by Harvill Press 1997. Translation copyright © John Brownjohn 1997. Reprinted by permission of The Random House Group Ltd.

Canetti, Elias *The Torch in My Ear*, first published in German in 1980 as *Die Fackel im Ohr* by Carl Hanser Verlag, Munich. Translation by Joachim Neugroschel © Farrar, Straus and Giroux, Inc. 1982. Reprinted by permission of Farrar, Straus and Giroux, and Granta Books.

Cole, Simon, blog entries at Bookpacking.com. By permission of the author. (Entries for 3/2/9 and 4/2/9.)

Collin, Beatrice *The Luminous Life of Lilly Aphrodite*, published by John Murray, 2008. Copyright © Beatrice Collin 2008. Reprinted by permission of John Murray (Publishers).

Collins, Ian 'Marlene Dietrich: RIP', copyright © Ian Collins. First appeared in the *Eastern Daily Press*, 1st August, 1992. Reprinted by permission of Ian Collins.

Deighton, Len *Funeral in Berlin*, published by Jonathan Cape

Ltd., 1964. Copyright © Pluriform Publishing Company BV 1964, reprinted with kind permission of Jonathan Clowes Ltd, Literary Agents, London.

Deutschkron, Inge *Ich trug den gelben Stern* ('I wore the yellow star') published by Deutscher Taschenbuch Verlag GmbH & Co KG, 1978. Translation copyright © Katy Derbyshire 2009. Reprinted by permission of Deutscher Taschenbuch Verlag.

Döblin, Alfred *Berlin Alexanderplatz* , copyright © 1929 by S. Fischer Verlag A.-G., Berlin. Translation by Eugene Jolas, first published in Great Britain by Martin Secker, 1931. Reprinted by kind permission of Continuum International Publishing Group.

Eugenides, Jeffrey *Middlesex*, published by Bloomsbury 2002. Copyright © 2002 by Jeffrey Eugenides. Reprinted by kind permission of Bloomsbury Publishing.

Fallada, Hans *Alone in Berlin* first published as *Jeder stirbt für allein* 1947. Copyright © Aufbau-Verlagsgruppe GmbH, Berlin, 1994. This translation published in the USA by Melville House Publishing and in Great Britain by Penguin Classics 2009. Translation copyright © Michael Hofmann 2009. Reprinted by kind permission of Penguin Books.

Figes, Eva *Tales of Innocence and Experience* published by Bloomsbury 2003. Copyright © 2003 by Eva Figes. Reprinted by kind permission of Bloomsbury Publishing.

Fontane, Theodor *Effi Briest* first published in book form in Germany 1895. This translation copyright © Hugh Rorrison and Helen Chambers, first published by Angel Books 1995. Published by Penguin Books 2000. Reprinted by permission of Angel Books.

Funder Anna, *Stasiland*, Published by Granta Books 2003. Copyright © by Anna Funder 2003. Reprinted with permission of Granta Books.

Gay, Peter *Weimar Culture: The Outsider as Insider*. First

published in Great Britain by Secker and Warburg, 1969. Copyright © 2001, 1968 by Peter Gay. Used by permission of W. W. Norton and Company, Inc. and the Random House Group Ltd.

Haffner, Sebastian *Defying Hitler*, published by Weidenfeld and Nicholson 2002. Translation copyright © 2002 Oliver Pretzel. Phoenix paperback 2003. Reprinted by permission of Orion Books Ltd.

Hare, David *Berlin*, published by Faber and Faber Ltd. 2009. Copyright © David Hare 2009. Reprinted by permission of Faber and Faber Ltd.

Harris, Robert *Fatherland*, published by Hutchinson 1992. Reprinted by permission of The Random House Group Ltd.

Haugaard, Mikka 'Hans Christian Andersen in love', copyright © Mikka Haugaard 2009.

Hein, Jakob *Gebrauchsanweisung für Berlin*, Copyright © Piper Verlag GmbH, Munich 200X. Reprinted by kind permission of Piper Verlag GmbH. Translation copyright © Katy Derbyshire 2009.

Hensher, Philip *Pleasured* published by Chatto and Windus 1998. Copyright © by Philip Hensher 1998. Published by Vintage 1999. Reprinted by permission of The Random House Group Ltd.

Isherwood, Christopher *Goodbye to Berlin*, first published by The Hogarth Press 1939. Copyright © Christopher Isherwood 1939. Reprinted by permission of The Random House Group Ltd.

Isherwood, Christopher *Mr Norris Changes Trains*, first published by The Hogarth Press 1935. Reprinted by permission of Curtis Brown Group Ltd, London, on behalf of the Estate of Christopher Isherwood. Copyright © Christopher Isherwood 1935.

Kaminer, Vladimir *Russian Disco* published by Ebury Press 2002. Translation by Michael Hulse copyright © Ebury Press.

Reprinted by permission of The Random House Group Ltd.

Kara, Yadé, *Salem Berlin*, copyright © 2003 Diogenes Verlag AG Zürich. Translation copyright © Katy Derbyshire. Reprinted by permission of Diogenes Verlag.

Kaul, Nitasha, 'Letter', copyright © 2009 Nitasha Kaul.

Kehlmann, Daniel *Measuring the World*, originally published in German as *Die Vermessung der Welt* by Rowohlt Verlag, Hamburg 2005. Published by Quercus Books 2007. Translation copyright © 2006 by Carol Brown Janeway. Reprinted by permission of Quercus Books.

Kerr, Philip *March Violets* first published by Viking 1989. Published by Penguin Books 1990. Copyright © Philip Kerr 1989. Reprinted by permission of Penguin Books

Kerr, Philip *The Pale Criminal* first published by Viking 1990. Published by Penguin Books 1991. Copyright © Philip Kerr 1990. Reprinted by permission of Penguin Books.

Lange-Müller, Katja 'Sklavendreieck', in *Neues aus der Heimat*, published by Verlag Kiepenheuer & Witsch GmbH & Co, 2004. Translation copyright © Katy Derbyshire 2009. Reprinted by permission of Kiepenheuer & Witsch.

le Carré, John *The Spy Who Came In From The Cold*, first published in great Britain by Victor Gollanz Ltd, copyright © 1963 Le Carré Productions. Reprinted by permission of David Higham Associates Ltd., on behalf of the author.

Lyon, Wenonah, 'The first time I saw Berlin … ' First appeared in *Unlikely 2.0.* Copyright © Wenonah Lyon. Reprinted by kind permission of the author.

MacLean, Rory, 'Rory's Berlin Blog', from the Goethe Institute website, reprinted by kind permission of Rory MacLean and the Goethe Institute, London.

MacLean, Rory *Stalin's Nose: Across the Face of Europe*, first published in Great Britain by HarperCollins, 1992. Copyright © Rory MacLean 1992. Republished by Tauris Parke 2008. Reprinted by kind permission of Tauris Parke.

Mak, Geert *In Europe: travels through the twentieth century* published by Harvill Secker 2007. Copyright © Geert Mak 2004. Translation copyright © Sam Garrett 2007. Reprinted by permission of The Random House Group.

Maron, Monika, *Animal Triste*, copyright © S.Fischer Verlag GmbH, Frankfurt am Main 1996. Translation copyright © Katy Derbyshire 2009. Reprinted with permission of S.Fischer Verlag.

McEwan, Ian *The Innocent*, first published by Jonathan Cape, 1990. Copyright © Ian McEwan 1990. Published by Vintage 1998. Reprinted by permission of The Random House Group Ltd.

Morris, Jan *A Writer's World: Travels 1950–2000*. Published by Faber and Faber 2003. Copyright © Jan Morris 2003. Reprinted by permission of Faber and Faber Ltd.

Nooteboom, Cees *All Souls' Day*, first published by Atlas Uitgeverij as *Allerzielen* in 1998. Copyright © Cees Nooteboom 1998. English translation copyright © Susan Massotty 2001. Reprinted by permission of Pan Macmillan, London.

Özdamar, Emine Sevgi, 'Mein Berlin' from *Der Hof im Spiegel*, Kiepenheuer & Witsch 2001. Translated as 'My Berlin' by Lyn Marven, in *Berlin Tales* (edited by Helen Constantine), Oxford University Press 2009. Reprinted by permission of Kiepenheuer & Witsch and Oxford University Press.

Parei, Inka *Die Schattenboxerin*, copyright © Schöffling & Co. Verlagsbuchhandlung GmbH, Frankfurt am Main 2000. Translation copyright © Katy Derbyshire 2009.

Pynchon, Thomas *Gravity's Rainbow*, published by Jonathan Cape 1973. Copyright © Thomas Pynchon 1973. Reprinted by kind permission of The Random House Group Ltd.

Rapp, Tobias *Lost and Sound: Berlin Techno und der Easyjetset*, first published by Suhrkamp Verlag 2009. Translation copyright © Katy Derbyshire 2009. Reprinted with permission of Innervisions GmbH, Berlin.

Richardson, C. S. *The End of the Alphabet* Published by Porto-bello Books 2008. Copyright © 2007 Dravot and Carnehan Inc., reprinted by permission of Portobello Books Ltd.

Rösinger, Christiane *Das schöne Leben* © S.Fischer Verlag GmbH, Frankfurt am Main, 2008. Translation copyright © Steph Morris 2009. Reprinted by permission of S. Fischer Verlag.

Rostropovich, Mitislav in *Mein 9 November: Der Tag an dem die Mauer fiel*, ed. Hans-Hermann Hertle and Kathrin Elsner. Published by Nicolai Verlag, Berlin November 1999. Trans-lation © Katy Derbyshire. Reprinted by kind permission of Nicolai Verlag, Berlin.

Roth, Joseph *The Wandering Jews* published by Granta Books 2001. Copyright © 1976, 1985 by Verlag Allert de Lange, Amsterdam, and Verlag Kiepenheuer & Witsch, Köln. Trans-lation copyright © 2001 by Michael Hofmann. Reprinted by permission of Granta Books.

Rothmann, Ralf *Hitze* published by Suhrkamp Verlag 2003. Copyright © Frankfurt am Main 2003. Translation copy-right © Katy Derbyshire 2009. Reprinted with kind permis-sion of Suhrkamp Verlag Frankfurt am Main.

Rüther, Tobias *Helden: David Bowie und Berlin*, copyright © der deutschen Ausgabe 2008 by Rogner & Bernhard Verlags GmbH & Co. KG, Berlin. Translation copyright © Katy Derbyshire 2009. Reprinted by permission of Rogner & Bernhard

Schley, Fridolin, 'Das Herz der Republik' from *Wildes schönes Tier*, published by Berlin Verlag 2007. Translated as 'The Heart of the Republic' by Lyn Marven, in *Berlin Tales* (edited by Helen Constantine), Oxford University Press 2009. Trans-lation copyright © Lyn Marven 2009. Reprinted by permis-sion of Berlin Verlag and Oxford University Press.

Schneider, Rolf, 'Ich bin kein Berliner' in *Berlin, ach Berlin*, published by wjs-verlag, Berlin, 2005. Translation copyright © Susan Thorne 2009. Reprinted by kind permission of wjs-verlag.

Sebald, W. G. *The Rings of Saturn* first published by Vito von Eichborn Verlag, Frankfurt am Main in 1995 with the title *Die Ringe des Saturn*. Published by The Harvill Press 1998. Translation copyright © Michael Hulse 1998. Reprinted by permission of The Random House Group Ltd.

Seiffert, Rachel *The Dark Room* published by William Heinemann 2001. Copyright © Rachel Seiffert 2001. Reprinted by permission of The Random House Group Ltd. and Toby Eady Associates on behalf of the author.

Simpson, John *Strange Places, Questionable People* published by Macmillan 1998. Copyright © John Simpson 1998. Reprinted by permission of Macmillan Publishers Ltd.

Tripathi, Salil 'Learning by the book', copyright © 2008 Salil Tripathi, reprinted by kind permission of www.livemint.com and the author.

Verhaeghen, Paul *Omega Minor*. Permission to reprint from *Omega Minor* by Paul Verhaegen is granted by Dalkey Archive Press, copyright © 2004 Meulenhoff / Manteau and Paul Verhaegen, translation copyright © 2007 Paul Verhaegen.

Vyleta, Dan *Pavel and I* published by Bloomsbury 2008. Copyright © 2008 by Dan Vyleta. Reprinted by permission of Bloomsbury Publishing.

Wagner, Bernd and Luise *Berlin für Arme: Ein Stadtführer für Lebenskünstler*, copyright © Eichborn Berlin 2008. Translation © Katy Derbyshire 2009. Reprinted by kind permission of Eichborn Berlin.

Walker Ian, *Zoo Station* First published in Great Britain by Secker and Warburg Ltd, 1987. Published in Abacus by Sphere Books, Ltd, 1988. Copyright © Ian Walker, 1987. Every effort has been made by us and the previous publishers to trace the current rights holder. We would be grateful to receive information that will ensure correct acknowledgement in future editions.

Walker, Tamsin 'Old Woman', copyright © Tamsin Walker 2009.

Weidermann, Volker *Das Buch der verbrannten Bücher*, copyright © Kiepenheuer & Witsch 2008. Translation copyright © Katy Derbyshire 2009. Reprinted by permission of Kiepenheuer & Witsch

Weiland, Rayk *Ich schlage vor, dass wir uns küssen* © Verlag Antje Kunstmann GmbH, München 2009. Translation copyright © Katy Derbyshire, 2009. Reprinted by permission of Verlag Antje Kunstmann.

Wildenhain, Michael *Russisch Brot*, copyright © Klett-Cotta Verlag, Stuttgart, 2005. Translation copyright © Katy Derbyshire 2009. Reprinted by kind permission of Klett-Cotta Verlag.

Winger, Anna *This Must Be The Place*, published by Riverhead Books, a member of Penguin Group (USA) Inc., 2008. Copyright © 2008 by Anna Winger. Reprinted by kind permission of the author.

Every effort has been made to trace and contact copyright holders before publication. If notified, the publisher will rectify any errors or omissions at the earliest opportunity.

city-lit

An exciting and unique travel series featuring the best-ever writing on
European and World cities

Praise for *city-lit PARIS*

'An essential guidebook ... It maps the Paris of the imagination beautifully'

Kate Muir, author of *Left Bank*

'It's terrific ... all the best writing on this complex city in one place'

Professor Andrew Hussey, author of *Paris: The Secret History*

'A great and eclectic set of writings ... an original book on Paris'

Sylvia Whitman, Shakespeare & Co, Paris

'Whether you're a newcomer to Paris or a die-hard aficionado, this
gem of a book will make you think of the city in a completely new
way'

Living France

'The ideal book for people who don't want to leave their minds at the
airport'

Celia Brayfield, author of *Deep France*

'The *city-lit PARIS* guide is essential reading for anyone remotely
interested in Paris, or planning a visit'

Mike Gerrard, best-selling travel guide writer

'This innovative guide takes us from Marcel Proust on that perfect
erotic moment to Gertrude Stein on the origins of the croissant to
Agnès Catherine Poirier on the lure of the Paris café'

Paris Voice

£8.99 ISBN 978–0–9559700–0–9

Praise for *city-lit* LONDON

'This treasure trove of a book ... a unique way to explore the ever-changing landscape of a city, through the voices of those that know it intimately'

Rachel Lichtenstein, author of *On Brick Lane*

'For those visitors to London who seek to do more than bag Big Ben and Buckingham Palace, this is the ideal guide, a collection of writings that expose not only the city's secret places but its very soul ... I can't imagine a more perfect travelling companion than this wonderful anthology'

Clare Clark, author of *The Great Stink*

'Brings London to life past and present in a way no conventional guide book could ever achieve'
Tarquin Hall, author of *Salaam Brick Lane*

'The latest offering in this impressive little series concentrates on the spirit of London as seen through the eyes of an eclectic selection of writers. Part of the joy of this collection is that the writers span several centuries, which means that multiple faces of London are revealed. It's an exciting selection, with unexpected gems from novelists, travel writers, journalists and bloggers. Keith Waterhouse, for example, writes with gentle pathos about the double life of a transvestite in Soho; Vita Sackville-West wryly observes a coronation in Westminster Abbey; Virginia Woolf promenades down Oxford Street; and Dostoyevsky strolls down the Haymarket'

Clover Stroud, *The Sunday Telegraph*

'For some time now, small publisher Oxygen has been producing the excellent city-lit series, which uses descriptions of a city penned by writers, both living and dead to illuminate the metropolis in question. The most recent is London, compiled by Heather Reyes. This includes Jan Morris arriving at Heathrow, Monica Ali on Brick Lane, Virginia Woolf shopping in Oxford Street, Barbara Cartland at a West End Ball, Dostoyevsky strolling down Haymarket and Will Self inside the head of a cab driver'

Giles Foden, *Condé Nast Traveller*

'We can't declare it with absolute certainty, but it's a fair bet that Dame Barbara Cartland and Diamond Geezer have never before snuggled up between the same covers. *City-lit: LONDON* places these strange bedfellows alongside Will Self, Virginia Woolf, Alan Bennett and sixty others in a frenzied orgy of London writing. You'll love it'
Londonist

'The second volume in this enticing new series includes extracts from the work of 60 wonderfully diverse writers, including Will Self, Monica Ali, Alan Bennett, Dostoyevsky, and yes, Barbara Cartland (writing about a West End ball)'

Editor's Pick, *The Bookseller*

£8.99 ISBN: 978–0–9559700–5–4
Discover city-lit Berlin, Amsterdam, Dublin, Mumbai, Rome and more – from Oxygen Books, a new publisher of surprising books about all kinds of journeys.
www.oxygenbooks.co.uk http://thecity-litcafe.typepad.com